Beyond East and West

Beyond East and West

by John C.H. Wu

Foreword by John Wu, Jr.

UNIVERSITY OF NOTRE DAME PRESS

NOTRE DAME, INDIANA

Original edition published by Sheed & Ward, Inc. © 1951

Library of Congress Cataloging-in-Publication Data

Names: Wu, Jingxiong, 1899–1986 author.
Title: Beyond east and west / by John C.H. Wu ; with a new foreword by John
  Wu, Jr.
Description: Notre Dame : University of Notre Dame Press, 2018. |
Identifiers: LCCN 2018000467 (print) | LCCN 2018000916 (ebook) | ISBN
  9780268103675 (pdf) | ISBN 9780268103682 (epub) | ISBN 9780268103651
  (hardcover : alk. paper) | ISBN 0268103658 (hardcover : alk. paper) | ISBN
  9780268103668 (pbk. : alk. paper) | ISBN 0268103666 (pbk. : alk. paper)
Subjects: LCSH: Wu, Jingxiong, 1899–1986. | Catholic
  converts—China—Biography.
Classification: LCC BX4668.W8 (ebook) | LCC BX4668.W8 A3 2018 (print) |
  DDC 282.092 [B] --dc23
LC record available at https://lccn.loc.gov/2018000467

To Mary, Mother of Divine Grace
and Queen of Peace

Contents

Beyond East and West

A Foreword

I

In April 1951, when Sheed and Ward published *Beyond East and West*, my father had already been credited with a number of works in Chinese and English that were published in China and in Hong Kong. His autobiography was the first of a series of books written in English that initially saw light in America and then within a relatively short time were translated into several major European and Asian languages, including French, Polish, Vietnamese, and Korean. For one reason or another, however, none of these books were rendered into Chinese, his native tongue.

As for *Beyond East and West*, a Catholic best seller in the States, when my father was asked why he had not pushed harder for its Chinese translation—despite requests for such a project—his usual reply was that the book was meant for a primarily *Western* reading public and therefore, in his opinion, a Chinese version was not appropriate. Then he would quickly add that if one day he saw fit to write of his life in and for the Chinese exclusively, he would present it from a more "Chinese" or personal perspective. Unfortunately for his people, this never came to be, though I have always believed that had he fulfilled his promise, the result could hardly have been more "Chinese" or more personal than the original

English version. Granted, perhaps it could have been more "Chinese," in some sense, but certainly it could not have been more *personal*, at least coming from the mind of a great legal and a budding mystical scholar.

The books that followed the autobiography included *The Interior Carmel* (1953), a study of the Christian path of perfection through meditations on the Beatitudes; *Fountain of Justice* (1955), a study in the natural law tradition; *Cases and Materials on Jurisprudence* (1958), a casebook used in law schools in America; *Chinese Humanism and Christian Spirituality* (1965), a fascinating collection of essays covering such diverse subjects as Confucianism, Taoism, and the Carmelite spirituality of St. Thérèse of Lisieux, the French saint whose thought was instrumental in my father's conversion to Roman Catholicism; and *The Four Seasons of T'ang Poetry* (1972), a rich poetic commentary on the poetry of the T'ang Dynasty (618–906 C.E.).

My father's book *The Golden Age of Zen*, initially published in English in Taiwan and translated into Chinese, French, and two separate Korean renditions, was published in America for the first time by Doubleday in 1996. Its Chinese translation by Wu I, my father's student in Taiwan, continues to sell. In addition, my father's Chinese translations of the Psalms and the New Testament, rendered into an exquisite modern classical Chinese form in the 1940s, continue to be read to this day in Taiwan, though they are no longer sold anywhere.

At this writing, unhappily, virtually all of my father's works in English, including the *Golden Age* and his translation of the *Tao Teh Ching*, the classic work of Taoism, are also out of print. Regrettably, too, *The Interior Carmel, Fountain of Justice*, and *Chinese Humanism and Christian Spirituality*—English writings done during what we might regard as the height of his intellectual and spiritual powers— remain untranslated for the Chinese reading public. This neglect on the part of Chinese scholars may be attributed to at least two factors: indifference to his thought and, possibly, intimidation by the scope of his scholarship and vision.

The Holmes-Wu correspondence (April 19, 1921–April 2, 1933) of III letters, which is preserved at the Harvard Law School Library and extensively documented in this autobiography in the chapters "The Story of a Friendship" and "'Law Is My Idol,'" provides the reader with excellent and copious examples of both men's intellectual, scholarly, and leisure interests, which were many. It is rather incredible that nearly sixty years separated them in age, not to mention that they had to overcome many cultural and racial differences.

One other important set of letters that has been preserved is my father's extensive correspondence with Thomas Merton, the American Cistercian monk and writer. These letters date from early 1961 to late 1968, up to Merton's sudden death by accidental electrocution in Bangkok on December 10, 1968, exactly twenty-seven years to the day the monk arrived at the Abbey of Our Lady of Gethsemani near Louisville, Kentucky. A good number of Merton's letters to my father can be found in the collection *The Hidden Ground of Love: The Letters of Thomas Merton on Religious Experience and Social Concerns* (the first of five volumes of Merton correspondence), selected and edited by William H. Shannon and published by Farrar, Straus and Giroux (1985). For a glimpse into the nature and scope of the Wu-Merton letters, see my essay "A Lovely Day for a Friendship," delivered in Rochester, New York, in June 1991 and printed in *The Merton Annual*, volume 5 (1997), published by AMS Press, New York. The most complete collection of their letters is found in the book *Merton and Tao: Dialogue with John Wu and the Ancient Sages* (Fons Vitae, 2013).

In the early 1960s, when my father was teaching in the Asian Studies Department at Seton Hall University in New Jersey, he first threw himself into the study of Zen (Ch'an) Buddhist literature. Through his exposure to Zen Buddhism, he came to a more solid and existential identification with the world. It further confirmed for him the necessity of studying such literature in the West as a prelude to, and as groundbreaking work for, a recovery of Western culture in general and Christian spirituality in particular.

Last but not least, my father was most interested in giving his own Chinese culture, which he viewed as a sleeping giant, a much-needed spiritual and intellectual impetus. He believed strongly and often affirmed, nearly litany-like, that the cultural recovery of Asia would come through the West. And especially while in the West, he saw this as part of his own calling. Though *Beyond East and West* is a deeply personal spiritual odyssey, it is also a work of vast cultural and intellectual importance. To miss this point would be to miss a good part of its original élan and intention—as it were, to mistake the trees for the forest, as Walt Whitman famously implied in his "Song of the Redwood Tree" (*Leaves of Grass*, 1881–82).

II

For years there have been requests to reissue *Beyond East and West* in its original English or in a Chinese translation. These requests come from many sources, not least from scholars who have taken a renewed interest in a twentieth-century man of letters whose specialization was the law but who, throughout his rich and, I think, saintly life, possessed an unquenchable interest in areas of knowledge that on the surface appear to have little or nothing in common. Yet in his person he seemed to have carried all these contradictions with grace and aplomb.

Requests also come from men and women of religion, particularly Christians of different sorts who are searching for a gentler and more expansive and generous form of their religion. They are sincere Christians craving to break out of the Western-oriented and *masculine* cultural biases of the Christian tradition and to find a more subtle and sublime, or, if I may put it this way, *feminine* vehicle of expression, one that would give their faith a truly universal and magnanimous tone. They seek a religion that is authentically a spirituality intended to redeem and give solace to *all* humankind, beyond any geographic or cultural bounds.

In a self-description to me, my father called himself an *anomaly*, and by this I suppose he meant a misfit, an abnormality, a person who deviates consciously or unconsciously from the expected norm. He was that, to be sure. Yet the passage of time and my rereading of his numerous writings now convince me that he was also that rare genius whose person and many achievements defy any facile classification. Could it be, I now ask, that his entire existence was dictated by an altogether higher law and providential will, one that is not fully graspable by those of us trying to fathom the roots of his often surprising and profound insights? He teases us with dreams and visions of something wonderful to come but which, to him, had most certainly *already* arrived because he was already living them to their very core.

In short, as a very serious follower of Christ (and, for that matter, of all the great paradigms of history, since he could not by nature reject anything or anyone true and good), my father regarded the Incarnation not as a mere footnote but as verbatim truth. He drew out its implications in every phase of his existence. It was because of his religious faith that he became such a sound and serious intellectual—because somewhere along the intellectual road, in spite of the fact that he himself was a first-rate thinker, he learned an all-important lesson about the limits of intellectualism. This is for me one of the greatest lessons of his life, and one, we might say, without which he could not have gone as far as he did, ironic as this may sound. Nothing else can quite explain the untrammeled and outright joy and divine hope that naturally graced every line he wrote and spoke, or the utter simplicity with which he learned to live his life, particularly as inspired by the "Sermon on the Mount," which he regarded as coming directly from the Heart of the Savior. That is why he spent an entire book, *The Interior Carmel*, dissecting this sermon's beauteous inner roads, which lead to its very center, to Christ Himself.

If one understands the simplicity of truth in my father's life, even the occasional lapses or unevenness in style in his autobiography nevertheless take on, I believe, a particular charm and beauty. He let things fall where they may, as naturally as possible. His words, one discovers, are simply the unabashed disclosures of an ingenuousness found only in persons of profound simplicity, unbridled by normal social conventions and not puffed up by the consciousness of their own achievements. In his case, the man and the style seemed perfectly melded together and *articulate* each other without fuss or artificiality. He never pursued goals that could lead to a false self or an inflated ego.

He wrote from the heart, from some secret chamber where the eternal Muse refused to let him be anyone but a *genuine man of Tao* who had come directly from the Mind of God. His writings—and I believe this to be especially true of the current book—were an outpouring of gratitude to his Divine Maker for the gifts that were given to him mysteriously and, to him, *always unearned*, at conception. His mature life was characterized by the full recognition that all his joys, sorrows, and sufferings were but divine acquisitions lavished upon him by an all-merciful Redeemer. His later piety was such that he was convinced that even particular qualities which had taken him a lifetime to cultivate were in the end not of his own making. He knew this implicitly from a relatively early age, when he was still struggling to understand both himself and God. Such piety might have belonged to a hermit; the great sinologist and friend, William Theodore deBary, once complimented my father by intimating that he was "a hermit at home in many traditions."

Viewing history as a continuous unfolding of the drama of salvation, my father seemed to be saying in his autobiography, "If Augustine of Hippo and Thomas Aquinas could make copious use of the Greeks in penetrating the Heart of Christ, I too am at liberty to see Christ through Confucius, Lao Tzu, and other Chinese sages!" Here he would be echoing Thomas Merton (see Merton's *The Way of Chuang Tzu*, which the Cistercian Merton dedicated to my father), although, at least chronologically, such a thought would have predated his cherished friend's sentiments by more than a decade.

Asian and Western scholars have long pointed out striking similarities between Asian sages and the Jesus of the Gospels. Few, however, have blatantly and unblushingly regarded the ancient sages as harbingers of the Good News, or done so in quite the same way and degree as my father. In coming to Christ through the East, he not only gave new blood and multidimensionality to Christianity but also may have unwittingly revitalized his own native traditions by placing them in an *eternal and universal light*, impregnating them with a transcendent and holy meaning that in their inception was of divine origin. To him, how could they be otherwise?

In this regard, he was following not some particular whim but the natural law itself, which for him is dynamically and continuously unfolding in man's consciousness in time, seeking after itself in an ever-developing process. Like the evolution that occurs in species, human knowledge evolves by gathering the most diverse elements, as though guided by a compassion, love, and mercy that refuse to cast away seemingly useless bits of humanity and human thought that may bring about a profounder whole, beyond the natural and human.

My father had an extraordinary gift for and faith in harmony. That holy instinct pushed him to investigate and salvage all knowledge, both sacred and profane. His developing theological and existential understanding of the Incarnation and Redemption and his penetrating studies into philosophical Taoism and Zen Buddhism—which contributed to his seeing the *extraordinary in the ordinary*—convinced him that *all* creation, regardless of how it may appear to our sometimes jaded minds and hearts, bore the unmistakable stamp of the Sacred Heart and Mind.

The proof of his convictions lies not so much in what he wrote, which was certainly eloquent and copious, but in the meticulous way he carried out his daily responsibilities, beginning with morning Mass and Holy Communion. As disarmingly chronicled in *Beyond East and West*, this was especially true following his religious conversion. We see in this spiritual classic that what was otherwise prosaic suddenly takes on poetry, and even the sweeping of a room—to borrow a George Herbert image—is alchemized into a romance. Among other things, the Roman Catholic Church, besides giving my father his raison d'etre, helped explode and dispel all the intellectual illusions and moral ennui that had plagued and enervated him for nearly two decades leading up to his fateful encounter with Christ.

And perhaps most ironically, in being given the gift of faith, he may have unwittingly fulfilled the one philosophical goal of the great Chinese sages: the inseparability of theory and practice, the blurring of the line between what one thinks and what one does. In this he was caught entirely unawares, for, in a sense, *grace* for the most part worked in him in a secret way. Thus his later achievements appeared to be effortless as well. As a profound mystic, he lived in mystery. And those in the past who have most appreciated this book and other books of his—even on ideas not centered on religion and the spiritual life—have been those who possessed a great sensitivity to and depth of religious feeling.

In the *Tao Teh Ching*, we have the deeply paradoxical thought that *going far is to return*. That is what I believe my father finally attained. Intellectually, he seemed to have pressed forward as far as he could, and in trying all the ways and byways, he had lost all taste for such travels and hit solid intellectual and moral cul-de-sacs. Nothing seems more obvious in this autobiography and his later books than his disenchantment with a pseudo-intellectualism that lacks fire and emotion and that, being stillborn, virtually has no place to go. But even more so in his pursuit of the religious life, he sought long and hard for a Christ whose signature was that of the *divine heart* rather than the brilliant mind, not because he disparaged the mind—he was, after all, a great intellectual himself—but because he felt a mind acting without a heart is absolutely incapable of penetrating deeply into the sublime regions of life itself.

At home, in our evening recital of the Rosary, our dear father nearly always stressed the importance of striving after a healthy moral life and never encouraged the kind of narrow moralistic strivings that would take us to the brink of forfeiting the very grace with which we have all been endowed. This was a formidable challenge, but, as we were growing up—all thirteen surviving siblings—we felt it as something that each of us had a deep obligation to fulfill, not toward our paterfamilias but to God Himself.

As for his conversion, there was no way my father could be satisfied with remaining outside, at the entrance, perceiving the hidden treasures within; he thirsted for at least a share in the way that the Perceiver himself perceived His creation. In short, he sought nothing less than to be engulfed by the contemplative vision. Hearing such a call from deep within, he thirsted to find a way back to what he regarded as his true home. That is why it was so important for him to have found in the very center of life a warm, throbbing, and knowing heart from which he knew all hearts emanate and go toward naturally, back to a nurturing Mother. In a letter to Thomas Merton dated September 6, 1966, my father wrote: "The beautiful thing about you is that your heart is as great as your mind. Thus in you love and knowledge [are] united organically. Herein lies your profound significance for this great age of synthesis of East and West." He might as well have been writing about himself.

Beyond East and West can be read in terms of a sojourner having once again recovered all the mislaid treasures and merriment that had sustained him as a child. That is the reason we can so readily view my father's faith in terms of a *spiritual childhood*—that which irresistibly drew him to St. Thérèse of Lisieux and made him love her so very much—and why unrestrained joy jumps off the pages of the book. It is, of course, a contemporary retelling of the story of the prodigal son.

III

Being an incurable bookworm, my father was a voracious reader of both ancient and modern classics. He also kept abreast of theological writings, from the old classics, *The City of God* and the *Summa Theologica*, to the moderns, such as the works of John Henry Newman, Reginald Garrigou-Lagrange, Jacques and Raïssa Maritain, Evelyn Underhill, Rudolph Otto, Bernard Lonergan, Paul Tillich, and Martin Buber, the great Jewish Hasidic. Moreover, being himself a mystic, he was especially attracted to the Spanish saints, St. Teresa of Avila and John of the Cross, as well as to Henry Suso,

John of Ruysbroeck, and Meister Eckhart, among others. Yet theology, including mystical writings, for all its grand structures and invaluable insights, was for him merely a support and buttress for, or a scaffolding of, that initial gift of faith. He knew that no amount of theological or intellectual wizardry and cleverness—though they could surely strengthen one's faith—could ever in and by themselves transport one directly to faith. In short, he could understand faith only in terms of an absolute *free gift* from God, especially as a *wholly undeserved gift* to one unworthy of God's love, which is given to each one of us, without exception.

The world's great books, while filling the cup of his ever curious mental life and continuing throughout his life to broaden the scope of his interests, nevertheless fell short in fulfilling his most basic spiritual needs. In Catholic converts such as Newman, Léon Bloy, the Maritains, and Thomas Merton, he happened upon the Divine Heart and Mind that gave weight to all knowledge and that helped fuse into a perfect unity what otherwise would have remained at best scattered and unconnected. The center in him held only because of the presence of this inexplicable faith.

Yet, if Christ were the beacon, then the ancient Asian sages were at least the doorway to his fateful return to Christ. For truly, as he acknowledged gratefully, the Chinese classics, notably Lao Tzu's *Tao Teh Ching*, had spontaneously, naturally, and matter-of-factly prepared him for this grand banquet at the foot of Christ. As one writer has put it: "It was not the intellectualism of Catholicism that attracted Wu; rather it was the simplicity of the Catholic message, its admission of the inscrutable mystery of God's love, and its demand for child-like faith."[1] In an age dictated by wild swings of values, he refused to give in to the temptation that had befallen so many intellectuals of his own day. In the face of a dire moral relativism, a life without the natural law and without an eternal law to

---

1. *Biographical Dictionary of Republican China*, ed. Howard L. Boorman et al. (New York: Columbia University Press, 1967–71), 3:421.

stabilize all of life, he sought all the more eagerly for an immutable scale of values to give value to all things.

The ultimate meaning and mystery of the Incarnation—of God stripping himself of divinity, of his taking on the qualities of the human person—lay for my father in this truth: When we resign ourselves to utter poverty of spirit, as Christ had chosen to do, we are led—as though our very nature compels us—into a garden of delights, a mystery of mysteries, which stands in opposition to a world that we had hitherto regarded as the only possibly perceivable world.

My father also had a wonderful gift for synthesis, evident even as a student. This natural penchant was all the more solid and convincing in view of his innate skills for analysis, of which he gained command as an academically trained jurist. He had a masterly grounding in the classical principles of rationality. In fact, one could easily maintain that his early discipline in the law gave his later writings on subjects as diverse as comparative mysticism and Zen the necessary structure and rock upon which to support his delightfully accessible intuitions, no matter what level of learning he was entertaining and perceiving.

Hence, rationality, rather than being placed in direct opposition to mysticism, was indeed the bedrock from which his mystical flights began. He seemed to have naturally adopted the *philosophia perennis* tradition of Thomas Aquinas. From this perspective, it should come as no surprise that he was a great legal thinker not *in spite of* but rather *because of* his mysticism. The subtle, dynamic, and living relationship between rationality and mysticism of this tradition and of his thought in particular is lost on most of us today, I daresay even among the religious, because of the security we find in compartmentalization and our resistance to viewing life in its entirety.

To my father, wholeness meant looking at life and the world in all its wonderful diversity and mystery. Having lived through dark times, he knew what great tragedies had already ensued due to our insistence in preempting Mystery from life or in relegating it to the merely esoteric and curious. For life to remain organically whole, he might say, mystery had to be returned to its rightful place, to the very interior core of life itself. It meant, if we could see clearly, that true rationality contained within itself the seeds of mysticism and mystery. For after all, God, not humankind, is the author of rationality.

This mystery of the wholeness of life he had initially encountered among one of the Four Books of the Confucian canon, the classic work *The Golden Mean*, where we are told that the author of human nature and the natural law is *T'ien*, or Heaven. From this classic, he had discovered the focal point at which East and West (an artificial geographical and cultural bifurcation) could meet and make dialogue possible and plausible. He saw his writings at least in part as a clearing away of conceptions that would make human unity and harmony difficult or even impossible, followed by a re-plowing of and making fertile again the entire field of human knowledge in preparation for future generations to reap, taste, and contemplate the fruits of true brotherhood and love.

As a jurist and academician, he understood the need for solid intellectual, rational, and spiritual foundations upon which any long-term, peaceable future is to be based. And, as a person whose life spanned the two great wars and who saw firsthand the atrocities that invading Japanese armies had inflicted upon his own people, he had few illusions regarding the full potential of humanity's infernal-like powers and the urgent need to harness them. He knew, too, that necessary as it is to create workable political and legal infrastructures, no healing among the peoples of the world could begin without a basic transformation of the human heart (a *metanoia*) that has been blighted by protracted wars, appalling holocausts, and countless other unconscionable social ills created by humankind. His return to basic human roots meant principally a recovery of the authentic self securely anchored on love. In fact, in his *Fountain of Justice* and other legal writings, he reminds us, as few other jurists have done—I might add, unabashedly—that *the true fulfillment of justice is nothing less than love itself.* To understand this process would be to understand the tightrope he had chosen to walk as a legal expert, a philosophical sage, and a thinker who no longer concerned himself with distinctions of East or West, North or South.

Still, for all his genius as a synthesizer of knowledge and experience—I find him as ambitious as Augustine and Aquinas in their times, and Pierre Teilhard de Chardin and Thomas Merton in ours—what marks his true greatness for me was his steadfast *fidelity to self.* This faithfulness stemmed from a natural and primitive honesty that, serving as an unfailing alter ego, refused to allow him to desert the true path. One is reminded of the true man of Tao, who gives up all other ways in order to follow the Way or, better put, in order to *lose himself in the Way.* Perhaps that is the reason why, retrospectively, it is impossible to classify my father simply as a thinker. He never slavishly followed any particular school of thought.

He was beyond doubt a major exponent of the natural law in an age when the menacing principles of utilitarianism, pragmatism, and positivism reigned supreme—as they continue to do today—in their many subtle or hidden shades and hues. He was, at the same time, both a rationalist and a speculative thinker. In his legal thinking, his neo-Kantian conceptual approach, mastered at the hands of the influential German legal philosopher Rudolph Stammler, was remarkably counterpoised and tempered by a perceptual, intuitive approach culled from Oliver Wendell Holmes's writings and correspondence.

If one were unfamiliar with the ancient wise men and writings of the East, one might mistakenly conclude that my father's intellectual background was firmly rooted in the West. After all, he even used the words "he had been born yellow and educated white." But obviously this was a gross exaggeration, and at best it is misleading. In his youth he was thoroughly schooled in and had mastered the Chinese classics. Had this not been the case, it would have been hardly possible for him to feel such love for and oneness with these classics in his mature years.

My father's initial brush with Mencius and more particularly with the classic work *The Golden Mean* sowed in him the seeds of the concept of natural law and with it a deep, irresistible craving for unity and harmony. Through such early affinity and contact he appeared to have grasped the knowledge that the universe contained within its center all the necessary elements prefiguring the fullness of life in all its many existential dimensions. Hence, when he subsequently came into contact with the basic Christian elements of the theory of natural law, he felt no rude, alienating break with his hallowed Asian past. Rather, Christian natural law concepts became an elaboration and development of ideas that had been instilled early in his life. In short, there was no mere unnatural transplantation of an idea but rather the growth of ideas planted long ago, which in fact ripened into the concept of the divine law itself.

Beyond East and West is the remarkable story of a soul coming home to rest after many surprising and dramatic turnings. Yet despite the circuitous bends, its transcendent quality lends a certain inevitability to what finally transpires in his more mature life, when a heightened contemplative vision and faith led him to ever closer encounters with his *divine companion* and ever blossoming self.

As a son and child—being the tenth and fourteenth, respectively—I shall always be grateful to both of my parents for letting us share in their charmed and saintly lives. I believe many of my siblings would share the sentiments I have expressed in these simple thoughts. I wish to dedicate these humble, perhaps even naïve, words to them. I only know I love them as much as they love me, in the way that my parents—through Christ—taught us to love at home. Much of what I know about love and compassion, which I confess is little, comes from the sharing of the family Rosary that followed our meal each evening. I do not know exactly what found their roots in us from our parents, but I am certain they were planted in us during the sacred rituals that we followed as a family. In time, everything we did both at home and away appeared to have strengthened each of us in ways that did not make complete sense, yet made sense in a *living way*, one that made strong both our individual and our collective lives, inside and outside the family.

John Wu, Jr.
January 31, 2017

A Note of Introduction

On a visit to Sydney in 1944 I first heard of John Wu. A Chinese-Australian lady told me of his conversion seven years before. She called him the Chinese Chesterton. When I met him, in Rome, five years later, it was not Chesterton who came into my head but Belloc, and not by way of similarity, but of contradiction. "The Faith is Europe," Belloc had said. Here, in John Wu, was the Faith, and here was not Europe.

This is the significance, for us of the Western world, of the man and of his book. He is at once so totally Catholic and so totally Chinese—so Catholic that you would think generations in the Faith must have gone to his making; so Chinese that you know he brought his whole racial and cultural heritage with him into the Church, intact; so both-together that you feel there must be a quite special affinity between that race and that religion; if one man of the race can be so quickly and so miraculously at home in the religion, then— But a Note of Introduction is no place for speculations on that scale.

The at-homeness is the thing. He has the run of the place and the feel of the place. He has not, as some converts have, a desire to reform the Church, but to rejoice in it. He is not, as some converts are, anxious to look like everybody else in the Church, but to be his own natural, unembarrassed and unembarrassable, self: at the tea-table, for instance, he will talk of the deepest things of the soul, without any Occidental blush or stammer.

So that there is a third totality to add to the other two. He is totally Catholic, totally Chinese, and totally himself. Of the self I need say nothing. It is all here in the book. Go ahead and meet John Wu.

F. J. Sheed

Illustrations

Drawing of John Wu by Jean Charlot, *frontispiece*

Gallery appears after page 188

Part One

Prologue

"How true is that saying, and what a welcome it deserves, that Christ Jesus came into the world to save sinners. I was the worst of all, and yet I was pardoned, so that in me first of all Christ Jesus might give the extreme example of his patience; I was to be the pattern of all those who will ever believe in him, to win eternal life" (I Tim. 1.15–16).

These words of St. Paul find a resounding echo in the depths of my soul. I do not know if he was the worst of all sinners. What I know for sure is that I was much worse than he. He was at least a Pharisee honestly trying to live up to his own lights. As for me, the case is quite different. Intellectually, I wobbled between scepticism and animal faith; morally I was a full-fledged libertine. I sneered at what I could not understand; I gave rein to the wanton appetites of sense. A slave to the world, I made myself an apostle of liberty. A well with no water in it, a cloud driven before the storm, I thought myself a clever man.

3

As I look back upon my past, the year 1937 stands out as the turning point of my life. It was in the winter of that year that I was converted. But in the spring of the same year I had published in the *T'ien Hsia Monthly* an article called "Humor and Pathos," which contains the following passage:

Happiness can make you sing, but it is not enough to make you write. Writing, especially creative writing, depends upon the convergence of so many contingencies that a successful author may be said to be more lucky than our Father in Heaven. Many an author must have felt as badly as God did when a little before the Flood his masterpiece, Man, was discovered to be such an addle egg. And I doubt very much whether the revised edition of the same book represents a marked improvement upon the first.

This is how I sneered at the works of God! Neither the Creation nor the Redemption impressed me. This is just the reverse of my present state of mind, for, now, I have come to love with a special predilection that beautiful prayer in the Holy Mass, which begins with: "O God, who in a wonderful manner didst create and ennoble human nature, and still more wonderfully hast renewed it." But had I heard these words then, they would have sounded more like irony than praise. Being mad myself, I would have considered all sober truths sheer madness. As I did not "see what the Church sees" [1] so I did not love what SHE loves.

But was I really happy and self-satisfied as I pretended, even to myself, to be? No, the contrary seems to be the truth. The fact is, having drifted away from God and lost hold on Eternity, I exposed myself to the merciless tides and torrents of Time. All my jolliness and buffoonery were but the hysterical laughter of a man in extreme distress. The seamy side

[1] F. J. Sheed, *Theology and Sanity*, p. 1.

of my apparent self-complacency reveals itself at the end of the same article which contains the terrible blasphemy I have already quoted. Here is a passage which presents nakedly the pathetic condition of my spirit at that time:

To be a Chinese of my generation is to be a very much bewildered person. I have been shocked from one haven of security after another. To be born is bad enough in any case. Didn't we all cry and shake our fists like little devils even before our umbilical cords were cut off? How I wish I had not come out from the womb of my mother! For to see the light and breathe the air is to incur annoyances. Yes, our birth is the beginning of all our troubles, and so far as this is concerned we are all in the same boat. But to be born a Chinese in my generation is to run the gauntlet of an endless series of births and deaths. Customs and ideologies have been changing with such feverish rapidity that sometimes I have a queer feeling as though I had always been carried along by a whirlwind and had never set my feet upon solid ground. The birds have their nests and the trees are rooted firmly in the soil, but where shall I find a cozy corner to rest my soul in? It seems as though you want to go to sleep, but just as you are dozing off, people come round to change the bed for you. Suppose such a thing happens a dozen times in a single night, how would you feel? Not very comfortable, I should suppose. But that is exactly what I have been up against. How many times have I found that the environment which I had taken to be a part of nature, and the majestic systems of thought which I had taken to be a part of the eternal order of things, were nothing more than illusions and bubbles! So many illusions have exploded, so many bubbles have burst, that my heart has become callous and chary of new enthusiasms. I have been shot through by the east wind and west, the south wind and north. One idol after another has fallen from its pedestal and gone to the fire, and the real god has not yet been found. The child in me is again proclaiming the coming of a new god, but the cynic in me is querying whether he may not turn out to be just another piece of wood. My spiritual life has never matured, but is still suffering from growing, or rather decaying, pangs. I only hope that the latter part of my life will find what its early part has been searching for so earnestly but in vain.

The awareness that I was nearing forty, but had not yet attained to the Truth to which I could give my heart without reserve, that awareness was at the source of my misery. I felt like a middle-aged maiden who had had many a disappointment in love affairs and was afraid that she would remain a spinster for life. So I wrote a poem on my thirty-ninth (Lunar) birthday, which tells its own story:

> Thirty-eight springs have come and gone,
> And all in the twinkling of an eye!
> One more spring and I shall be forty,
> When life should begin and illusions die.
> But illusions are still tarrying with me,
> Although I've bidden them a hearty Goodbye.
>
> My soul spreads its wings over nature and man:
> O what a prolific source of sorrow is love!
> I want to fly and carry the whole brood on my back,
> But I have found no roads in the skies above.
> If you are not as powerful as the eagle,
> What boots it to be as harmless as a dove?
>
> Life is short, and art is long;
> And wisdom is as rare as gold.
> With ardent hopes I set out at the peep of dawn;
> Now the sun is setting, and it's growing cold.
> My heart is heavy with the emptiness of my hands:
> O, let me return home, as I am getting old.
>
> At home, I hear my children laughing and playing,
> They hail me with "Daddie" like a singsong.
> I send all my worries to Hell,

And say, "Boys, let's play pingpong!"
I'll cudgel my brains no more over life and death.
Who can know the meaning of the cosmic ding-
    dong?

Don't you see Confucius as worried as a dog in a
    house of mourning;
With Jesus, wearing a crown of thorns, he forms a
    good pair.
And Buddha, his talk of Nirvana was mere gibble-
    gabble,
For he too was snuffed out in Time's Electric Chair.
An ephemera attempts to stop a gigantic wheel;
It is crushed to dust, and what does the Cosmos
    care?

Don't you see Tu Fu shedding an ocean of silent
    tears;
Homeless and forlorn, in spite of his poetic skill?
Peh-yung sang bitterly of the miseries of the poor,
But now the poor are more miserable still.
O God, if You are there,
I wish to know Your secret will!

It seemed as though God was playing hide-and-seek with
me. But my failure to find Him was due entirely to my fault.
Instead of seeking Him according to His way as revealed by
Christ, I was seeking Him according to my own way. Instead
of making myself better, I was desiring more power for good.
I savored not the things that are of God, but the things that
are of men. I saw the material miseries of the poor, but I
did not realize my own spiritual wretchedness. I was per-
verted to such an extent that I would spend days and nights
in chambering, and would think myself charitable by giving
to the poor girls twice as much as they could get from others.
This was like a man jumping into a well in order to save

another, with the result that both of them are drowned. I did not realize then that to save others presupposes the salvation of oneself. Nor did I realize as St. Augustine did, that the value of a single soul is greater than the whole material universe.

To sum up, a wrong-headed and vicious philosophy of life had poisoned whatever good qualities I had inherited from my parents or acquired through my first rather superficial acquaintance with Christ. I was homesick for God, but I had forgotten that Christ is the Way to return to Him. I had sympathy for the poor, but I had forgotten that men have souls as well as bodies. I desired wisdom, but I had forgotten that wisdom can only be acquired by renunciation, not by a self-centered possessiveness as evidenced by the line:

"My heart is heavy with the emptiness of my hands."

I desired power, but I had forgotten that goodness, and nothing else, is power. I desired freedom, but I had forgotten that freedom can only be won by obeying the commandments of God. I desired life, but I was running in the broad road that leads on to perdition. Because of my moral turpitude, I was lost in the labyrinths of life. The more I tried with my own effort to be disentangled from the snares of sin, the more entangled I was in them. The very universe became a prison to me, and I constantly bumped my head against its iron walls—all in vain.

"An ephemera attempts to stop a gigantic wheel;
It is crushed to dust, and what does the Cosmos
care?"

This was a faithful portraiture of my soul.

It is to be noted that when I wrote these things, I was,

from the worldly and material standpoint, in the most prosperous period of my life. So my unhappiness and restlessness
could not have been due to external adversity. So far as I can
see, they were entirely due to sin, which is nothing else than
estrangement from God. Only God in His infinite mercy
could have lifted me from the living hell that I had made
for myself. Only the Truth could have freed me from the
slavery of sin and tyranny of error, and given me a joy and a
peace that taste of heaven. The more I consider my life, the
more I am convinced of the truth of St. Augustine's *aperçu*
that God has made us for Himself and that our hearts are
restless till they rest in Him.

Grace is all. Nobody can come to Christ without first
being drawn to Him by the Father (John 6.44), nor can any
one come to the Father except through Christ, nor can any
one be sanctified except through the Sacraments of the
Church, which are the regular channels of grace. It is no
more than the truth to say that ever since I became a
Catholic, my life has been a continual feast, a feast that
satisfies without satiating. Adversities and tribulations there
are aplenty, but even these are sweet, or rather they serve
to bring out the marvellous sweetness of God. Whenever I
read the beautiful parable of the prodigal son, I am inclined
to say to Jesus, "O my Love and my All, You have under-
stated the case!" To anyone who has tasted the infinite
goodness and wisdom of God, the whole New Testament is
an understatement of the Truth.

1. THE GIFT OF LIFE

I was born under the Lunar Calendar. It was on the seventeenth day of the Second Moon in the year of *chi-hai* (1899) that I first saw the light in the city of Ningpo. The spring was fresh and young, and the day was dawning. It was the "Budding Moon," in which, according to the old lore, "the plants on the mountain are changed into jade." Every little leaf and bud was making ready to greet the sun; willow-tips were turning green; orchids were sending forth their fragrant blooms; and in every orchard fruit-blossoms were eager to burst their sheaths. In short, the year had passed out of the dark tunnel of winter into the brightness of spring. This is precisely the season when the bride in *The Canticle of Canticles* hears the voice of her beloved:

> Behold, my beloved speaketh to me:
> Arise, make haste, my love, my dove, my beautiful
> one, and come.

> For winter is now past, the rain is over and gone.
> The flowers have appeared in our land, the time of
> songs is come.
> The voice of the turtle is heard in our land.
> The fig tree hath put forth her green figs.
> The vines in flower yield their sweet smell.
> Arise, my love, my beautiful one, and come.

It was God who chose the season and the day of my birth, and called me out of the womb of my mother. And I was so eager to see the light that, as my folks told me later, I arrived before the midwife!

The seventeenth of the Second Moon is as good a birthday as any. It finds itself between two popular festivals. In the old folklore, the birthday of Lao Tse, "the Old Boy," the apostle of the Tao fell on the fifteenth; and the birthday of Kuan Yin, the Buddhistic goddess, was celebrated on the nineteenth. Thus, I was comfortably sandwiched between Taoism and Buddhism. Add to this the fact that the Second Moon was specially dedicated to the remembrance of Confucius, and you will note that the three great religions of China seemed to have come together to serve as my spiritual nurses. I have profited by all of them, although the light that I finally saw was the *Logos* that enlightens every man coming into the world.

My present attitude towards these three religions or schools of thought may be described by borrowing the following lines from Walt Whitman:

> I dared not proceed till I respectfully credit what
> you left, wafted hither:
> I have perused it, own it is admirable (moving
> awhile among it);
> Think nothing can ever be greater,—nothing can
> ever deserve more than it deserves;

> Regarding it all intently a long while,—then dis-
>   missing it,
> I stand in my place, with my own day, here.

No, nothing human can be greater than these, but Christianity is divine. It is a mistake to regard Christianity as Western. The West may be Christian (I wish it were more so), but Christianity is not Western. It is beyond East and West, beyond the old and the new. It is older than the old, newer than the new. It is more native to me than the Confucianism, Taoism and Buddhism in whose milieu I was born. I am grateful to them, because they have served as pedagogues to lead me to Christ. Christ constitutes the unity of my life. It is thanks to this unity that I can rejoice in being born yellow and educated white.

According to certain superstitions, under which I was brought up, I was born under an extremely happy conjunction of the stars. These superstitions I have, by the grace of God, outgrown, but the fact remains that due partly to their influences I had from my very childhood a deep-rooted faith in my high destiny. As a boy I felt as though some day I should be great in a political way and my country and even the whole world would be the better for my existence. Thus I started with high hopes, but my later life has proved how groundless they were; and whenever I compare my ideals with what has actually happened, I feel quite tickled by the glaring contrast. Perhaps this is why I have become so humorous and so chastened. For, what is humor but a certain spontaneous tendency to laugh at one's own follies and failings, with the humility of a frank recognition of the stark truth? Indeed, God has a knack of drawing good from evil.

As it was, the day of my birth corresponded, in the Solar Calendar, to March 28, 1899. It is a great consolation to know that St. Teresa of Avila, for whom I have a special devotion, had seen the light at about the same hour and on the same date in 1515; and that St. John Capistrano, the lawyer who became a holy man, had gone to Heaven on the same date in 1465. All this does not guarantee that I too shall become a saint, but it does serve as a stimulus to my spiritual life. I suppose I would have been even happier if I had been born on Christmas or Easter or on any feast of Our Lady. But who am I to question the wisdom of God? Has He not an infinitely better right than Pontius Pilate to say, "What is written is written"? As for me, I accept most gladly and in the fullest exercise of my free will whatever God has written for me from all eternity.

Some of my friends have observed that since I became a Catholic, I have somehow lost my ambitions. The fact is that I am now more ambitious than ever. I have had my share of worldly glory, but I have found it very hollow. To be contented with perishable things is not to be ambitious at all. To me the whole world no longer offers anything worth coveting; my only ambition is to be a docile child of God, and this is open to everybody who sets his heart upon it. If this ambition were not the noblest of all, my heart would not have rested in it; but if it were not open to all men, my mind would not have entertained it for a single moment. Since the supreme privilege of becoming a child of God is open to all, what is the use of enjoying any other privileges short of that?

God not only gave me a good birthday, but also a good birthplace. I was born in the city of Ningpo, at a place called "The Twenty-four Mansions." "Ningpo" literally means "peaceful waves." I do not know exactly why it is so called. Probably because it was built on the bank of the river Yung which connects it with the sea, and which ebbs and flows with such regularity that people in my generation used to tell the time of the day by its tides.

Now, the Ningponese are not refined people, but they are warmhearted and honest, full of vitality and the spirit of adventure. They take to business and industry more than to arts and letters; but they are brainy and prolific, perhaps because they feed mostly on fish and other kinds of sea food.

The best thing about the Ningponese, so far as I can see, is that they enjoy life wholeheartedly. God created the Ningponese, and the Ningponese saw that it is good to live. It is true that they are of the earth, earthy; but they never forget that the earth belongs to God, and they accept whatever grows on it as a gift from Him. In other words, they have a good appetite for the feast of life as it is offered by God for their enjoyment. I think it is not unreasonable to suppose that God likes such people more than those who show a finicky taste, as though they were invited to pass judgment on the dishes God has to offer them. A Ningponese enjoys the gift of life as a hungry school boy in America would enjoy a hot dog.

There is something rugged and untamed about a Ningponese. He is not sissy and suspicious. He is full of animal faith, full of horse sense. He is humorous, although his humor takes the form of practical jokes rather than subtle stories. He is attached to the good earth, and smells of the soil. He finds himself at home in the universe. Nay, the sun, the moon, the stars, the winds and rains, the dogs and cats, the birds and flowers, seem to be more human in Ningpo than anywhere else. They seem to constitute familiar members of each household. In my childhood, one often heard such talk as: "Look, the sun has already walked down the third step, it is about time to cook the lunch"; or "The chickens have entered their cage, your Daddy will come home soon"; or

"Look at the red clouds, tomorrow will be hotter than today"; or "Hark! the magpie has cried three times just over your head, tomorrow there will be some good news for you." If it happened to be a crow that cried above you, it was a warning that some misfortune was coming, and the most effective way for you to ward it off was to spit on the ground and say, "P'ei!" Why, your very body was one divining rod. If you sneezed, it was a sure sign that some friend in a far-distant place was speaking kindly of you. If, on the other hand, your ear was itching, you might be sure that some-one was backbiting you. We had invented a system of psy-chical communications long before radio was heard of in the West.

Thus I spent my childhood in fairyland. I remember how amazed I was when for the first time led to see a cotton mill at work. I said like a wise man, "I am sure the witch is in it!" I felt like a very courageous boy indeed to be able to hold my own in such a haunted house.

On another occasion, our neighbor invited me to listen to a newly bought gramaphone. "What a pity!" I thought, "the soul of the dying man must have been caught and put into a box by a malicious magician, so that the poor man must repeat what he said whenever the magician uses his talis-manic spells!" Those were the most thrilling days of my life, days when the unadulterated oriental imagination came into first contact with the Western scientific inventions. Those days will never come back for me or for any boy in Ningpo or any other part of China. Science has discovered many won-ders of the universe, but it has killed the sense of wonder.

Fourteen years ago I wrote some words which expressed faithfully how I then felt about the material civilization of the West and its contact with China. To some extent they still represent my present feelings.

The sweet soul of old China haunts me like one of those half-forgotten melodies that used to enrapture me in my childhood days. How I wish to live again in the bosom of my old Mother! As I look back to her, my heart leaps, for

> She was a soft landscape of mild earth,
> Where all was harmony, and calm, and quiet,
> Luxuriant, budding; cheerful without mirth,
> Which, if not happiness, is much more nigh it
> Than your mighty passions.

Now China has changed. She has been dragged into the swirl and whirl of the world. Like a leaf in the west wind, like a flower fallen upon the ever-flowing Yangtsze, she is no longer herself, but is being swept along against her will to an unknown destiny. I know she will survive all the storms and currents, and emerge victorious over all her trials and tribulations, but she will not recover the original tranquillity of her soul and sweetness of her temper. Her music will no longer be flute-like, reverberating with clear wind and running water; it will be turned into something metallic and coarse, like the Wagnerian masterpieces. To her sons, she will no longer be the tender Mother that she was, but will be transformed into a stern Father, a Father who will be as severe as the Summer sun. China my Motherland is dead, long live China my Fatherland!

At present, the soul of China is undergoing the most painful period in her history. Melody is over, and harmony is yet to be. She is now in the midst of heart-rending discords. In my own case, God has resolved all the discords for me and infused a supernatural harmony into my soul. But when will this happen to my country and my people? My own harmony can never be complete so long as this does not happen, so long as discords are still raging in the world.

At any rate, I cannot think of Ningpo without intense nostalgia, which consists partly in homesickness and partly in wistful memories of my childhood days. The last time I was in Ningpo was in the spring of 1949. I made it a special point to seek out the house in which I was born. (For we had moved from that house when I was a boy, and I had never entered under its roof since.) Accompanied by my elder brother, I knocked at the door, and the present tenants were kind enough to let us in. My elder brother pointed out the room of my birth, the hall where our mother's body had lain after her death, the sections occupied by our erstwhile neighbors, all of whom had gone the way of the flesh. It was all like a dream.

There is one thing about my birthplace that I cannot convey in writing. The Ningponese dialect sounds like jazz music at its worst, so much so that there is a popular saying in Shanghai, "It is better to quarrel with a Soochowite than to make love with a Ningponese." But the strange thing is that, vulgar and jarring as it is, its accent sticks to one for life, so that a Ningponese can never speak the national dialect without his native place being discovered. I think that it has been so since time immemorial. One of the most famous poets of the T'ang Dynasty, Ho Chih-Chang (b. A.D. 659) was a Ningponese; and he testified in an immortal poem how he retained the native accent after several decades of absence from Ningpo. Let me present the poem in Ruth Chun's version:

> As a young man I left home;
> As an old man I return.
> My native accent unchanged,
> My temples have turned grey.
> The village boys, seeing me,
> Know not who I am.
> Smilingly they ask:
> "Honorable guest, where are you from?"

The Ningponese call father "appa," and this is very near to the Aramaic that Jesus spoke. Great was my delight when for the first time I read in St. Mark's Gospel the prayer of Jesus: "Abba, Father, all things are possible to thee. . . ." (14.36) After all, it is not such a far cry from "appa" to "Abba."

The streets of Ningpo are dirty. The river of Ningpo is as muddy as ever. Yet there is something healthy and invigorating in the very air. The sky itself seems to be more lively and cheerful than elsewhere.

As I read over my past writings, I often come across passages which, for good or for ill, only a Ningponese could have written. Take this, for instance:

Taking a bath in one of the cordial bathing-houses in Shanghai is certainly a great pleasure in life, only a little too aristocratic. One boy rubs your back, another massages your feet with his fingers between your toes, and a third taps and raps lightly all over your body with skillfully trained fists. All you need to do is lie down comfortably in the bath-tub and let the "back-rubber" wash and rub you clean, as a cook would do to a plucked chicken. In order to show his efficiency, he would gather together all the dirt in the form of thin vermicelli in one part of your body. My experience tells me that the size of the heap is in direct proportion to the length of the interval between your last bath and the present one. This law applies in normal cases. I have also discovered another law, which I would like to call Wu's law of marginal dirtiness. When you have not had a bath for a sufficiently long period, say a month, your dirtiness has reached its utmost limit beyond which it refuses to grow. This law is the saving grace of our race. We are not half as dirty as some foreigners seem to imagine. There is such a thing as nature-bath, as there is such a thing as nature-cure. I for one prefer healthy dirtiness to finical cleanliness. Many people seem to forget that they are made of dust, and to dust they will

return. The great earth doesn't care a damn for your encar-
mined nails.

Whether you like it or not, this is the spirit of Ningpo,
and I am an embodiment of it. A Ningponese can be anything, but he cannot be a whited sepulchre. I prefer a healthy
dirtiness to a finical cleanliness. If I am clean now, it is Christ
who has cleansed me, I have not cleansed myself. Only
grace could have cured the dirtiness of my nature. No amount
of purism can really purify a man.

I have taken to heart these words of our Lord:

But when the unclean spirit has gone out of a man, he
roams through dry places in search of rest, and finds none.
Then he says, I will return to my house which I left; and
when he has come to it, he finds the place unoccupied, swept
and decorated. Then he goes and takes with him seven other
spirits more evil than himself, and they enter in and dwell
there; and the last state of that man becomes worse than the
first (Matt. 12.43–45).

This is not the way of keeping pure. The proper way is, after
the unclean spirit has gone, to welcome Christ, with a Ning-
poish heartiness, to occupy the centre of your soul and
allow Him to purify and transfigure it by His radiant presence.
Then only will you rejoice in discovering the full significance
and purport of what Our Abba spoke through Isaias:

If your sins be as scarlet, they shall be made as white as
snow; and if they be as red as crimson, they shall be as white
as wool (1.18).

2. MY FATHER

I hardly know anything about the early life of my father.
His name was Chia-Ch'ang. Most people called him "Master
Ch'ang." He was born in Ningpo on February 13, 1847. He
was born poor. He had only three years' schooling in classical
education. He began as an apprentice to a rice dealer. In his
forties, he became a banker. In his fifties, he was the general
manager of a native bank, and served as the first chairman
of the newly opened Chamber of Commerce. He died in
1909.

His life was uneventful enough. But if there was ever a
man possessed by the passion for goodness, it was my father.
I do not remember his ever telling us what good he had
done to others. All that I know about his extraordinary
benevolence has been told me by his beneficiaries, his friends,
our elder relatives, my mother and my elder brother.

One morning, as we were taking our breakfast, somebody
knocked at the door. I ran to open the door, and there came

20

in a very old man. Without speaking a word, he threw himself upon his knees before my father. My father, startled by this unexpected behavior of the stranger, rose instinctively from his seat and helped the old man to his feet, asking in the meantime, "What is it? What is it?" After being seated, the old man told my father how grateful he was to him for his having helped his good-for-nothing son, how his son had reformed and how good he was now to his parents, and so forth. My father, instead of appearing puffed up, became humbler than ever, and said something to the following effect: "Your son was really never very bad. Furthermore, with a good father like yourself, how could he have remained in his erring ways? Heaven has eyes, and rewards your virtues. What have I done? What have I done?"

After the old man had gone, I asked my father what he had done for that family. "Om, om!" he said with a gentle frown, "a little boy should not be too inquisitive. It is time for you to go to school."

There was a hiddenness in all his good deeds. He did not even tell everything to my mother.

But one cannot hide one's goodness any more than one can hide one's wickedness. In the case of my father, his whole personality radiated, with unconscious spontaneity, a warm sympathy for all. He was rather fat, breathing slowly and smiling benignly. One imagines that his bosom was as vast as an ocean in which boats of all tonnages could sail freely, from ocean-liners to little fishing-boats. An ocean truly pacific, with no navy fleet nor submarines. There was really a heavenly atmosphere about him.

How many good deeds he did to others, only God knows. It was only after his death that people began to tell anecdotes about him: how he would stand guarantee for the same person after he had failed him several times; how he interceded for the poor peddlers with the magistrate who wanted to levy taxes upon their meagre income; how many business concerns he helped to start in order to give jobs to the jobless; how he mediated controversies and patched up the hostile parties at the expense of his own pocket. It has also been alleged that two years before my birth, there being a prediction of a forthcoming famine, my father provided against it by importing many bags of rice from the rice-producing districts at a cheap price, so that when the bad year actually came (1898), my father sold the rice at a fair price, with the result that many lives were saved from starvation, at the same time that he managed to make sufficient profits to cheer up his partners. For what the people of Ningpo lacked was not money, but rice. By sheer foresight, he benefited others and himself! I wish all charities were like that.

As it happened that I was conceived that very year and born the next year, some friends suggested for me the cognomen "Teh-Son," which means "born of virtue"! A pretty name for a future sinner!

My wife has told me some things about my father, which she had heard from her father. On certain days of the year—days which the fortune-tellers picked out as especially auspicious for weddings—my father had to attend twenty or more parties successively on a single day. He went to the rich one first, and excusing himself gracefully after a few minutes' stay he went his way. Invariably he dined at the poorest home. "The reason was," so my wife philosophized, "that he would not be missed by the rich, while his presence was a great consolation to the poor."

On one New Year's Eve, a young man came to borrow money from my father. He nodded his head and said, "I will send it to you by and by." The young fellow gave thanks, and went his way, but he did not appear happy. After a while, my father sent a man with the money wrapped up in a napkin, and said to him, "Be sure to hand the money to Mrs. So and So." As I learned from my mother, that young man was a notorious play-boy, and apparently he borrowed money to pay his gambling and flowery debts. His wife was the last person in his mind, for he had been neglecting her all the time. My father was good, but he was not a fool.

Once an old man in our neighborhood was sick. That was a peculiar sickness. His head was swimming, and lying in bed he saw the furniture of his room whirling around him. My father visited him and sat by his bed. They talked for about an hour. The sick man told his wife, "As soon as Master Ch'ang entered the room, the furniture ceased to move; but as soon as he went away, they have begun to whirl around again!"

My father was not a Christian, but I am quite sure that Christ has said to him: "Come, blessed of my Father, take possession of the kingdom prepared for you from the foundation of the world; for I was hungry and you gave me to eat; I was thirsty and you gave me to drink; I was a stranger and you took me in; naked and you covered me; sick and you visited me; I was in prison and you came to me" (Matt. 25.34-36).

One day a well-known Confucian scholar of Ningpo, Mr. Huang Ts'u-huei (God bless his memory!), after recounting to me many anecdotes about my father, remarked in conclusion: "The life of your father was like a beautiful essay, in which words and sense, ideals and facts, emotions and reason, tenderness and strength, the yin and the yang, are formed into a perfect harmony. Among scholars I have not found such a wonderful personality, though they may be able to write beautifully. In the case of your father, although he could not write so well, his life was in itself a marvellous essay." That conversation must have taken place more than thirty years ago. But these words impressed me so profoundly that they have been ringing in my ears ever since.

The life-motto of my father was: *Help others even when you have not enough to spare.* For, as he often told us, "If you delay in helping others under the pretext that you are not sufficiently rich, then you will never be helping others." There was something quixotic about him; yet, being a banker, he could calculate well, although in his calculation he took into account the imponderables as well as dollars and cents.

His death was a great experience for me.

My father died at sixty-three, when I was ten. I have not seen such a beautiful death in my life. On his death bed, he seemed to be in ecstasy during several hours, casting glances from time to time at the windows and saying constantly, "Behold, eight *busa* (gods or angels) to conduct me to Heaven! What a condescension! How unworthy I am of it!" His countenance was illumined by a truly celestial smile. He breathed his last with a wonderful peace.

Seven days after his death, it was reported to us one evening, a peddler possessed by a spirit had seen a vision of my father sitting in the city temple of Ningpo. So there was a widespread rumor of his becoming a city god. I do not vouch for the truth of this, but I vouch for the prevalence of such a rumor.

Some years later, I had an embarrassing experience. I was attending a feast, and someone who did not know me at all was praising in the warmest of terms a living leader in the business world, and finally concluded by saying, "He is so good that he may be called Wu Chia-ch'ang the Second!" Now, it was not very polite of him to pronounce my father's name so nakedly in my presence. When somebody pointed out to him that I was the son of Master Ch'ang, he blushed and so did I. But that is beside the point. The point is that for many years, my father was thought of as the pattern of goodness. How sweet it is to be the son of a good man! I only hope that my children will enjoy half as much happiness in their father as I in mine.

In relation to my father, I often recall the words of St. James: "Religion clean and undefiled before God and the Father is this: To visit the fatherless and widows in their tribulation and to keep one's self unspotted from this world." In this sense, my father is a Catholic, a citizen of the spiritual Jerusalem. I also remember what St. Peter said in the house of Cornelius: "In very deed I perceive that God is not a respecter of persons. But in every nation, he that feareth him and worketh justice is acceptable to him." Finally I remember what St. Paul wrote to the Romans: "For not the hearers of the Law are just before God; but the doers of the Law shall be justified. For when the Gentiles who have not the Law, do by nature those things that are of the Law, these having not the Law are a law to themselves, who show the work of the Law written in their hearts."

3. MY LITTLE MOTHER

God gave me two mothers, one to bear me and another to bring me up. The one who bore me I shall call here my *little* mother; the other who brought me up I shall call my *big* mother.

When my father was already in his forties, he was still without issue; for my big mother, who was four years his junior, had never borne any child after twenty years of married life. Now, according to the old Chinese ethics, to die without issue was considered as the gravest sin against one's ancestors. This was, no doubt, bound up with the whole institution of ancestor-worship. So my big mother pressed my father to take a little wife for the bearing of children. My father found my little mother in the house of a poor lady, who had adopted her from a still poorer family by the name of Yu. My little mother's personal name was Kuei-yuen, which means "Cassia-cloud" or "a cloud of cassias." My father found her in 1889. She was then barely sixteen, being born in 1873. He took her home, and next year my elder brother was born. In 1894 came my elder sister. I was the last and least of the family. When my little mother died in 1903, I was only four, and she was only thirty.

I have no recollection whatever of how she looked, and she has left no photographs. The only thing I can faintly remember is that she could revive the flame of a candle by blowing at it after it had been blown out. This must have struck my infantile fancy with a special force. Even now, whenever I think of resurrection the image flows up from my subconscious regions.

Another memory I have of her is this: when she was propped up for her funeral coiffure, I did not know that she had died, and I was struck by the pair of red shoes that people had put on her feet. I said, "Mommy going to a wedding feast?"

Some years ago, I wrote a poem, "Thinking of My Mother," which has been rendered into English and published in the *T'ien Hsia Monthly* (March, 1939). As this poem represents my true feelings, I want to reproduce it here:

> When my mother bore me,
> She was only twenty-six.
> Four years after I was born,
> She passed away.
>
> Her features have left
> No imprint on my mind.
> Often have I wept
> In the depth of night.
>
> But I can never forget
> That day,
> When she was propped up

> For her last coiffure,
> How I still clung
> To the skirts of her robe,
> How I thought that she was going
> To a wedding feast.

I have been told that her life was not at all happy. Suffering made her a philosopher. She could not watch the spider weaving its web without uttering a sigh. She would say, "Why so much ado about nothing? Does the little animal know that tomorrow, when the wind comes, all its elaborate cobwebs will be swept away without leaving a trace?" I suspect that I inherited from my mother a streak of pessimism, which makes me respond readily to the Shakespearean note that there is nothing serious in mortality. The strings of my heart vibrate sympathetically to the wise words of Solomon: "Vanity of vanities; all is vanity." When my good friend Wen Yuan-Ning recited to me a passage from the Talmud:

> Life is a shadow, saith the Scripture, but is it the shadow of a tree or a tower that standeth? Nay, it is the shadow of a bird in its flight. Away flyeth the bird, and there is neither bird nor shadow.

it sounded like a familiar refrain to my interior ear.

In my psychical make-up, there are two strains: one negative, which I inherit from my mother, and the other positive, which I inherit from my father. The negative strain helps me to be detached from the things that pass; while the positive strain helps me to be attached to the One that remains. The result is that I look at the world as a stage on which the actors are constantly making their entrances and exits. To me, a man whose portion is in this life, however successful he may be, is more to be pitied than to be envied, for he is but

A poor player,
That struts and frets his hour upon the stage,
And then is heard no more.

There is only one thing that has permanent value, and that is to do the will of God.

The spirit of my mother helps me to understand Taoism; the spirit of my father helps me to appreciate Confucianism. The Taoist in me looks at the vicissitudes of fortune as the succession of day and night, spring and autumn, in the natural order of things. The Confucian in me urges me on in the cultivation of Love, which alone lasts. Thus, I am prepared for the worst but hope for the best.

St. Paul wrote to the Corinthians: "But this I say, brethren, the time is short; it remains that those who have wives be as if they had none; and those who weep, as though not weeping; and those who rejoice, as though not rejoicing; and those who buy, as though not possessing; and those who use this world, as though not using it, for this world as we see it is passing away" (1 Cor. 7.29–31). This is the quintessence of Taoism! Whenever I read and meditate on this passage, there rises an interior echo in my mind. The spirit of my mother is at work.

On the other hand, when I read St. Peter's words: "As obedient children, do not conform to the lusts of former days when you were ignorant; but as the One who called you is holy, be you also holy in all your behaviour; for it is written, "You shall be holy, because I am holy" (1 Pet. 1.14–16), I respond "Amen" from the bottom of my heart. The spirit of my father is at work.

The truth is that only Christianity has satisfied all the aspirations of my heart and confirmed all the insights of my mind, and woven the two strains of my inborn nature into a perfect harmony, which is the music of the spheres rather than that of the earth or of man.

But where am I? I am afraid I am anticipating and digressing too much. Let me pick up the thread of narration.

As I have been told, the last words which my little mother said to my father were to this effect: "I came to your house to pay my debt. Having given you three children, I am acquitted and now I go. Take good care of yourself." In saying goodbye to my big mother, she expressed her sorrow at dying so soon and leaving her with the burden of rearing the children.

But what did she mean when she said, "I have come to your house to pay my debt"? In order to understand this, we must refer to Buddhism, which believes in the transmigration of souls and the law of spiritual causality. If someone receives a favor from another in this life, he must return it in a future life. On the other hand, when he renders a good turn to another, he considers that he is merely paying a debt which he had in some way contracted in a previous existence.

This is not my belief. All the same, the feeling that the meaning of life consists in acquitting oneself of a debt is fundamentally sound and salutary. It is a good sentiment wedded to what I consider a false ideology. We need only to pass all the pagan ideas through the sieve of the true Faith in order to discover the grains of gold and to purify them from every alloy.

For me, the vague sense of being a debtor, which I had inherited from my mother, was transmuted by grace into the sentiment of gratitude to God. How often I have said with the Psalmist:

"What shall I render to the Lord
For all the things he has given to me?"

When I recite this, it is with the spirit and faith of a Catholic, but also with the heart of a Chinese who has absorbed with the milk from his infancy the sense of a debtor! Let every man consider himself a debtor—debtor of God and of his neighbors for the love of God. In fact, we can never acquit ourselves of the debt of love until death, and even in heaven. Woe to them who consider themselves creditors, because there is only one Creditor!

Before I take leave of my little mother in this chapter, let me relate a dream which she had on the eve of my birth. As my elder brother and many others have told me, she saw in her dream an old man with a white beard leading a young man on horseback as far as the threshold of her chamber. The old man stopped right at the threshold and said to her, "Madam, this is your son." Then he left. The horse entered and went directly towards my mother; and at the same time the young man was continually somersaulting on the back of the horse, until finally he entered the womb of my mother. This awakened her from her sleep, and early in the morning I was born.

There were quite a few attempts on the part of my elder relatives to interpret the dream. Some said that I was to die young; others surmised that I might turn out to be a revolutionary. But my elder brother, than whom there could be no better brother, said, "A-Pao is going to be a great general!"

Let me add here, parenthetically, that "A-Pao" means "the precious one": and that was a pet name by which all my home folks called me. Sometimes they called me "Pao-Pao," which means "the doubly precious."

To return to the dream, my own interpretation was that I was destined to be a circus actor, for the Chinese word for circus was "horse-play." It happened once that I was led to see a newly arrived circus, and I was very deeply impressed

by a woman walking a tightrope with a pole for balance.
She did it so well that it appeared as though she were walking
on the plain ground. When I returned home, I tried to emulate her. I tied a rope between a pillar and a millstone about
the height of my body. I took a pole in my hands for balance.
I set my feet on the rope. Everything was bidding fair; but
suddenly the rope snapped, and I fell headlong to the ground,
remaining unconscious for a few moments. That was my first
fall, and, physically speaking, my greatest fall. From that time
I ceased to entertain any ambitions along athletic or acro-
batic lines, and I dismissed the dream from my mind.

When I was in Rome, the Gregorian University invited
me to give a public lecture on my spiritual Odyssey. I began
by recounting the dream of my mother, and I continued to
comment on it:

But why have I related to you my mother's dream? I
scarcely believe in the meaning of dreams. However, this
dream can serve as a convenient synopsis of my spiritual
Odyssey. The womb of my mother symbolizes the Catholic
Church. The boy is myself. The constant jumping and somersaulting symbolize all the changes, commotions, and upset-
tings which I had to experience during the long, restless
night before I embraced the true Faith. Perhaps the threshold symbolizes the Baptism which I received in the Methodist sect. But who could the old man be? Well, for me he
represents Confucius and all that is good in the old oriental
culture. As for the horse, I think it represents Providence,
because it comes directly towards my mother, in spite of all
the movements of the uneasy child.

Hardly had I finished this when I heard applause from my
audience. That was a tremendous encouragement to me. I
thought to myself, "This time I have got it right!"

4. MY BIG MOTHER

It is not easy for me to write about my big mother. If I am asked who of all human beings is dearest to me, I would answer without the slightest hesitation that it is my big mother. I have dreamed of her more often than of any other person. I have wept more tears in memory of her than of anyone else.

I remember that in the winter of 1935, I was in Nanking, writing an article for the *T'ien Hsia Monthly* ("Some Random Notes on the Book of Poetry"). I quoted for comparison with a Chinese song the two touching stanzas from A. E. Housman:

> When first my way to fair I took
> Few pence in purse had I,
> And long I used to stand and look
> At things I could not buy.
>
> Now times are altered; if I care

> To buy a thing, I can;
> The pence are here and here is the fair,
> But where is the lost young man?[1]

Immediately, it made me think of my mother, and I wrote:

At least, this is exactly what I have felt and am still feeling. For, let me confess once for all, I used to filch a dime or two from the private hoard of my beloved mother, in order to buy kites. Now I have money enough to buy thousands of kites, but I have no use for them any more. Not even an aeroplane can give me anything more than a ghostly taste of the wild ecstasies that a little kite used to kindle in me. The world no longer contains for me anything that is worth the trouble of my stealing. And where is my mother? And who else will appreciate my peevish art of pilfering?

As I was writing the last few sentences, tears gushed suddenly from my eyes like a geyser in Yellowstone Park. It happened that my servant came in just then bringing tea to me; and I was so ashamed to be seen crying like a baby that I said to him, "Wen Chi, a speck of dust has entered into my eye. Give me a towel. Go quick!" This was one of the few lies I have told in my life. If such a thing happened today, I would have put it more abstractly by saying that there was something wrong with my eyes instead of mentioning such a specific thing as a speck of dust. You see I have learned casuistry. But this is beside the point. The point is that more than twenty years after her death I still found myself weeping in memory of her. You can imagine how dear she is to me.

Yet, dear as she is, I should be lacking in candidness if I were to portray her as a perfect woman. Nobody is perfect, and my big mother had her faults, the chief of which was

[1] From *The Collected Poems of A. E. Housman*, Henry Holt and Company (New York), p. 142.

her intense jealousy of my little mother. She wanted the children but she did not like the mother. I remember how my sister, who was five years older, disliked our big mother. She used to tell me how she had made our poor little mother suffer; but I simply did not want to hear about it. People have told me that when my little mother died my father, in consideration of her childbearing, wanted to dress her as one equal to the big wife. That was too much for my big mother. She went away to a nearby Buddhist nunnery in protest. Strictly speaking, she was right, that is, according to the Procrustean rules of propriety that prevailed then. My father had to yield and to go personally to the nunnery to bring her back.

I have mentioned this episode because, as I think of it now, it had some unconscious influence on my juristic thinking in later life. Although I am a lawyer, I have always preferred equity to strict law, the spirit to the letter, and mercy to justice. Nobody appreciates more than I do the Roman maxim: "The height of justice is the height of injustice." This also explains my predilection for the sociological and humanistic jurisprudence of Holmes, Wigmore, Cardozo and Roscoe Pound, as against the mechanical jurisprudence of the nineteenth century. More important still, it influenced me to entertain a great dislike for Confucian ritualism, and to sympathize wholeheartedly with the mighty struggles of Christ against the strait jackets of Phariseeism. When I first came across St. Paul's words: "The letter killeth, but the Spirit giveth life," I knew that I was destined to be a Christian. The experience was just like falling in love at first sight.

But to return to my big mother, so far as I know, jealousy was her only fault. As a mother, she was simply wonderful.

When my little mother died, my big mother was already

fifty-two, being born in 1851. In age, therefore, she could have been my grandmother. One cannot imagine what a blessing it is for a child of four to have a grandma to take care of him. Mother may spank you, but grandma, never.

I slept in the same bed with my big mother from the age of four up to her death, when I was fifteen. (This was not such a rare thing as the Western reader might think. Our beds were large, and different beddings were used in one bed.) No mother could be more tender to her own children than she was to me. She loved me, she adored me, she served me like an old maidservant, she waited for me every day to come from school, she made my clothes, she prepared special dishes for me. I do not remember that she ever chastised me or scolded me. How I repent that I was so unkind to her! I often scolded her, kicked her, and threw things at her. Once or twice I was so cruel as to say to her, "Do you think you could have borne me? No, I am not your son!" She only sobbed, and said, "How I wish I had died before your little mommy, that I might be spared all this!" That touched me to the quick, and I cried and would not stop crying until she retracted that statement and promised to live on. Of course, we were soon reconciled and became better friends than ever.

After the revolution of 1911, it became a fashion to cut off queues. But my mother did not know it. One day, my queue was cut off by my schoolmates; when I returned home holding the queue in my hand like a dead snake, my poor mother was so frightened that she burst out wailing loudly. My elder brother said that she thought I had been caught in the act of adultery! (It was a practice under the Old Regime to cut off the queue of the adulterer.) I never ascertained the reason why she wailed so loudly, but I suspect that it was because I looked so miserable without the queue, the queue she had so tenderly combed and braided every morning for a period of ten years.

Although she was illiterate, she did everything to encourage me in my studies. She was happy to see me practising calligraphy. She was proud to hear that my English was making progress. She boasted to others, "Some day, Teh-Son may become a manager of a foreign company!" Her ambition for me was low enough, but her love was genuine.

I sinned against her more than against anyone else. But to her mind I was a good boy! She said to her relatives, "Teh-Son's temper is like fire, but his heart is like gold!"

When I was fifteen years old, I had typhoid fever. She nursed me for twenty days. Finally, she collapsed. Upon my waking one morning, I was surprised to find that she had not yet got up. It was not usual, for she was an early riser. When I looked at her, I saw her eyes wide open, but she could not speak. One of her blood vessels had burst on account of her excessive worry and labor during my sickness. She could still recognize me, and shed tears silently. She remained in that state for ten days before she died. It was the most pitiful sight I have ever seen. Truly it can be said that she sacrificed her life in saving me from death.

I have never known such great sorrow. For several months after her death, I was almost out of my senses. Every time an old lady visited us, I would address her, "O mommy, you have come back?" Ladies who understood would weep in pity of me; those who didn't would say, "What a lunatic!" I was not entirely out of my senses, I knew that I was saying nonsense, but I was simply like a drunken fellow who cannot resist the impulse of saying things which he knows should not be said. When I was walking on the streets and happened to see an old woman looming in the distance, I would say to myself, "This time it must be my mother." I simply could not reconcile myself to the fact that she would never come back again to pet her little A-Pao. If I were not actually insane, I was at least bordering on insanity. But one day as I was looking at myself in a mirror, a thought suddenly shot through my mind and I was cured at once. "After a few decades at the most, I too shall die, and then I shall be reunited with my mother." That thought alone made it bearable for me to live without a mother. But who could have foreseen that even before my death, God would give me a Mother who does not die?

I have written some little stanzas on my big mother:

> Motherly love blinded her to my faults;
> She only saw the good in her dear Teh-Son.
> How often she bore the cruel taunt:
> "Was it you who bore the darling one?"

> Nursing her boy's sickness,
> She fell sick and passed away.
> O Jesus, since I am wholly Thine,
> I beg Thee my mother's love repay!

> Since I was admitted into Thy House,
> Thy Mother then became mine.
> As Thou hast deigned to come under my roof,
> Make my humble mother also Thine!

ſ. THE PHILOSOPHY OF THE NURSERY

It was G. K. Chesterton who said, "My first and last philosophy, that which I believe with unbroken certainty, I
learnt in the nursery." This may be an exaggeration, but who
can deny the deep-seated influence of one's childhood
impressions upon one's philosophy of life? One of my earliest
impressions was the sight of a fat maidservant weeping pit-
eously because her lower jaw was disjointed! I could not
have been more than five, but I remember that I was standing before her with my heart melting in compassion. I asked
somebody standing behind me, "What has happened to
Amah Lin?" I was told that it was because she was too happy,
that she had laughed so violently that her lower jaw got out
of joint. A doctor came and by his skilful manipulation she
could move the jaw again. But my sense of humor had been
awakened, and I burst into laughter with my hands carefully
holding my lower jaw. With the sense of humor came also

a vague idea of the irony of life: laughter, when it was too violent, could lead to weeping! When later I came upon the wise saying in one of the Chinese classics: "When a thing is pushed to its extreme, it moves to its opposite," it sounded quite familiar to me. When I read Shakespeare's dictum: "The web of life is of a mingled yarn, good and ill together," I said, "How true it is! For instance, Amah Lin's laughter led to weeping and her weeping led to laughter again." In short, I was early initiated into the mysteries of paradox, and my paradoxical turn of mind played no small rôle in my acceptance of Christianity.

When I was six, I began to study at home under a private tutor, who was a Confucian scholar. By seven I had mastered a sufficient number of characters to embark upon a little book called *The Twenty-four Models of Filial Piety*. Being the first book I ever read, it impressed me most deeply.

The first lesson was drawn from the legends of Emperor Shun, supposed to have reigned in the twenty-third century B.C. He was of humble origin. His father was stupid, his mother perverse, and his younger brother insolent. He was ordered by his father to cultivate the hills of Li in the modern Province of Shansi. There came to him elephants in great crowds to plough his fields, and countless birds flocked together to weed the grain for him. One day he was commanded by his father to descend into a well, and his brother cast down stones upon him; but he came out miraculously through another opening. His virtuous life caught the ears of Emperor Yao, who gave him two of his daughters in marriage. He loved his parents and his brother in spite of their maltreatment of him. His perfect sincerity was effectual in renovating his family; his parents became pleasant and his brother transformed in character. The whole lesson was summed up in a charming quatrain:

Elephants came in crowds to plough his fields;
For the weeding, numberless birds did their part.
He succeeded Emperor Yao on his throne,—
Ah, how his filial love moved Heaven's Heart!

This was the first poem that I ever learned by heart. Although I did not believe the whole story in its literalness, I did not doubt, nor ever have doubted, that a good man, whatever hardships he might have to undergo at the beginning, would never suffer any harm in the end. "*Heaven has eyes.*" "*Heaven is just.*" "*Heaven blesses the good, and punishes the wicked.*" These were some of the proverbs known to everybody in my generation. Although my conception of blessing and punishment has been etherealized, or spiritualized, in the course of time, the fundamental principle of the justice of Heaven has been confirmed by my observation and experience.

Another story which touched me profoundly concerned the well-known disciple of Confucius, Min Tse-ch'ien. Tse-ch'ien lost his mother when he was a child. His father married another wife, who bore two sons. She petted her own children, but loathed Tse-ch'ien. In winter she clad him in garments made of rushes, while her own sons wore warm cotton clothes. One day as Tse-ch'ien was driving his father's chariot, his body shivered so violently that the reins dropped from his hands, for which apparent carelessness he was chastised by his father; but he refrained from making any explanation. Later, his father came to know the actual circumstance, and he was so angry at his wife's cruel partiality that he determined to divorce her. But Tse-ch'ien pleaded, saying, "If mother remains, only one son is cold; if mother goes away, three sons will be destitute." The father desisted from his purpose; and the mother was led to repentance and began to love her stepson.

I cannot help believing that this story was based upon facts. At any rate, the above words of Tse-ch'ien were on the lips of every Confucian scholar that I knew. The generosity and wisdom of this great disciple of Confucius makes one think of some of the Christian saints.

Another story I liked because it tickled my sense of humor. A six-year-old lad by the name of Lu Chi once was a guest of the celebrated general Yuan Shum, who gave him some oranges for a treat. Two of them the lad put in his bosom. This evidently was against social etiquette; for the things offered by the host to a guest were supposed to be eaten, not to be taken away secretly. As it happened, when the lad took leave of the general, bowing courteously to him, the two oranges fell out on the ground. When the general saw this, he said, "Why does my young friend, who is now a guest, put the fruit away in his bosom?" The lad, bowing again, replied, "My mother is very fond of oranges, and I wished to let her have a taste of them." The general marvelled at the filial love of the lad. But when I read the story I marvelled at his audacity in brushing aside social etiquette. I remember the book was well illustrated, and whenever I looked at the picture of the two oranges lying on the ground, I could not help chuckling over it. What a denudation!

But somehow the story which impressed me most of all was that of the old man Lao Lai Tse. He was already more than seventy years old, and had lost nearly all his teeth. But his mother was still living. In order to amuse her, he would dress himself in gaudy-colored garments, frisking and cutting capers like a child in front of her. He would sometimes take up buckets of water and try to carry them into the house; and, feigning to slip, would fall to the ground, kicking and wailing like a baby. His mother was delighted, and even his children and grandchildren were amused. Thus the whole house was

filled with the spirit of joy. I regard Lao Lai Tse as the pro-
totype of such Christian Saints as Philip Neri, the "Mystic
in motley," and Francis of Assisi, the *"jongleur de Dieu."*

I took a great fancy to this story and tried to emulate the
old boy. I too would feign to slip and fall to the ground,
cutting capers and turning somersaults, in order to amuse
my mother. But I forgot that I was not yet seventy, and
that the floor was dirty and apt to soil the new clothes which
my mother had made for me. Instead of being amused, she
used to beg me to stop it; but she knew that my intentions
were good, although my particular way of manifesting them
left much to be desired.

Unfortunately, a habit which was formed so early in life
is not easily broken. Even now, whenever God favors me with
either little crosses or great consolations, I feel an almost
irresistible impulse to throw myself on the ground and imitate the actions of Lao Lai Tse in order to win a smile from
our Blessed Mother. My dear friend Paul K. T. Sih once
caught me in the midst of such acrobatics in my bedroom,
and drew the conclusion that I was imitating Francis of
Assisi. In fact, I was only adapting the homespun style of
Lao Lai Tse to the field of spiritual life. Jokes aside, I marvel
at anyone who could serve God with a sulky face and a heavy
heart.

Another book that delighted me tremendously was *The
Book of Songs*. I did not exactly study the songs; I heard
them chanted by my elder brother. He sang them with such
spontaneous gusto and joy that even when I did not understand their letter, I imbided their spirit. One song enchanted
me most of all—*"The Song of the Quince."* No translation
can do it justice, for the simple reason that an essential part
of its charm consists in its tune. But the wording can be
faithfully rendered:

She threw a quince to me;
I requited her with a girdle-gem.
No, not just as requital,
But as a pledge of eternal love.

She threw a peach to me;
I requited her with a greenstone.
No, not just as requital,
But as a pledge of eternal love.

She threw a plum to me;
I requited her with an amulet.
No, not just as requital,
But as a pledge of eternal love.

For more than forty years this poem has been haunting me, and its meaning has grown richer and deeper for me with the passing of time.

What a beautiful sentiment is here embodied! It is "simple in conception, abounding in sensible images, and informing them all with the spirit of the mind." It fulfills the Chinese ideal of art: the impression should be as unfathomable as the ocean, while the expression should be as clear as crystal. In these few lines, the whole philosophy of love and friendship, which is the purest form of love, is shrined. For love does not count in terms of material gifts. Love is lavish. Love is generous. Love is the infinite, in the presence of which all mathematical and worldly distinctions melt and vanish into the air. Do you call it extravagant to return a greenstone for a peach? No, he says, it is not enough. She gives me a peach, because she loves me. I can only repay her love with my love.

From nine to twelve I studied at a primary school called "Han Hsiang." In those days, the *Analects* of Confucius was still used as the regular textbook for ethics. What impressed me about Confucius was his sincerity, his love of learning, and his spirit of joy. The very opening paragraph shed an atmosphere of gladness.

The master said, "Is it not a true pleasure to learn and constantly to practise what we have learnt? Is it not a real joy to have friends come to us from afar? Is it not the mark of a gentleman not to feel sad even when his merits are not recognized by others?"

This set the tone to the whole book. The great thing about the *Analects* is that the more you study it, the better it tastes. The enamored student is often like a dog gnawing and chewing at a piece of juicy bone. I want to reproduce here some of the passages which used to fascinate my mind:

The Master said, "Yu, shall I teach you what knowledge is? To know is to know; and not to know is not to know. This is knowledge."

The Master said, "In the old days man studied to cultivate his own character; nowadays men study to impress other people."

Tse-kung asked, "Is there a single saying that one can follow as the motto of life?" The Master said, "Perhaps the principle of fair dealing and consideration: 'Never do to others what you would not like them to do to yourself.'"

The Master said, "With coarse food to eat, water for drink, and a bent arm for a pillow,—even in such a state I could be happy. As for wealth and honor obtained by improper means, they are like the fleeting cloud to me."

The Master said, "What a good man was Hui! A single bamboo bowl of millet; a single ladle of cabbage soup; living in a miserable alley! Others could not have borne such

distress, but Hui never lost his spirit of joy. What a good man
was Hui!"

The Master said, "To know it is not so good as to love it.
To love it is not so good as to enjoy it."

The Duke of Shê had asked Tse Lu what he thought about
Confucius, but Tse Lu made no answer. "Why did you not
say," remarked Confucius, "that he is simply a man so eager
for improvement that he forgets his food, so happy therein
that he forgets his sorrows and the coming on of old age?"

Confucius' love of learning, so vividly painted in the pages
of the *Analects*, was infectious to me. When I was eleven,
which was twelve according to our way of reckoning age,
I came across the sentence: "I was bent upon learning at
fifteen years of age"; I was so inspired as to write on the
upper margin of the page, "I am bent upon learning at
twelve!"

The old method of teaching, which still prevailed then,
was to make us memorize and recite the whole book, word
by word, sentence by sentence, paragraph by paragraph. The
meanings were only half digested; but, like the ox, we often
found ourselves ruminating over them, chewing the cud, so
to speak, of the classics. Thus the philosophy of the ancient
sages was gradually digested and absorbed and turned into
the living tissue of our mental make-up. The great maxims
were applied in social life just as legal currency is used in
the world's commerce. I frequently heard them quoted by
my schoolmates when they were at loggerheads with each
other. When, for instance, a boy kicked at another, the latter
would say, "Has Confucius not told us not to do to another
what you do not wish to have done to yourself? Would you
like to be kicked yourself? But this is what you are doing
to me!" If the boy was not exceptionally foolhardy and irra-

tional, he would cease kicking right away. The extraordinary thing about the words of Confucius is that they are so ordinary, and therefore acceptable to average people. The great problem for the Confucians was how to be ordinary without being mediocre.

From twelve to fourteen I found myself in a secondary school, where, besides the rudiments of the natural sciences, I continued to study the Confucian classics, especially the works of Mencius, whose position in Confucianism is comparable to that of St. Paul in Christianity. What impressed me most in the works of Mencius was his doctrine of heavenly nobility as distinguished from merely human nobility. He said, "There is a nobility of Heaven, and there is a nobility of man. Love, justice, loyalty and faithfulness, with persistent and joyous cultivation of goodness,—these constitute the nobility of Heaven. To be a duke or a prime minister or a great officer,—this is but the nobility of man." The nobility of Heaven is intrinsic, and not subject to the vicissitudes of fortune. The nobility of man is extrinsic, because the honors which man can confer on you man can take away from you. The wise man, therefore, cultivates the intrinsic nobility, but remains indifferent to the extrinsic honors.

Mencius had a wonderful insight into the workings of providence. He said, "Whenever Heaven wants to confer a great work on anyone, it first drenches his heart with bitterness, submits his nerves and his bones to weariness, delivers his members and his whole body to hunger, reduces him to the most extreme indigence, thwarts and upsets all his enterprises. By this means, it wakens in him good sentiments, fortifies his patience, and communicates to him what was still lacking in him." He illustrated this principle with the events of history. "From these things," he concluded, "we see how life springs from sorrow and tribulations, while death results from ease and pleasure." One can hardly imagine how deeply this philosophy of suffering has influenced the Chinese outlook on life. During the last war, the most popular poster seen on the walls in China was: "When you hear of victory, don't be elated. When you hear of defeats, don't be disheartened." This, I submit, is the secret magic that has pulled China through so many national crises. Any philosophy that keeps one humble in prosperity and hopeful in adversity cannot be very far from the spirit of Christianity.

Perhaps the most celebrated aphorism of Mencius was: "The great man is one who has not lost the heart he had as a child." This prepared my mind to appreciate the words of Christ: "Believe me, unless you become like little children again, you shall not enter the kingdom of Heaven."

On the cultivation of the interior life, Mencius has said something which has influenced me profoundly:

What belongs to the superior man cannot be increased by the largeness of his sphere of action, nor diminished by his dwelling in poverty and retirement . . . What belongs to his nature are love, justice, propriety and knowledge. These are rooted in his heart; they manifest themselves as a mild harmony appearing in his countenance, a rich fullness in his back. They spread even to the four limbs; and the four limbs seem to understand without being told.

This tallies very well with the spiritual doctrine of St. Benedict and St. John of the Cross.

Whenever I think of Confucius and Mencius, Buddha and Lao Tse, I am inclined to call them—as St. Justin Martyr called Socrates, Plato, and Aristotle—"Pedagogues to lead men to Christ."

Monsignor Kolbe, in his little book on *The Art of Life*, has written:

The light that enlighteneth every man coming into this world must have shone with special strength into the souls of those who so earnestly felt after the Truth, Goodness and Beauty, which, whether they knew it or not, is God: and every human response to this Divine shining is of the nature of faith. "The Spirit of the Lord hath filled the whole earth"; and I cannot but think that it is with some degree of the virtue of faith helping their natural insight that such men as Buddha and Plato reached their moral level. There is something very touching in these early efforts after perfection, and like all early art they sometimes produce simple effects which are beyond our reach in these more conscious days.

What he says about Buddha and Plato applies also to Confucius and Mencius.

Before concluding this chapter, I want to give some glimpse of my school life. In those days, the Western influence had already made itself felt in the schools. Side by side with the old classics, we were taught the rudiments of the natural sciences, such as geography, botany, zoology and even bits of astronomy. I still remember the thrill of joy I experienced in knowing that the earth was a round ball rather than a square block resting on the back of the fabulous Tortoise. When the teacher illustrated to us how the eclipses of the sun by the moon happened, I felt as though I was introduced into an entirely new Universe fresh from the hands of the wonderful Creator. When I learned how the tadpoles were transformed into frogs, and caterpillars into butterflies, I felt as though I was living in a fairyland.

The school curriculum was actually a hotch-potch of the old and new. The new subjects were taught by the new method of experimentation, while the old were taught by the traditional method of memorization. I was more and more attracted by the new, and I acquired a kind of aversion for the old. Aside from a few sentences which I could understand and apply in daily life, the bulk of the old classics was simply rammed down my throat, in the same way as a laxative medicine, to my great resentment.

English was already the second language in all schools. I began to learn it in the primary school at the age of nine. After teaching the alphabet, the first sentence the teacher taught us was: "Fie, is that so?" In fact, the teacher himself was not an accomplished scholar in English. I suspect that he learned that sentence from books, or composed it by consulting the dictionary. The Chinese are a people addicted to sighing, sighing over the events of the world or the vicissitudes of life. But this is beside the point. The odd thing is that I liked English from the very beginning. It takes a great deal more memory to learn Chinese characters than to master the English ones. In the case of Chinese, there is no spelling system, with the result that although you know the meaning of a word you often do not know how to pronounce it. The experience is just as embarrassing as if you were to meet the familiar face of an acquaintance whose name has slipped your memory. With English it is different. Although you may put the accent on the wrong syllable, as I so often do even now, you can at least pronounce it in such a way as to make yourself understood. Then you have grammatical rules to go by. The Chinese language has its own grammar, but we were never taught it in the schools. Anyway I loved English at the first sight. Later my interest in it grew by reading the English translations of Chinese classics and essays which I loved so much. For instance, I loved the essay of Tao Yuan-ming on "The Peach-Blossom Fountain." Then

I read Herbert Giles' version of it in order to see how the same things were presented in English. When I was impressed by some of the pithy sayings of Confucius, I referred to the version of James Legge to see how Confucius would speak if he had been an English gentleman. Thus, curiosity was the nurse of my English. I still think that this is the best way to learn English, or any foreign language, for that matter. The only drawback was that when I began to talk in English, people remarked that I talked like a book. I said, "Oh, no, you are too polite with me." I thought it was a compliment, because to a Chinese student, it would be a great thing to talk like a book. Later, in 1918, I learned French under the tutorship of the Jesuit Father Tosten. He also used the French translations of some of the famous Chinese essays and poems for instruction. But I have never mastered French in the same degree as English, because I am afraid of its conjugations, genders, modes and liaisons. The English language is becoming more and more popular in Europe. It is *the* language of the commercial world.

Of course, I have not forgotten my mother-tongue. I *think* in English, but I *feel* in Chinese. That is why I have produced only Chinese poems. I sometimes sing in French and make jokes in German. As for Italian, my children speak it fluently, but I have not mastered a single sentence. You simply cannot teach an old monkey new tricks.

As I have said, ever since my falling from the tightrope, I had given up my ambitions to be an athlete. At the secondary school, I did not participate in football or the high jump. But I was one of the champions at the kicking of shuttlecocks. For that reason, my schoolmates nicknamed me "Wooden Rooster." This expression they took from a parable which we had learned in our class in Chinese Literature.

The parable, a selection from the writings of Chuang Tzu, is as follows:

Chi Hsing-tzu was rearing a fighting cock for the king. Being asked after ten days if the bird were ready, he said, "Not yet; he is still vain and quarrelsome, and relies on his own vigor." Being asked the same question after another ten days, he said, "Not yet; he still responds to the crow and appearance of another bird." After ten days more, he replied, "Not yet. He still looks angry, and is full of spirit." When a fourth ten days had passed, he replied, "Nearly ready. Though another cock crows, it makes no change in him. To look at him, you would say he was a cock of wood. His quality is complete. No other cock will dare to meet him, but will run from him."

From that I infer that I must have looked very dull to my schoolmates. On the other hand, I must have played better than they had expected from my appearance. It is significant that the parable should have come from the hands of the great Taoist master Chuang Tzu. Perhaps I am a Taoist by nature, covering my discretion under the coat of folly. But my poker face is not an affectation; I was born that way.

6. ADAM AND EVE

After the death of my mother, I stayed at home for several months. Thenceforward my elder brother and his wife took care of me in lieu of my parents, until my marriage in 1916, when my wife became a mother to me. But before my marriage, whenever I was home from school, on holidays and during the summer and winter vacations, my elder brother always kept me company by sleeping together with me in the same room. We occupied two beds, with some of our manservants sleeping on the floor. It is to the credit of my sister-in-law that she never complained about it. She is by nature high-tempered, but she certainly treated me very well. My brother is one of the kindliest men I have known. Whenever he was not drunk, he was always cheerful and full of genial humor. He treated our servants like brothers, and he treated his brother like a king. Each night, even after we had gone to bed, we cracked jokes at each other, and whenever we heard the servants snoring or talking in dreams, we had a jolly time of it. I remember once we laughed so loud over the dream-talk of a boy that our laughter was somehow woven into the texture of his dream; so he howled at us, "Damn it, what are you laughing about?" The joke was on us.

In China elder brothers do not bully their brothers. On the contrary they exercise a kind of protective care over them. But an elder brother like mine is a rarity even in China.

Nine years my senior, he was brought up as a child in the pure Confucian tradition. After several years of intensive study of the Chinese classics under the private tutorship of a first-rate Confucian scholar, he was sent by my father to St. Joseph's School in our native town. It was a Catholic school run by French Lazarists. The language they used in instruction was, however, not French but English. This throws a sidelight on the stress laid upon English even then. My brother did not become a Catholic till 1946, but his impression of those kind priests who taught him was so deep that he never wearied of praising them. He regretted very much that that group of missionaries had to return home for some reason or another. He told me how touching the scene of their departure was. With tears in their eyes, and waving their hands from the departing boat, they called out to the boys, "Adieu!" He told me that he did not understand what "Adieu" meant, but that the way they said it attested their deep emotions. It was not until many years later, when I began to learn French, that I came to know the meaning of that word, and I told my brother about it.

After that group of priests went away, I think St. Joseph's was closed down. At any rate, my brother did not graduate from the school, and his education ended, for he was sent to a native bank as an apprentice. As my father was getting old, it was but natural that he should desire his eldest son

to learn business, so that he could take care of all his interests
in the sixty-odd partnerships, in case he should pass away.
My father was not an enterprising businessman. He had
helped to organize those partnerships for the principal purpose of securing jobs for his friends and relatives. But at
that time all business concerns were of unlimited liability,
as the modern laws of corporations had not yet been introduced. I remember on two occasions my father was made to
pay a hundred times the capital he had put in. After his
death, my brother had the good sense to withdraw our shares
from the less dependable partnerships, and we had enough
money to live on and to pay for my tuition. Without such
an unselfish brother, I would never have been able to receive
a university education and to pursue my advanced studies
abroad. When I reflect how much he has done for me and
how little I have done for him, I feel utterly confounded.

By the time I was fifteen my interest had taken a turn for
natural science. So I went to Hsiao Shih Junior College in
my native town, which laid a special emphasis on such
courses as algebra, geometry, chemistry, and physics, in order
to prepare the students for the study of engineering. I won
good marks in all of these; particularly in physics I always
stood at the top of the class. During the hours of self-study,
many of my classmates used to flock to my desk with "Mil-
likan and Gale" in their hands to ask me to explain to them
some of the more obscure passages. I remember this with a
certain sense of pride, because some of them whom I used
to coach in the elementary principles of science have actually
turned out to be engineers, although I, who to all appearances
was cut out for engineering, have ended by being a philosopher building castles in the air.

After two years' stay in that school, I was admitted to
the Baptist College of Shanghai, where I continued to pur-

sue the study of the sciences. One day, as I was in the chemistry laboratory experimenting on hydrogen, my curiosity got the better of me. I wanted to see how the hydrogen would burn in the bottle. I tried to light it with a match, but immediately the bottle burst into pieces. Somehow I did not get hurt, although I was peeping closely into it. On the very next day a similar accident happened to a classmate, but he was not so lucky, for one of his eyes was so badly hurt as to become blind. I suddenly realized that I had got away with it by sheer luck, and began to wonder if a peeping Tom like myself who could not control his whimsical curiosity was fit to handle the elements and atoms so full of potential explosive energies. It seemed to me to take a ton of patience and self-control together with one ounce of imagination and logical reasoning to make a scientific discoverer or inventor. Just as I was speculating on my life career, another classmate of mine, Hsu Tse-mou, came around and announced to me his decision to go to the Peiyang University in T'ientsin to study law. He asked me whether I would like to join him. My heart leaped on hearing the word "law." To my mind, law was the science of society just as science was the law of nature. "A good idea!" I said. So we decided to take the entrance examination which was being offered in Shanghai. Both of us passed the test. That was in the winter of 1916. In April 1916 I was married.

In *The Merchant of Venice*, Shakespeare makes Nerissa declare:

> The ancient saying is no heresy:
> "Hanging and wiving goes by destiny."

I don't know about hanging; as to wiving I am perfectly sure that it goes by destiny. In fact there was a current

Chinese proverb which I knew as a child: *Every marriage was predetermined five hundred years before its consummation.*

My wife and I had never seen each other before our wedding, which occurred on April 12, 1916. Both of us were pagans and brought up in the old Chinese way. It was our parents who engaged us to each other, when we were barely six years of age. In my early 'teens, I came to know where her house was. I had an intense desire to have a glimpse of her. In coming back from school, I sometimes took a round-about way so as to pass by the door of her house at the foot of the T'ai Ho Ch'iao, or the "Bridge of Celestial Harmony," in the hope that she might be leaning at the door. But I never had the good fortune to see her.

I have compared notes with my wife and have concluded that our engagement happened this way. When I was six, I was brought by my father to his bank to spend a day there. The manager of the bank next to my father's sent a boy to fetch me to his bank, and he feted me with fruits and everything. I took supper with him, and all the time he was silently beaming at me. I certainly had lived a day as a prince. At night I returned home in my father's sedan-chair.

I did not know why that friend of my father had treated me with such kindness and had smiled at me with such sweetness. It was only later that I came to know that he had chosen me to be the husband of his second daughter! My wife recollects that on the very day when he had seen me, he returned home in the highest spirits, telling her mother, "I have found a husband for Ah-Yu." He even teased his six-year-old daughter by saying, "Ah-Yu, I have got a boy for you. He is handsome and clever!" My wife did not have any reaction at all, because she did not know what "husband" was, thinking that it was humbug.

Nor did I know what "wife" was. I only knew that whatever my father did for me could not but be good. Later I came to realize that I was betrothed to the daughter of that sweet elderly man who had treated me like a prince. I met him many times, and I called him "father-in-law." A genuine affection developed between us. I had such love for him that later, whenever I was angry with my wife, I needed only to remind myself that she was the daughter of her father in order to turn my anger into something like tenderness.

Although I was engaged not by my own will, I had absolutely no doubt that the one to whom my parents had matched me was predestined to be my wife. In one sense, such a betrothal had a greater dignity than the civil engagement by the free choice of the parties; because it was, as it were, registered in Heaven. If one has chosen one's own fiancee, one is liable to wonder at times if one has made the right choice. If, on the other hand, one believes, as we did, that every marriage is made in Heaven, there could be no room for regret, any more than Adam could have regretted that only Eve and none other was given to him.

You can easily imagine then how eagerly I was looking forward to meeting my predestined wife. At long, long last, the day of the wedding arrived. My wife arrived in the flowery-chair. As soon as she got out of the chair, we had to undergo all the complicated marital rites of the old days, including among other ceremonies the *kowtowing* to the tablet on which were written the five characters: Heaven, Earth, Nation, Parents, Teachers. During the ceremony, as we were standing side by side, I tried to look at her through the corner of my eyes, but I did not see her face, because it was heavily veiled. I remember that some of the guests, espying my furtive looks at her, put their fingers on their cheeks, signifying that I was a cheeky bridegroom.

When the ceremony of *kowtowing* was over, we were led into the bridal chamber, where we were placed in front of our bed and made to drink to each other the "love-wine" out of twin cups carved from the same piece of wood. It was only then that I looked my wife in the face, and I loved her at the first sight. She did not see me even then, for she was too bashful to lift her eyes.

After the drinking of the love-wine, we were again led out into the hall to perform many other ceremonies, such as bowing to the elder relatives and friends, and receiving the homage of our nephews and nieces. At the banquet, which was offered in the evening, we served the wine to all the guests. It was not until midnight that we were again led into the bridal chamber and left alone. At last, the door was closed and the guests were shut out, although the more curious ones still tarried in the antechamber to listen to our conversation. May God forgive their itching ears!

As soon as I found myself alone with my wife, a fit of bashfulness overcame both of us. We remained silent for some moments, which seemed very long. She was too shy and too good to open her mouth first, because she knew that for a wife to speak first would be an omen that the husband would be henpecked. On my part, I was fumbling in my mind for some appropriate subject-matter of conversation. Suddenly I remembered her father, who had been so kind to me when he was living. So I started the conversation stutteringly, thus: "It is too bad, isn't it, that Father-in-law has died? Otherwise how happy he would feel today!"

She looked at me ominously, and answered, "Oh yes, Father was so fond of you."

Another embarrassing silence ensued. I made an attempt to resume the conversation by remarking, "It is too bad, isn't it, that my father should have died so early?"

She looked at me with visible sadness on her face, but remained silent. I thought she was not too easy to talk to. After some moments, I said, "It is too bad, isn't it, that my mother should have died two years ago, when we were scheduled to be wed?"

This time she did not even look at me. I thought it was about time to change the subject, so I asked, "Do you know how to read and write?"

"No," she answered. "Just as I was starting to go to school, your mother sent word to my mother that she would not like to see her future daughter-in-law educated in the modern way."

"Ugh, ugh, that I did not know," was my curt comment.

But I wondered why the bride was so sulky. Did I offend her by mentioning our dear parents? How could that be? The truth is that her mother had taught her that in her first conversation with me there should be no mention of death or anything of that sort, as that would augur ill. I did not know that kind of superstition, as I had no mother to teach me. As it happened, I mentioned death three times in "opening my golden mouth," as a bridegroom's first words to his bride were popularly called in those days. It was only later that my wife confessed to me what she thought of me at the first conversation. She took me for a lunatic, and I don't blame her for that.

Humanly speaking, no marital life could have begun more inauspiciously. But Christ, Who is the Light, has swept away all the cobwebs of superstition in which we were caught like a pair of butterflies struggling in a spider's web. Truth has made us free, and freedom has made us happy.

To the Western reader, the old Chinese marriage system must appear inconceivable. I remember that when I told my dear friend Dom Edouard Neut, the Belgian Benedictine, about it, he simply could not believe it. All amazed and amused, he asked me, "Do you mean to say that you actually had not seen your wife before you were married?! How could that be?" On my part, I was amazed by his amazement and amused by his amusement. I said to him, "Father, did you choose your parents, your brothers and your sisters? And yet you love them all the same."

God has given a good wife to me, just as He has given me good parents, a good brother and sister, a good body and a good mind, good children, and a good country. I am not trying to justify the old system of marriage, but to make you understand the psychology that made it possible. The same thing is true with the education of women. In the old days, there were no schools for women. The few women writers we have had in history were educated at home, and they were the exceptions. In my childhood days, a girl from a respectable family seen walking on the streets would be talked about in the whole city of Ningpo. So it was quite natural that my wife did not learn to read. But she was *educated* in the family tradition, though not through the reading of books. She was taught by her mother how to behave like a woman, how to perform the domestic duties, etc., with the result that she is full of common sense, which after all is so uncommon. As to her religious faith, she was brought up in exactly the same kind of spiritual atmosphere as I was: the anonymous indigenous religion of the Chinese people, the religion of Heaven and good conscience, the faith that God sees everything, that He prospers the good and punishes the wicked, that all the minor deities are His emissaries, that all religions have but one purpose—to make men good, that to help others is in the long run to help yourself and your children, for God is just and merciful. This is the fundamental faith of the Chinese people. It is the ocean in which they swim freely, whereas the three religions are but the waves of the ocean.

In other words, it was in the atmosphere of a simple and sincere natural religion that both my wife and I were brought up. We even regarded our children as gifts from God. My wife became pregnant in the latter part of 1917. But after three months she had a miscarriage. Again an inauspicious beginning! It was not until the winter of 1918 that our first child Tsu-ling (later baptized Thomas) was born. We were still under twenty and we became parents! There was a real thrill in the experience. This was the first of our fourteen children, of whom thirteen have been preserved and adopted by God through baptism, and one boy is in limbo through my negligence.

My wife and I have often speculated together as to what kind of children we would have had if the first one had not miscarried, for it would have been impossible for Thomas to have come at the time he did, and that in turn would have affected our second boy, Edward. Then we have said to each other, "Oh, let us not speculate vainly on these mysteries. Whatever God does cannot be but for our good." The fact is, the more you procreate, the more mysterious birth and life appear to you. How is it that each child has his own individuality and personality? Certainly we parents are only junior partners with God in the matter of creation. It is an ever-growing wonder to me that all our children are so good and filial to us. They seem to take great pleasure in serving me, their unworthy father. In my youth, I often wished that I had a younger brother; now God has given me thirteen younger brothers and sisters in my children, and I am still the baby of the house! Once I went with Thomas to see an aged friend of mine, Mr. Yu Ya-ching, a prominent businessman of Shanghai. The old man asked, "Is this your

brother?" I said, "No, he is my son." The old man laughed
and said, "I thought he was your elder brother!"

The fact is, due to my lack of practical ability, all my
children have to take care of themselves, they have to work
hard, and therefore easily get old. As for me, who am a carefree mystic, the currents of time have touched me but
slightly. Even in my darkest days, I have felt a secret joy
bubbling from the fountain of my heart, so much so that I
have often recalled the striking words of St. Paul: "as dying
and behold, we live, as chastised but not killed, as sorrowful
yet always rejoicing, as poor yet enriching many, as having
nothing yet possessing all things" (2 Cor. 6.9–10).

7. JOHN IS MY NAME

Just after my marriage in 1916 I had an altercation with my brother. By that time the Western influence had begun to work on my mind. Among other things, Emerson's essay on "Self-Reliance" had wakened me to my individuality. I proposed to my brother to have our property divided and to set up separate kitchens. That sounded like a family revolution to my brother's ears, and you can imagine how deeply offended he must have been then. His ideal was for brothers "to live together in the same hall for five generations," to quote a current saying. My maxim was that "there should be no two women in one kitchen." I said to him, "It is better to be small men in the beginning and gentlemen in the end than vice versa. Brothers should help each other in times of need, but each must help himself first. If our families share one kitchen together, in the long run the togetherness will be merely physical, while the hearts will be wide apart. On the other hand, if we live separately, we shall continue to love and help each other to the end of our lives."

Emerson was not entirely responsible for this philosophy of mine; I had witnessed with my own eyes how unpleasant were the relations between my mother and my sister-in-law. At last my brother yielded to my wishes, and we set up separate kitchens in the same house and had our property divided. But he was so generous as to continue to take care of the shares we held in common, making detailed accounts to me at the end of every year. It was thus that I was able to pay my way through the university and even to pursue my further studies in America.

In the spring of 1917, my old companion Tse-mou and I found ourselves in the Peiyang University, studying law. Before the semester ended, however, the announcement was made that the law school was going to be amalgamated with the law school of Peking University as from the next academic year. Well, T'ientsin was far enough from home, and Peking was farther north. Wasn't I newly married? I would not go to Peking, but would rather go to school in Shanghai, where it would be feasible to have my wife come to join me. Now it happened that the Comparative Law School of China had recently been opened in Shanghai under the auspices of the American Methodist Mission. The school enjoyed quite a reputation. In the fall of 1917 I registered myself as John Wu.

Nothing could be more casual than the way I came to adopt the name "John." As I have said, in the Spring of 1917 I was a student of law at Peiyang University. Now in those days there was a vogue among Chinese students to adopt Western names. Some of us, at any rate, worshipped the heroes of the West such as George Washington, Abraham Lincoln, William Shakespeare, and many others. One day, my fellow-student Hsu Tse-mou and myself decided also to pick up some names for ourselves. Tse-mou chose for himself "Hamilton," because he aspired to be a great Constitutionalist and economist. Thereafter he was to be called Hamilton Hsu. But later he turned out to be a poet of no mean order; and I think that was the reason why he dropped the adopted name.

As for me, I worshipped so many heroes that I could not decide upon any one. So I referred to the "Proper Names" section of Webster's Dictionary. I was running through the section alphabetically. When I came upon "John," I felt there was something arresting about it. I read it aloud many times, "John, John, John. . . ." "Why," I said to myself, "this sounds exactly like my Chinese name *Ching-hsiung!*" The fact is, when my schoolmates called me Ching-hsiung, they said it so quickly that the two syllables were merged into one, sounding very much like John. Therefore, this name suited me like a glove. What if the glove was imported, so long as it fitted my hand? I did not care which John I was following. Anyway there were John Marshall, John Keats, John Wesley, John Webster, John Falstaff, and King John. So I thought I was in fairly good company. But the interesting thing is that a name that was adopted so casually should have come to stay. From thenceforward, I have been known as John Wu, and I hope I shall be John Wu to the end of my life.

The Dean of the Law School was Charles W. Rankin from Tennessee. He was about forty then, still a bachelor. Besides being a good teacher and dean, he was full of the spirit of love and self-sacrifice. His asceticism impressed all his students. Taken all in all, he was one of the most devout Christians I have seen in my life. He called his students "Brother Chang," and "Brother Wu." We called him "Brother Rankin."

The classes were held in the evenings, from five to eight.

There were no regular professors except Rankin himself, but practically all the famous lawyers in Shanghai, including Judge Lobingier of the U. S. Court for China, were on the faculty as lecturers on particular branches of the law. The students were mostly grown-up people who had work to do in the daytime. One of them was fifty years old. I was the youngest. I remember an interesting thing happened on the day of my registration. I went to see the dormitory and met a sophomore student, who asked me, "What are *you* doing here?" I told him that I was just admitted. "What!" he said. "Look at these big textbooks and case-books. We have to read about a hundred pages a day. How can you catch up with the assignments, a young boy like you?" Neither he nor I could foresee that I would be the first honor man for six terms consecutively. Still less did we dream that I was some day to be the Principal of that very school. Life is certainly full of surprises, pleasant as well as unpleasant.

Besides the courses on legal subjects, there was a class on religion, taught by Rankin. We were required to read the Bible, and I fell in love with it. Also, the edifying example of Rankin made me search for the living source of his spirit of purity and love. And then the textbook we used on religion, James Orr's *The Christian View of God and the World*, impressed me deeply. The author gave a bird's-eye view of the Christian philosophy; he wrote beautifully of Christ; he had a clear idea of the doctrine of the Trinity. I still have the book with me; my underlining in blue and red, which was done more than thirty years ago, looks still as fresh as if it were done yesterday. Here is what he wrote about the Incarnation:

Incarnation is not simply the endowment of human nature with highest conceivable plenitude of gifts and graces;

it is not mere dynamical relation of God to the human spirit
—acting on it or in it with exceptional energy; it is not simply the coming to consciousness of the metaphysical unity
all along subsisting between humanity and God; it is not
even such moral union, such spiritual indwelling and oneness of character and will, as subsists between God and
the believer; still less, of course, is it analogous to the heathen
ideas of sons of the gods in human guise—or even of temporary appearances of gods in humanity, as in the case of
the Avatars of Vishnu. The Scriptural ideal of the Incarnation is as unique as is the Biblical conception as a whole. It
is not, to state the matter in a word, the union simply of the
Divine nature with the human,—for that I acknowledge in
the case of every believer through the indwelling Spirit,—but
the entrance of a Divine Person into the human.

There is an immanent presence of God in nature, but there
is also a transcendent existence of God beyond nature. So the
Divine Son took upon Him our nature with its human limits,
but above and beyond that, if we may so express it, was the
vast "oversoul" of His Divine consciousness.[1]

On Christianity as a lever of civilization, James Orr had the
following to say:

We know something of what Christianity did in the
Roman Empire as a power of social purification and reform;
of what it did in the Middle Ages in the Christianizing and
disciplining of barbarous nations; of the power it has been
in modern times as the inspiration of the great moral and
philanthropic movements of the century; and this power of
Christianity is likely to be yet greater in the future than in
the past.[2]

Writing in the last decade of the last century, he affirmed:

Like a bark above the waters, Christ's religion will ride in

[1] Scribner's (New York, 1893), pp. 241, 243.
[2] Ibid., p. 330.

safety the waves of present-day unbelief, as it has ridden the
waves of unbelief in days gone by, bearing in it the hopes of
the future of humanity.[3]

At the close of the book, I wrote in pencil: "I thank the
author for his edifying words."

To make a long story short, thanks to the influence of the
Bible and this book and to the edifying example of Brother
Rankin, I was brought into my first contact with Christ, and
was baptized in the Methodist Church in the winter of 1917;
and it was only then that I knew I was named after the
Beloved Disciple.

When, twenty years later, I came to embrace the Catholic
Faith, the same name was retained at my conditional Baptism. But only recently have I come to know that "John"
means "God has been gracious," which sums up the story
of my life.

After I became a Catholic, I naturally began to take interest in the Daily Missal. My birthday being March 28, I was
curious to find out which saint it was whose feast happened
to be on that day. To my greatest astonishment, I discovered
it was St. John of Capistrano! What is more interesting still,
he was by profession a lawyer just like myself!

It is evident that I could not have chosen my own birthday. Nor did I really choose my own name John, because
had my parents given me any other name than "Ching-
hsiung" or rather "Ching-yong," as it is pronounced in my
native place, Ningpo, I could hardly have arrived at "John."
The long and short of it is that God has been gracious and
arranged everything sweetly for me.

Those who have not got the faith would, perhaps, think
that all this is a mere coincidence. But to me it is more than
that; it is Providence. Can it also be a mere coincidence, for

[3] *Ibid.*, p. 347.

instance, that the saintly Abbot Dom Pierre Celestine Lou, who gave the *Nihil Obstat* to my Chinese version of the New Testament, should have taken a special fancy to my translation of the Gospel of St. John? I myself felt most at home in translating the Epistles of St. Paul. But the Abbot thought that the version of St. John's Gospel was my masterpiece! In his posthumous book, *La Rencontre des Humanités*, he has written something which puts me under an eternal debt to him. "The whole evangelical account and exposition of St. John," he writes, "attains for us Chinese, in this so faithful version of Mr. Wu Ching-hsiung, a beauty and a profundity that the versions in alphabetic languages could never equal—for us!" As if this were not enough, he continues to say, "It offers to us the announcement of the Good News in such a manner that, as I am intimately assured, St. John himself would have presented and written it, if God had disposed that he should be a Chinese and had made him one." He might be wrong, but I have the greatest respect for the sincerity and judgment of a man who had the courage to stand against the whole world in refusing grimly to sign, on behalf of China, the Versailles Treaty at the conclusion of the first World War.

I have quoted these words not to glorify myself, but to reveal the mysterious ways of God in guiding one of his little children. As the holy Abbot has so well put it, "My friend Wu Ching-hsiung and myself, we have, furthermore, only one thing to desire and to look forward to: that the eyes and hearts of all men should open themselves more and more, in order to see and receive Jesus, as much as He deigns to reveal and give Himself,—and as for us, let us disappear." This is highly suggestive to me; for, although I am named after St. John the beloved disciple, I have also a particular veneration for St. John the Baptist, who was sensible enough

to say, "*He must increase: I must decrease.*" In fact, all
apostles of Christ are His harbingers like the Baptist. Anyway, it does no harm to follow the Beloved Disciple in the
spirit of the Baptist. I myself do not know which of the two
is dearer to me. Sometimes I think of myself in terms of the
one, at other times the other. I choose both to be my patron
saints. In fact, I regard all the saints in heaven as my patrons.
Christ being our sole Love, we can make friends with all His
friends without being an idolater or an eclectic. The universality of our love is a necessary consequence of its integrity.

   In this connection, let me introduce a letter which I
received years ago from one of my dearest friends, John C.
Ferguson, who was a Quaker and a great sinologue. I had
published, in January of 1940, an article in the *T'ien Hsia
Monthly* called "Thoughts and Fancies," under the pen-
name of "Lucas Yu." Dr. Ferguson read the article in Pei-
ping, and he was so moved by it that he wrote to my friend
T. K. Chuan in the most glowing terms. "I am enclosing a
note for Lucas Yu," he said, "whom of course I recognize at
first glance. He has written beautifully and in most appealing
words. This is an article which is bound to be immortal and
will be quoted when every other article in *T'ien Hsia* has
been forgotten, for it treats of an immortal theme." Whether
this is true or not I have no way of judging. Nor can such
praises swell my head; because ever since my becoming a
Catholic all praises of my work have sounded in my ears like
words addressed to another person. If there is anything good
in what I do or in what I say, it belongs to the Holy Ghost;
and the rest is the earthenware. What interests me here is to
show that the John in me could not be hidden even under
the name of Lucas. As you will see, he took me to be named
after the Baptist. Another touching thing is to see how the
Johns loved each other. John Ferguson has gone to his reward.

John Wu is still a pilgrim in this valley of tears. I treasure the memory of Dr. Ferguson so dearly in my heart that I beg my reader's indulgence in reproducing the whole note, which was the only letter he ever wrote to me:

> 3 Hsi-Chiao Hutung,
> Peiping, China,
> Jan. 30, 1940.

Lucas, my fellow labourer,
    (Philemon 24)

Your "Thoughts and Fancies" in the current number of T'ien Hsia has touched me deeply. I heard that, like Chesterton, you had gone to Rome but could not have guessed from your recent translations of poetry and of the Tao Teh Ching that your conversion would have put you in such a glow. Your state of mind reminds me of many persons whom I saw in my boyhood. They had a sudden Enlightenment of spirit which radiated in their faces. It was then called conversion or turning to the Lord. Not that I have ever believed the delusion of so many occidentals that your countrymen are stolid; my observation is that they are highly emotional, and I am glad that your decision to be a Christian has affected your heart for it seems to me that no religious truth is ever actually understood or appreciated unless it stirs the heart.

I like your article for it opens a long-hoped-for era in the long struggle of Christianity in China. I have lamented its failure to reach some one who could express his convictions in language which would carry its own appeal, and as far as I know you have done so for the first time among Christian converts in your great country. Hsu Kuang-chi was more or less a governmental convert and Li Chih-tsao a scientific one. Ma Hsiang-pe had a deep religious experience but he was fickle. Now that you have expressed yourself in English in sentences which will prove immortal can you not also turn yourself to do so once again in your own language?

The pity of the revolution and the rise of a modern China has been that its leaders who have mostly been Christians and have owed their inspiration to Christian teachings have been dumb as to their religion. Sun Wen, and his son Sun Fo, could have increased their influence many fold if they had given expression to their religious convictions in the same way as one of their followers J. Usang Ly. It is a great pity that instead of meeting Joffe or Borodin, Dr. Sun had not met an Augustin or an Ambrose of Milan and that Gen. Chiang instead of Donald had not had a man like Gordon or Lawrence. Our recent history would have been different.

As a Christian I welcome you into the Christian Church and pray that you become "a burning and a shining light" like an earlier John (John 5.35). Whether as John or as Lucas I salute you with mine own hand. The grace of our Lord Jesus Christ be with you always.

Your brother in the Gospel

John C. Ferguson

Let me mention another thrilling experience that I owe to my name. It was after the death of my beloved friend Justice Oliver Wendell Holmes that I became a Catholic. I have often thought of him and remembered him in my prayers, especially on his birthday, which is March 8. What was my happiness to discover that March 8 is the Feast of St. John of God! He possibly did not know it himself. But who can tell that St. John of God had nothing to do with drawing us together? After the fashion of Holmes, I am inclined to say that while my reason tells me that such things do not matter much, "my feelings still have some of the illusions of youth."

Since my coming to Honolulu, I have come to know two other Johns, or rather three, whom I hold nearest to my heart. One is Father John Francis Linn of the Sulpicians. He is the head of the St. Stephen's Seminary, which is hidden in the midst of mountains. But when he comes to town, he often drops in at my house. He is one of the most charming personalities I have ever met, a man of burning charity and profound wisdom. I met him about a year ago; I was drawn to him from the very start, and he has been my spiritual director ever since. But until recently I did not know his first name, as I always called him Father Linn, which, by the way, sounds very Chinese. About two weeks ago, as I was musing on the friendship of this holy priest which had meant so much to me, an intuition flashed through my mind. I said to myself, "I wonder what is the name of Father Linn. I bet that it must be John!" So I phoned Father Eugene Morin, Chancellor of the Diocese, to inquire about it; and my hunch was confirmed! He is not only John, but Francis, another name for which I have a special predilection.

The second John is a layman, Jean Charlot. I admire his art, but I admire his personality even more. In fact, his art and his spiritual life are inseparable. He prays with his brush. In his case, genius is duly subordinated to grace. Both Jean and his wife Zohmah are so dear to me that I cannot help thanking God for giving me their friendship. Of their children, I am partial to John Charlot, Jr. Once Zohmah brought John to my class on Christian Mysticism. After the lecture, John remarked to his mother, not in my own hearing, "I like Dr. Wu. He is so wise!" It was the first time in my life, so far as I can remember, that I was called "wise." Indeed, it takes a John to recognize a John!

8. THE HOUND OF HEAVEN

For the first few years after my conversion to Methodism, I was quite a zealous Christian, praying constantly and visiting the poor. I graduated from Law School in the summer of 1920, and in the autumn I found myself sailing on board the S.S. *Nanking* to the United States. I used to steal out from my cabin when my roommates were fast asleep to the stern of the ship, where I would pray on my knees for an hour or so. I did it for fifteen nights, and I was not seen by anyone but God. On the Pacific Ocean I was praying for the meeting of the East and the West and for the peace of the world. When the sky was clear and the moon shining, and the stars scintillating above and around me, I felt as though I were no longer in this world, and enjoyed some moments of eternity. I would recall what I had read in the Psalms:

> When I consider thy heavens, the work of thy
> fingers,
> The moon and the stars, which thou hast ordained;

What is man, that thou art mindful of him?
And the son of man, that thou visitest him?
For thou hast made him but little lower than the
        angels,
And hast crowned him with glory and honor.
Thou makest him to have dominion over the works
        of thy hands;
Thou hast put all things under his feet:
All sheep and oxen,
Yea, and the beasts of the field,
The birds of the heavens, and the fish of the sea,
Whatever passes through the paths of the seas.

Oh, the joy of it! I felt as free and happy as the birds of the
heavens and the fish of the sea. Although away from my
home, I did not feel homesick; I saw my spiritual horizons
opening boundlessly before me. That maiden trip of mine
was really like a honeymoon with Jesus. But alas! the honeymoon was not to last very long. Soon afterwards I was to
desert Him for a long, long period before I came to be united
with Him again. I sneaked away from His house, as it were,
by the back door. When I returned, He opened the front
gate to welcome me back, and this time he introduced me
to His Mother! He said, "John, behold thy Mother!"

But where am I? I am anticipating too much.

In the fall of 1920, I found myself pursuing my post-
graduate work in the Michigan Law School at Ann Arbor.
I was engrossed in my studies, and by imperceptible degrees
my interest and faith in Christianity waned. I ceased to pray
and to go to church. In the meantime I was scandalized at
hearing my American schoolmates swear in the most irreverent manner by the name of Christ. In the janitor's quarters
they were wishing one another to become millionaires in
the future. Now Mr. Rankin had given me to understand
that the American civilization was founded on Christianity.

By this time I was completely disillusioned about this observation. I found to my greatest surprise that the almighty dollar was America's God! I believe that the situation is much better now; but there is no denying that a generation ago, practically every young man that I met was aspiring to be a millionaire, and the more ambitious ones wanted to be multi-millionaires. I asked myself, "Is this the America of Washington, Lincoln and Emerson?"

As my own faith was not firmly rooted, I gradually drifted away from my first love for lack of a congenial religious *milieu*. Moreover, my juristic and philosophical preoccupations diluted more and more what little faith I had got, with the result that I forgot all about the doctrine of the Trinity, and became a Unitarian without my knowing it. I began to look at Christ as a mere man, a human teacher whose extraordinary personality and lightning-like flashes of moral insight continued to fascinate me. I adored Him in the spirit of hero-worship, which I had imbibed from Thomas Carlyle. As a freethinker I no longer cared whether He was born of a virgin, or whether He rose again from the dead, or whether He actually worked miracles. If He was not God, He was all the more admirable and worthy of imitation. All questions of dogma were relegated to the background.

In the meantime I was sorely disappointed with Rankin, who, as I heard, had become more narrow and intolerant in outlook, and more rigid and stiff, sombre and gloomy in spirituality. He had quit the Law School of which he was the founder, and established an independent institute in the neighborhood of Shanghai, called "The Bible University." To him all Truth was contained in the Bible, and no other courses were necessary to constitute a university. Being a fundamentalist himself, he could not tolerate other missionaries who happened to hold more "liberal" views. He wrote letters in criticism of this one and that one. His intentions were good, but his views seemed to me too narrow. To my mind, the Bible was only a part of the living Truth, but in the hands of Rankin it had become isolated from the rest of God's universe, like a poor fish taken out of water and gasping for life. In reaction against the fundamentalists, who believed literally everything in the Bible, I went to the other extreme and became a modernist. I used to say, "The fundamentalists are incidentalists, as they regard the incidentals as the fundamentals." What was fundamental to me was the moral teachings of Christ, His beautiful spirit of love and self-sacrifice. He might not have been the Son of God in the beginning; He certainly became the Son of God par excellence by virtue of His perfection as a man. The differences between Christ and the founders of other religions were differences of degree, not of kind. I could not understand why people plunged themselves into meaningless theological controversies, while neglecting the one essential lesson of fraternal charity. It seems to me that such persons had wandered far from the royal way of Love to lose themselves in a *cul-de-sac*.

Meanwhile my oriental mentality had got the better of me. I could still imagine man being divinized; I could no longer imagine God being humanized. The whole doctrine of the Incarnation went overboard. What I thought of Jesus may be gathered from a fanciful passage which, though written only two years before my conversion to the Catholic faith, had actually begun to take shape in my mind during the twenties:

All the great men must have felt like Saul who set out to seek for asses but found a kingdom. They must have watched with curiosity and wonder the scroll of their own lives unfold itself with ever-varying and unexpected sceneries from day to day. Our great Mother, Nature, had painted the whole scroll long before our great-grandfathers were born, but She will reveal to us its hidden beauties only inch by inch, lest we should become too elated over them. O the wonder of it! What are really *faits accomplis* in the realm of eternity appear only as potentialities to us creatures of time. We may be born great, and yet at every step we feel as though an ordinary reptile were being constantly transformed into a dragon. The reptile rides on the tides surging both within its bosom and outside its body, and some day it wakes to find gigantic wings growing from its sides and magical scales covering its back. When Jesus began to preach, golden sentences dropped from his mouth like ripe plums, and people were surprised and said, "No man has taught like that before." But no man was probably more astonished than Jesus himself. He didn't expect so much wisdom and courage from himself. He humbly ascribed them to God. Nay, all greatness is due to God. Whoever by taking thought has ever added a single cubit to his stature?

Did I still read the Bible? Of course I did. But I approached it as a freethinker: I absorbed from it whatever suited my taste, while rejecting whatever repelled me. I relied upon the inner light, which as the direct inspiration of God in the individual soul stands above the Bible and is the ultimate norm of religious faith. Here is what I wrote in the thirties:

In the sphere of religion, my mental wheel has swung a full circle. I began as a fanatic, I passed through the stage of complete scepticism, and now I have come upon a religion which I can believe in not only with all my heart, but also with all my mind; not only with all my soul but also with all the organs of my body. I am no longer impressed by miracles, which are no miracles to me. Jesus had to stoop to them because he was born in a superstitious and sign-seeking generation. He is divine not because of them, but in spite of them. He grows to his full stature by constantly

eliminating whatever is unessential and addressing himself
directly to the heart. His life is an endless struggle against
the strait jackets of the legalistic formalism of the Pharisees.
In his eyes the scribes and the Pharisees are infinitely worse
than the publicans and harlots. The earmark of his divinity
is to be found in those supreme moral insights which flashed
through his whole being like electric sparks. What a man
who says, "All manner of sin and blasphemy shall be forgiven
unto men: but the blasphemy against the Holy Ghost shall
not be forgiven unto men"! And what is the Holy Ghost but
the never-dying spirit of revolt against the spectres of tradition and convention? In law, it takes the form of an insur-
gence of justice and equity against antiquated precedents.
In literature, it takes the form of a revolt against rhetoric
and squeamish over-refinements. In all branches of culture
we find two tendencies eternally antagonistic to each other:
the tendency toward spontaneity and sincerity, and the
tendency toward formalism and hypocrisy. The former
belongs to the kingdom of God; and the latter belongs to
Hell.

I believe that God has not died since the New Testament
was written. I believe that the Bible is only the *letter* of
Christianity, not its *spirit*. I believe that the kingdom of God,
or what the Buddhists call the Lotus Land of Purity, is within
you, and not within the covers of the Bible, although it may
be gold-edged and bound with the choicest leather. I believe
that you are God in as much as you love, and a devil in as
much as you hate. I believe that the same heart that beat in
Jesus is beating in you, and that moral intuitions of the same
quality, though of different scopes of application, will flash
through your heart so long as you keep it in order as a radio
receiver for the messages of God, waiting for a chance to plop
with oily plops in the inner chambers of your heart.

In fact, I was tending toward the founding of "a New
Religion"! Here is what I wrote in December of 1936 to a
lady missionary, who must have been greatly scandalized
by the letter:

Recently I have been thinking upon the fundamental problems of life, and have come to some terms with myself. On the question of religion, for instance, I have found that the Bible reveals its truth to the literary-minded, not to the literal-minded. I have found that parts of the Gospels are mere gossips, but they are *divine* gossips. Justice in the soul of the people demanded that Christ *ought to* have been resurrected, and therefore he was resurrected. A wish became a fact, but the wish is in itself of infinitely greater value than any parade of facts. The foolishness of God is wiser than the wisdom of man. A divine gossip is truer than all the true news that have appeared since the first newspaper was out.

I'll whisper into your ears that the Religion I have in mind will be to Christianity what Christianity was to Judaism. It will represent a step toward further etherealization.

Thus, my romantic tendencies urged me to exalt Goodness above Truth, and Beauty above Goodness. I went to the extent of writing in my diary: "Christ is Buddha, Buddha is Christ; this is all you have to know!"

As I think about it now, all my restless wanderings were a long and unconscious protest against the gloomy and sombre outlook on life on the part of certain Protestants, against the heavy and oppressive atmosphere of Puritanism. I missed the gaiety and festivity, the spirit of joy and spontaneity, which I thought should characterize one's spiritual life. At the same time, the pragmatism of James, Nietzsche's Dionysian "will to power," Vaihinger's philosophy of "as if," Bergson's "*élan vital*" as the motive force of evolution, Freud's "libido," Havelock Ellis' esthetical conception of life as a dance, Holmes' humorous dig at "the solemnity with which men of the 'Nonconformist conscience' like Spencer take themselves," and Goethe's *Faust* and Lessing's *Laocoön*, —all these conspired to reinforce my romantic and Promethean tendencies. Having lost the worshipper's freedom,

I was searching for "a free man's worship"! Genius was placed on the pedestal formerly occupied by grace. In fact, I was thinking of installing a chapel in my house, with the human Christ in the center, and all the great men of the world in all fields of human activities surrounding Him, leaving empty niches for the new heroes. The project was frustrated by the unaccountable opposition of my wife; but the interior pantheon was already built until it was transformed by the grace of God into a regular cathedral.

Protestantism carries the seed of disintegration within its own bosom. It began by protesting against authority; it is bound to end by protesting against itself. At least this was what happened to me. My individualism, together with my irrationalism and sentimentalism, had reached such a point that I had become like a lonely disembodied soul wandering through an empty universe and trying agonizingly to find a new body for itself. I was completely denuded; only the grace of God could have re-clothed me with Christ, with the whole Christ: True God and True Man. Else I should have done away with my life like another Werther.

The influence of Goethe's *Faust* on me was especially strong. I was so completely enchanted by it that I identified myself with Doctor Faust, and became a close friend of Mephistopheles. I adopted him as my guide in the world. I desired to have all knowledge and all power. I desired to experience everything, including Hell itself! At the same time, I had a mysterious confidence that God would finally triumph over me and my dear friend Mephistopheles. When I read in the Prologue what the Lord said to Mephistopheles:

> That a good man, by his dim impulse driven,
> Of the right way hath ever consciousness.[1]

[1] Translated by Albert G. Latham in *Everyman's Library*, E. P. Dutton & Co., Inc., p. 10.

My heart leaped with joy, but my feet lightly followed the steps of the devil. Imitating Faust, I was playing with my soul. The romantic strain in me readily responded to his heroic words:

> And in myself I'll gratify each yearning,
> Assigned in sum to the whole race of mortals.
> All heights and depths my mind shall compass single;
> All weal and woe within my breast shall mingle;
> Till mine own self to mankind's self expanded,
> Like it at last upon Time's reef be stranded.[2]

As could have been expected, the result was exactly as he described:

> Outlawed and homeless, man no more I wander!
> I have no goal, I have no peace!
> I am the cataract! From crag to crag I thunder
> With hungry frenzy, headlong to the abyss.[3]

Objectively speaking, Goethe's *Faust* is one of the most spiritual pieces of literature. It is a colorful footnote to the wonderful insight of St. Augustine: "*Thou hast made us for Thyself and our hearts are restless till they rest in Thee.*" It is a dramatic illustration of Jeremiah's prophecy: "*Be astonished, O ye heavens, at this, and ye gates thereof, be very desolate, saith the Lord. For my people have done two evils. They have forsaken me, the fountain of living water, and have digged to themselves cisterns, broken cisterns, that can hold no water.*"

Mankind is actually stranded upon the reef of time; and like Faust himself, it is thundering from crag to crag with

[2] *Ibid.*, p. 55.
[3] *Ibid.*, p. 115.

hungry frenzy, headlong to the abyss. God has long ago thrown a living and lifesaving Bridge from Heaven to earth, but man has ignored the divine Bridge while trying hectically and in dead earnest to build his own bridge from earth to Heaven! Man now has too much cleverness, and too little wisdom! How can one reach the Infinite by finite means? Faust himself realized this:

> I feel it! vainly have I every treasure
> Won by man's mind, raked up my hoard to swell!
> When I sit down at last, my gains to measure,
> I feel no new-born power within me well;
> Not by a hair's breadth am I higher,
> Nor to the Infinite am nigher.[4]

This is the underlying philosophy of the whole drama. But in my youth I was more fascinated by the process than by the conclusion. However, even the conclusion left a deep impression on my mind, so deep that I was not conscious of it. It is most significant that Goethe should have concluded the heart-rending drama of man with the appearance of the Blessed Virgin. All is well that ends well:

MATER GLORIOSA

> Come, soar to higher spheres! Divining
> Thee near, he'll follow on thy way.

DOCTOR MARIANUS

> Tender penitents, your eyes
> Lift where looks salvation.
> Gratefully to bliss arise
> Through Regeneration.

[4] *Ibid.*, p. 54.

Each best power, Thy service in,
Prove it efficacious.
Ever, Virgin, Mother, Queen,
Goddess, be Thou gracious!

CHORUS MYSTICUS

All things corruptible
Are but reflection.
Earth's insufficiency
Here finds perfection.
Here the ineffable
Wrought is with love
The Eternal-Womanly
Draws us above.[5]

I have often caught myself humming the *Chorus Mysticus*
with joy welling up within me. I had been searching for a
Mother, and I have found her in the Catholic Church. Nay,
the Church itself is the Mother of the faithful. In her
motherly hands, severity is tempered by mildness; discipline
conduces to a healthy freedom; inebriation and sobriety,
feeling and dogma, emotion and reason are duly balanced;
the Sacraments are the regular channels of grace and the
Holy Spirit; the Bible is a part of a living tradition, the
liturgical year is a tree planted by the streams of water, bearing flowers and yielding fruits for each season; asceticism
becomes a source of gaiety and festivity; sanctity becomes the
true romance of life; and mysticism is transformed into a living fountain of virtues. There is unity in diversity, and diversity in unity. True individuality is realized in catholicity. St.
Thérèse has said it for me, "Fear makes me shrink, whereas
under love's sweet rule I not only advance—I fly."

By embracing the True Church of Christ, I have lost

[5] *Ibid.*, p. 422.

nothing, but gained all. Truly, as the Hound of Heaven said it:

> All which I took from thee I did but take,
>   Not for thy harms,
> But just that thou might'st seek it in My arms.

However, before I reached this Haven, this Home, I still had a long, long way to travel like a wandering son. My period of *Sturm und Drang* extended from my early twenties up to the time of my conversion in the winter of 1937.

9. THE STORY OF A FRIENDSHIP

There is a Chinese proverb giving a good caricature of the irony of life: *Flowers intentionally cultivated have not flourished, but the willows casually stuck in the ground have grown into a shady grove.* This seems to be a faithful portraiture of the course of my life. Things that I had planned out for myself have not ripened, but things that I did not even dream of have flourished and borne fruit.

Nothing could be more casual than the beginning of my friendship with Justice Oliver Wendell Holmes. In 1920, as I have said, I was studying as a post-graduate student in the Michigan Law School. In the following year I published an article in the March issue of the *Michigan Law Review* under the title of "Readings from Ancient Chinese Codes and Other Sources of Chinese Law and Legal Ideas." As I had so often heard my professors speak of Justice Holmes in the most laudatory of terms, I sent him a complimentary copy of the *Review.* In the meantime I wrote him a letter telling him

that I was sending the *Review*, and that knowing his interest
in comparative jurisprudence I was sure he would be glad to
read something on the legal ideas of ancient China, some of
which were akin to his own views. All that I expected was a
polite acknowledgment written by the hand of a secretary.

Now it happened that my letter reached him before the
Review, and he was so good as to answer me without seeing
the article. That letter is dear to me, because it was the beginning of a lifelong friendship. As it is very brief, I want to
quote it in full:

Your article in the Michigan Law Review is not within
my reach at this moment, but I shall try to get a sight of it
at the Capitol tomorrow. What you want, I take it, is a word
of sympathy. I only venture one bit of caution that very
possibly you do not need, but some young men of generous
ideas do need. One cannot jump at once to great ends. Therefore I hope you will not shirk the details and drudgery that
life offers, but will master them as the first step to bigger
things. One must be a soldier before one can be a general.
(Dated April 19, 1921)

When I received this note, I was already very happy,
because it was a letter from a great man and was written in
his own hand. The handwriting was simply beautiful, making
me think of the running-hand of some of the Chinese masters
in calligraphy. As to the advice, although it was couched in
the most general terms, it was very sound anyway. In short,
the response was more than I had expected, and I thought
that it was the end of it.

What was my surprise when I got another letter from him
the next morning! It began with an apology. "Yesterday's
letter," he said, "evidently was written under a misappre-
hension. I thought I was writing to a beginner, as the heading
of your letter was the Law School. I have now your article

before me and have nearly finished reading it and perceive that I am addressing a scholar who already knows so much that he probably smiles at elementary counsels. I trust that you will take my ignorance in good part." What humility! I thought, only America could have produced such a truly democratic judge. The letter continues to discuss my article and the art of translation in general. The grand old man of eighty had begun to take a serious interest in a young man of twenty-two.

As that article on Chinese law was my maiden work in jurisprudence, I want to reproduce here the opening paragraph, which reflects faithfully the mental physiognomy of the young John Wu:

With the legal profession today there is a growing interest in the study of universal legal ideas. Legal ideas, it would seem, gain strength by extension both in time and in space. As *jus gentium* is necessarily more congenial to human reason than *jus civile*, so it may be said that the laws of all ages are more deep-seated in human nature than those of a particular generation. The scope of comparative jurisprudence, therefore, embraces all the length and breadth of legal scholarship, so that it cannot afford to ignore any materials that may give us light upon the legal notions of the ancient world.

My stay in Ann Arbor was among the happiest periods of my life. My teachers, Dean Henry M. Bates, Professor Joseph H. Drake, and Professor Edwin Dickinson, took a personal interest in me. They were so cordial and kind to me, and I was so intensely interested in my studies, that I had no time to feel homesick, although it was the first time that I was ever abroad. Professor Drake called me a "prodigy," and Dean Bates used to say to me, "Are you again working in white heat?" There was a certain homelikeness and coziness about

Ann Arbor, and a warm sympathy about its people. There were also quite a number of Chinese students there, and a nice Chinese restaurant on the campus. My landlady, one Mrs. Hutchinson, was very kind to me. Once she had a good laugh over my stupidity in handling the telephone. Someone wanted to talk to me over the phone, and she called me to it. I said "Hello" at the top of my voice for five minutes, but I did not hear a thing. She came down to see what was happening and found me talking to the listening end and listening to the talking end! It was the first time that I ever handled a telephone.

Some time in May 1921, as I was reading in the library, Professor Edwin D. Dickinson, who was my teacher in International Law, approached me with an application form in his hand. He asked me, "Do you want a fellowship in International Law?" "Of course, I do!" I said. "Then fill up this form, which I have just received from the Carnegie Endowment for International Peace. It will be a travelling fellowship. You have a good chance of getting it, and you can choose any school in the world except this school."

I got the fellowship, and I chose to go to the University of Paris. When I was settled in Paris, I wrote a long letter to Holmes. I want to reproduce it here with few omissions, because this was the first of my letters to be preserved by Holmes to the end of his life.

My dear Mr. Justice Holmes:

Last Spring I was in Ann Arbor; now, I am in Paris. Time and space may change, but my love and respect for Your Honor remain still the same.

Now, let me tell you what has brought me to this Continent. When I was in Michigan, I studied International Law and Comparative Law. The Professors being satisfied

with my work recommended me to a Fellowship offered by
the Carnegie Endowment for International Peace. The Fellowship left me free in choosing the institution in which I
was to study; and I chose the University of Paris. So that the
fact that I am in Paris is the result of my own free choice:
this reminds me once more of Your Honor's doctrine that
there is no determinism with human affairs, and that "mankind yet may take its own destiny consciously and intel-
ligently in hand." I shall get the best out of Paris; I shall
read and write as much as I can; I shall observe and think as
profoundly as possible. As a Chinese I have a country to save,
I have a people to enlighten, I have a race to uplift, I have
a civilization to modernize. To me, therefore, the writings
of such a creative genius as Your Honor cannot fail to be a
source of comfort and encouragement; for Your Honor tells
me among other things that continuity with the past is *only*
a necessity and not a duty and that we have to reduce this
necessity like all other necessary evils to a minimum. One
of the principal causes of the stagnation of the Chinese civilization is a wrong conception which regards continuity with
the past as a sacred duty, and which ignores the fact that the
divine right of the past is no less baseless than the divine right
of kings. By the way, I beg to tell Your Honor that I am going
to review Your Honor's *Collected Legal Papers* both in English and French magazines. My reviews, of course, are not
going to be simple praises sung in honor of a great soul and
a comprehensive mind; they will rather be analysis and synthesis of the author's views together with criticisms if there
be any; for I try to be a man who "should be able to criticize
what he reveres and loves." It seems to me that one can get
into the background of Your Honor's views and theories by
a single key: I mean that throughout all Your Honor's views,
writings and decisions, there sounds an undernote, there
whispers the small, still voice, which yearns, so to speak, for
the general welfare of the nation. Another point which strikes
me is that Your Honor is a born idealist, but Your Honor's
idealism is seasoned by pragmatic considerations. This, perhaps, can be better expressed by saying that Your Honor has
a Platonian foundation with an Aristotelian superstructure.

Does Your Honor approve of this opinion? Give me some
hints so as to let me taste the Fountain of Truth, for I am
always thirsty for the living water.

As a student of International Law, I am quite anxious to
find out both the past traces, the present stage and the future
tendencies of its evolution. It has often been remarked that
International Law will probably be evolved in a similar manner as the Municipal Law has been evolved. If this is true, as
I believe that it is, what stage of evolution does Your Honor
think the modern law of nations is in? Is it in the stage of
blood-feuds? If so, what can we do to accelerate its advancement? If the advent of Nationalism contributed to the
removal of the blood-feuds between families, would it be
improbable that the growth of Internationalism will help
put an end to wars between nations which to my mind are
nothing more nor less than blood-feuds on a large scale? I
think that it is the duty of the older jurists to prepare a program for the development of the *Jus Gentium* to obtain in
the generation to come; and being a universally recognized
jurist no one is better qualified than Your Honor to undertake
this task, and no man's words will carry a greater weight.
Your Honor's *Collected Legal Papers* will be incomplete, if
they are silent upon a law which is destined to rule the whole
world. I supplicate Your Honor on behalf of the younger
generation and in the interests of humanity to leave us a
testament, a bequest which is not to be measured by dollars
and cents, but which will be instrumental in saving countless
human lives and souls from unnecessary destructions. I wish
Your Honor could see how my heart burns with enthusiasm!

Inclosed please find a photograph of mine. I was born in
the closing year of the last century, or, to be a little fantastic,
in the year when Your Honor delivered the address, "Law
in Science and Science in Law," which I now read with such
an immense joy. Our ages are widely separate, but what has
Eternity to do with years and centuries? Our birth-places are
far removed, but what has Universality to do with oceans
and continents? I desire Your Honor's friendship, because
Providence has made us kindred spirits; Your Honor being
an old man endowed with a child's heart, and I being a boy

provided with an old man's mind. I wish that Your Honor would favor me with a photograph to crown my album. In Your Honor's last letter to me, it was very kindly stated, "I have not a good photograph to spare at present and I should not like to send you a poor one." If Your Honor can spare a good one now, please send that to me. But even a poor one is far better than none; for, the value of a photograph does not exist in itself, but in the person that it represents; and so long as it represents Your Honor, I shall be satisfied all the same. (Dated Nov. 23, 1921)

In those days, the memory of the first World War being fresh in my mind, my heart was burning like a live coal for international peace. I would rather have my own body torn into a thousand pieces than see humanity being torn by another war. In Paris I used to watch lovely French children spinning tops in the public squares. When I was in Berlin, I saw lovely German children spinning tops in the public squares. I can still remember how my heart was pierced as by a sword when the terrible idea shot through my mind that some day when these children had grown up they might find themselves shooting at those others, whereas if they had met and known one another, they could easily have become the best of friends! A tragic sense of life had begun to dawn in me. I think it was partly due to the letter Holmes wrote me in answer to the above. I will quote a part of it:

Your very kind letter which comes this morning deserves an immediate answer, and luckily I have no case to write this week and am able to send one. By a coincidence, the moment I came upstairs to my library I had been talking about war with a guest who served in France. I am afraid that my talk was a little more sceptical than you would approve, perhaps because I am old and have seen many wars. It is shortly this. We all try to make the kind of a world that we should like. What we like lies too deep for argument and can be changed only gradually, often through the experience of many generations. If the different desires of different peoples come in conflict in a region that each wishes to occupy (especially if it is a physical region) and each wishes it strongly enough, what is there to do except to remove the other if you can? I hate to discourage the belief of a young man in reason. I believe in it with all my heart, but I think that its control over the actions of men when it comes against what they want is not very great. A century ago Malthus ran his sword through fallacies that one would have thought must die then and there, but men didn't like to believe him, and the humbugs that he killed are as alive as ever today. I will not go on with a subject which is rather a sad one.

I have written to the Harvard Law Review to send you a copy of the number you asked for, if one is to be had. I am afraid that I cannot venture into the realm of self-criticism to which you invite me, but may I say that I think that what you say about Platonian and Aristotelian is pretty keen. The two little pieces, *Ideals and Doubts* and *Natural Law*, indicate some of my starting points. (Dated Dec. 12, 1921)

This did not dampen my idealism, but only made me think more seriously. It opened my eyes to the realities; but the realities only furnished to me the necessary foundations upon which I was to build my idealism. In the following letter, it will be seen how I tried to induce Holmes to adopt my point of view under the disguise of adopting his. Here is a boy attempting naively to lead a grand old man by the nose! I wrote:

Your talk about war has made me think like a real jurist. It has reminded me of an interesting passage in your "The Path of Law," which reads, "But if we take the view of our friend the bad man we shall find that he does not care two straws for the axioms or deductions, but he does want to know what the Massachusetts or English courts will do in fact. I am much of his mind. The prophecies of what the courts will do in fact, and nothing more pretentious, are what I mean by the law." If we substitute "the bad *nation*" for "the bad man," we would have a pretty clear idea of what international law is. Now, the remarkable thing is this. Christ our Saviour took upon himself the form of a sinner in order that he might learn to be sympathetic towards the real sinners. It was in such a noble attitude that he said to his disciples who were asleep when they ought to have been waking, "The spirit, indeed, is willing, but the flesh is weak." Likewise, you have stepped into the shoes of "the bad man" in order to get his viewpoint, and you might as well have said, "Reason, indeed, is at work, but its control over self-interest is weak."

Just now, I am planning to write a thesis on the subject "La methode du droit des gens: Essai de la critique juridique," my object being to make international law a true legal science. Professor François Geny of Nancy has written me to say that I should lay special emphasis upon the sanction of international law, law without sanction being no law at all. This, certainly, is no easy job, as the sanction of international law is more or less intangible,—it is in the air. But your conception of law as a matter of prophecy has cleared away the fog that besets the early wayfarer in the path of international law. The sanction of law is psychological, and if the *probabilities* of its being enforced in the court, which in the case of international law is the forum of international public opinion, are so high that no serious doubt could arise in a *normally* constructed mind, we have a law, no matter what sanctions it,—be it army, navy, police power, legislative morality, superstition, tradition or what not. Indeed, the idea of *normality* is the one great safety-value in the whole mechanism of legal science. We find in such phrases as "beyond reasonable doubt," "probable cause," "ordinary prudent man," etc., some practical expressions of the idea of normality. Of course, normality of one epoch is not the same as that of another epoch; and when you say in your address on "Law and the Court," "For most of the things that prop-

erly can be called evils in the present state of the law I think
the main remedy, as for the evils of public opinion, is for
us to grow more civilized," the "us" expresses the idea of
normality, and it is applicable to nations as well as, if not
more than, to individuals.

You say that the two little pieces "Ideals and Doubts"
and "Natural Law" indicate some of your starting points. I
am glad to tell you that I have adopted them as mine. Thus,
what you have by nature I incorporate into myself by choice.
But there is one thing that I cannot digest very easily. In
your "Natural Law" you state that "the jurists who believe
in natural law seem to me to be in that naive state of mind
that accepts what has been familiar and accepted by them
and their neighbors as something that must be accepted by
all men everywhere." This is true. You did not hint, however, that what makes the jurists or any other man, for that
matter, believe such things to be natural law is itself a natural
law, which is very real and which we may term "psychological
natural law." And psychological natural law is not the highest
form of natural law either. The highest form, to my mind,
is Natural Law in the philosophical sense. When the jurists
—I mean the sociological school—say that there is no such
thing as an immutable, unchangeable natural law, they are
unconsciously proclaiming a principle which is itself valid
in all times and places. In other words, their statement denying existence to the pseudo natural law is really establishing
the genuine Natural Law, which requires change and growth
in human institutions and makes possible the evolution—the
conscious evolution—of mankind. Your later remark, "We do
know that a certain complex of energies can wag its tail and
another can make syllogisms" comes very near to the point
I am driving at; and your question "Why should we employ
the energy that is furnished to us by the cosmos to defy it
and shake our fist at the sky?" expresses my conviction in
other terms. I take "cosmos" or "sky" as an embodiment of
what I insist to call Natural Law. But why should I split hair
with the terms, while I am sure that we have exactly the same
thing in mind? Well, the simple reason is that jurists, in
general, are conservative in their use of terms, and they will

not yield up their "natural law" unless we show them that they have only visualized the back of Natural Law—as Moses only saw the back of God—and that our vision of Natural Law, which, like the face of God, is ever-glowing, vivid, expressive of internal feelings, responsive to external changes, and looking forward to the welfare of Humanity, is a truer vision of Natural Law. The habit of the lawyers has been to preserve the form while changing the contents. (Dated Jan. 8, 1922. Berlin)

Thus, I was trying to save the notion of "Natural Law" in the very teeth of Holmes' scepticism. He wrote:

No criticism occurs to me upon your letter, only a suggestion. I just now have finished reading Lévy Bruhl, *La morale et la science des moeurs*, and I think you will find that it falls in with the line of your thinking and may be of some use. It is a short book, easily read, and I think could be made much shorter if the author did not feel it necessary to argue things that I should take for granted. (Dated Jan. 28, 1922)

From the very beginning, it was not so much Holmes the philosopher as Holmes the man that captivated me. As a philosopher, he was not always consistent. Sometimes he talked as though he were a libertarian. He says, for instance, "Philosophy does not furnish motives, but it shows men that they are not fools for doing what they already want to do." That flabbergasted me when I first read it. But it was immediately followed up with another sentence which marks him down as a mystic: "It opens to the forlorn hopes on which we throw ourselves away, the vista of the farthest stretch of human thought, the chords of a harmony that breathes from the unknown." If this is true, then philosophy is not as neutral as Holmes thought. The fact is that Holmes was an unconscious philosopher. To do him justice, we must not judge him intellectually as a philosopher, *but esthetically as a personality*. At bottom, he was a poet become judge.

When I was in Germany, studying under the great Neo-Kantian philosopher of law, Rudolf Stammler, Holmes was worried lest I should be too much influenced by systematic thinking, which to him was barren and empty. For him, insight is the valuable thing, but system kills insight. I, however, attempted a synthesis between the two.

Stammler's emphasis was on the conceptual or logical aspects of law, whereas Holmes' emphasis was on the perceptual or psychological aspects. They were, thus, diametrically opposed to each other. Neither of them satisfied my mind perfectly. I was convinced that their views could be brought to a higher synthesis. Form without matter is empty: matter without form is blind. In the Preface to my *Juridical Essays and Studies*, which was published in 1928, I stated my position in the following words:

My whole philosophy may be looked upon as an attempt to reconcile the Holmesian with the Stammlerian in legal thinking, the perceptual with the conceptual, the becoming with the become, the matter with the form, the theory of interests with the theory of justice, the empirical with the rational. This point may be illustrated by the parable of the pot and the beer.

In a letter to me dated September 2, 1923, Holmes wrote: "Just after sending my last letter to you a further thought occurred to me with regard to the forms of thought. Whatever the value of the notion of forms, the only use of the forms is to present their contents, just as the only use of the pint pot is to present the beer (or whatever lawful liquid it may contain), and infinite meditation upon the pot never will give you the beer."

Stammler, on the other hand, would say, in a characteristic way, that beer without the pot could hardly be preserved in a permanent form, and it is the part of philosophy to furnish the permanent forms. Thus, for the former, the subject-matter of philosophy is primarily the beer, and for the latter it is primarily the pot. I would say, however, that the subject-matter of philosophy is neither the beer alone, nor the pot alone, nor yet the beer and the pot added together, but the beer-in-the-pot.

In fact, in an article on "The Juristic Philosophy of Justice Holmes," which was published in the *Michigan Law Review* (March, 1923), I presented both the conception of law and the perception of law, and concluded by suggesting a synthesis. Both Stammler and Holmes were pleased with the conclusion. Stammler published a most generous comment upon it in the May issue of the *Michigan Law Review*. Holmes wrote me a very encouraging letter, in which he said: "Your second instalment moves me, and commands my sympathy. I am glad to see you on the side of the *Ding an sich*, which seems to me to follow, the moment we admit that the world is not a dream. . . . I like your rapture over the law. I only fear that it may be dimmed as you get into the actualities (in the sense of the hard side) of life. But if, as I hope and as what you write indicates, you bear the fire in your belly, it will survive and transfigure the hard facts." (Dated Feb. 5, 1923)

I want to reproduce here two paragraphs from that particular section which delighted both Holmes and Stammler, not only because it is a sweet souvenir to me but also because, being "a rapture over the law," it reveals some interior qualities of my soul and represents a stage in my spiritual pilgrimage.

The perception and conception of law are, to my mind, merely two aspects of law, the former being nothing but law perceived, and the latter nothing but law conceived. In both cases, the law as a thing-in-itself seems to be posited, as it would be absurd to think that there could be a perception or a conception without something which is perceived or conceived. It is clear, then, that perception and conception both point to a unity which is manifested in their very difference, and to a substance which gives birth to both of them.

For the fundamental core and kernel of reality which pervades everything pervades law, so that law is but one of the portals through which we come to Truth; and the unity of nature and mind is so close that whatever touches the utmost reality of things stirs also the innermost core of our feeling. Emerson says rightly that man must attain and maintain that lofty height where facts yield their secret sense, and poetry and annals and, we may add, music and law are alike. The higher our point of view is, the more deeply we penetrate into ourselves, till we see with our mental eye that the ultimate ground of law is identical with the ultimate ground of all being, and that law derives its meaning from the first Whence and last Whither of the universe. The universe is a mystery, and what is true of the whole is true also of the parts. The so-called things-in-themselves are but the different forms under which the Thing-in-Itself appears, in which lies the possibility of all experience, and which constitutes the living principle in all things, including the law. Upon this hypothesis of utmost reality depends the innermost unity of thought, without which our perception and conception would remain meaningless discrete pieces, but with which they become at once vital parts of a living whole. This living whole does not represent a mere abstract unity of ideas external to each other, but, to borrow an expression from Edward Caird, "an organic unity of transparent differences, a self-differentiating, self-integrating unity, such as seems to be presented to us in pure self-consciousness." It is only when we are in possession of such self-consciousness that we can say without self-contradiction that law is at once one and many, and that it is always and never the same. Know thyself and thou knowest law.

In the fall of 1923, I returned to America from Europe to

join the Harvard Law School as a research scholar under the direction of Pound. Holmes and I continued to correspond, and our friendship was growing constantly. But it was not until December 20 that I went to Washington, and saw him for the first time. I spent several evenings with him, "twisting the tail of the cosmos together," according to his happy phrase. He was in the most cheerful of moods. He showed me around his library, picking up one book after another, commenting on them casually but most interestingly. He showed me his collection of the woodcuts and engravings of Albrecht Dürer. Finally, he said, "My dear boy, I have not yet shown you the best books in this library." I pricked up my ears and asked, "Where are they?" He pointed at an upper corner; and I saw that it was an empty shelf! I understood him immediately and burst out laughing. I said, "How characteristic of you! You are always looking ahead!" He smiled most sweetly.

In those days, we had come to understand and love each other as profoundly as any friends could. On one occasion, Mrs. Holmes came to join us. I rose from my seat to meet her halfway, and pointing to Holmes I said to her, "Madam, may I present to you my friend Justice Oliver Wendell Holmes?" "With great pleasure!" she said. The three of us looked at one another, and had a good laugh together. The Buddhists would say that right at that moment we had a Zen experience, for what is a Zen experience but a momentary, unexpected transport of mind from the realm of time to eternity, so that one looks at the familiar as if it were strange and at the strange as if it were familiar? Mrs. Holmes, two years older than Holmes himself, was one of the most charming, quick-witted and lively ladies I have ever met.

After my return to Cambridge, I wrote a letter which reads more like a love letter than anything else:

Dear and much honored Mr. Justice Holmes,

It is not likely that you would derive any substantial pleasure from my praising you. Nevertheless, the fact is that I "can't help" praising you; and while my "can't helps'" are not cosmic "can't helps," yet I "can't help" believing that the same Energy that made you so worthy of praise makes me praise you so.

You seem to represent a perfect harmony of the most contradictory qualities. You are old, yet you still remain in merry childhood; you are a jurist, yet no poet has a sweeter nature; you are tough-minded, going by solid facts, yet there is in you a lightness of heart which makes one forget or even enjoy the burden of existence; you are energetic, yet show no sign of vulgar strenuousness. A certain indefinable simplicity combined with greatness of character makes your life a work of art which is at once sublime and beautiful. If Carlyle was right in describing genius as "the clearer presence of God Most High," then I can certainly boast of having at last seen a genius.

My life has become infinitely richer now than before I had seen you; my views of human possibilities are broadened. Your warm friendship with me has become one of the formative influences in my intellectual and moral development; it is a powerful impetus which drives me toward ever higher aims. Your influence is not like a sharp spur which soon spends its virtue, but is a gentle stimulus which acts as a spontaneous initiative within me.

I can assure you that your advice with regard to the mastery of details will not be given in vain. I shall attempt to overcome my constitutional idleness, and to rise up early and go to bed late so as to watch carefully the actualities passing before my eyes. I shall direct my gaze toward the external world, and enjoy the natural scenes with a sort of disinterested curiosity. And yet, even when I shall have known enough of the world, I shall not deprive myself of the divine pleasure of seeing the beauty of my own ideals, which are all the more precious because they cannot be suddenly realized or made popular. If they can become a common possession of mankind, then they will not be mine. The ideal-ists are awkward and dry because they betray a lack of humor by expecting promptitude of results. They are gratuitously generous, inasmuch as they want to distribute their wealth, the ideals, equally among the masses without regard to their deserts. And excessive or ill-placed generosity is ugly and even irritating. This is why such men as Fichte, Bentham, Thibaut, Spencer and other hasty reformers and generalizers have not the classical beauty possessed by such scholars as Montesquieu, Savigny and yourself. But how about Jean Jacques Rousseau? He was an idealist of the most radical type, and yet there is something graceful about his person. This is probably because he did not take his own idealism seriously, nor does he expect others to do so, though some do in spite of him. In his case, idealism was an amusement, and as the author amuses himself, we spectators rejoice with him instead of getting uneasy over him.

How about Socrates and Christ who died for their ideals, and yet their personalities are so attractive? This is probably because they didn't take death seriously. They played, in the fullest sense of the word, with their lives. We feel pleased with their deaths because they themselves were pleased. Did Socrates not say, "The time has come for us to depart—I to die, you to live. Which of us is going to the better lot God alone clearly knows!" What cynicism, what a good humor! Suppose he had said, "Ye people, I am disappointed with you. I entertained high ideals which ought to have been realized but for your wickedness; I am now disillusioned." He would not be Socrates. Same thing is true of Christ. He did not die disappointed; his death he knew was a necessary step toward bringing the Kingdom of Heaven to the Earth. His idealism is therefore beautiful, because it did not assert more than was the case and could support the solid facts without trembling. There was an enormous "waste" or "more than enough" in his idealism; and as you said, "waste" is an essential constituent of beauty.

With my best wishes to you, and to Mrs. Holmes, at whose quickness of insight I "can't help" marvelling. I am, Sir,

Your "dear boy"

John C. H. Wu

His reply was no less warm and cheerful than my letter, although he wrote it during a toothache:

Your truly remarkable letter leaves me speechless so far as it refers to me. I only hope that I shall manage to die before I disappoint those who think so kindly of me. I am much pleased with your suggestion concerning Rousseau. I don't know whether to accept it or not, but it sounds very plausible. Certainly he is an amusing contrast to the solemnity with which men of the "nonconformist conscience" like Spencer take themselves—a solemnity that even some of our literary men have not been free from. I can write but a line as I must go out to drive in a few minutes. The dentist spoiled most of my promised leisure of this last week, but I have trifled with literature a little and have cleared the deck —I ought to say the desk—for action which begins on Wednesday. I can't forbear saying that you delightfully satisfied my hopes when I came to see you here. A happy New Year to you and many happy and efficient years thereafter. (Dated Dec. 31, 1923)

In one of my letters written in the spring of 1924, I have come across some words which indicate the influence of Holmes on my outlook on life: "Ever since I saw you, I have got, as by contagion, a peculiar sense of humor which I did not possess before. You seem to have imparted to me the gospel of relaxation, of looking at life esthetically, of taking oneself not too seriously." (Dated Feb. 9, 1924)

Time passed quickly, and I soon found myself returning to China after four years of absence from home. On May 15, 1924, I wrote him a farewell letter, which even now, as I read it, touches me profoundly:

My dearest Friend:

I know not in what words to bid you Farewell.
It is four years since I left home and my dear ones and

journeyed forth in quest of the "unknown end" in the West.
I had then no idea of the marvellous things that the world
had in store for me. I dreamed merely of academic honors
and other low vanities; they exhausted my ambition and
vision. Never did I expect to enter into such a close communion with such an overwhelmingly great jurist and philosopher as yourself.

You, Sir, have not only fulfilled the highest ideal of public
justice, but have also deepened the meaning and enriched
the content of human friendship. As I re-read these beautiful
letters you have written me during the past years, I experience
a continual thrill of gratitude, love and admiration. You have
been true even to the most unworthy of your friends. Whenever I was dejected, you comforted and encouraged me, and
lo! there emerged a ray of fresh hope. When I was over-enthu-
siastic, you, so far from being bored, sympathized with me,
and what an echo of sweetness—a sweetness bringing moder-
ation without recommending it. You have enlightened me on
a great variety of topics, ranging from War to Bacon-Shakes-
peare controversy, from the theory of Style to Dürer's etch-
ing, from the doctrine of consideration to Frazer's Golden
Bough, from police power to the analogy of pint pot, from
Spinoza's Ethics to my own Sonnet.

The life of reason consists in overcoming barriers. The
fact of our friendship has overcome at least three formidable
barriers: Time, Space, and Society. I am two generations
your junior, and as to Space I was born in a sphere whose
morning is your evening. The most cruel of barriers is probably conventionality. I am an insignificant scholar, and yet
you have taken me into your bosom. You would judge only by
quality and care nothing for qualifications. Our friendship,
my dear Friend, is age-forgetting, distance-nullifying and
society-transcending. It enlarges human possibilities, and I
give you the whole credit for it. You are the *dominus* and I
the *servus* of the relation.

Since you wrote me the last letter (which gives me an
interesting account of your dash into some more classics,
and contains a wonderful critique of Santayana) I have

known two more of your admirers, Cardozo and Cohen, both through the good offices of the amiable Frankfurter. They courted me because I am beloved by you, and you love none but choice spirits. Nor indeed could anyone but a choice spirit entertain a genuine admiration for you. Cardozo, the apostle of "the method of Mansfield, Marshall, Kent and Holmes," is a charming person. His character is not merely good, but beautiful. (By the way he is publishing a new book, *The Growth of the Law*, in which he quotes a long passage from my essay on your Philosophy of Law. He elaborates your "prediction theory of the law.") Cohen called on me two weeks ago, and we had a stimulating talk. We agreed that you, dear Sir, have the power of expressing what is inexpressible, and that you are the most original juristic philosopher we had known (both in history and among the living). I find Cohen a real thinker, and shall try to get him to China.

I know not how to bid you farewell! In five or six days I shall leave for Canada (my ship sails from Vancouver on June 5). I find myself returning home, probably never to come abroad again! Such is life and such its limitations! I wish I had never been born—how sweet would then be my rest! And why should I be born in this dark world, and in its darkest part? I tremble before my heavy task. To enlighten, to ennoble, to bring joy to the joyless, to procure minimum wages for the laborers, to provide human homes for human creatures, to take in hand Life and direct it to purer channels—these are some of the problems toward the solution of which I shall contribute my part. I don't regard them as a bitter cup, no, they are amusements to while away a life time. Given existence what is there to do except to bear it goodhumoredly and improve it? Farewell to Mrs. Holmes! Farewell! my dearest Friend!

Eternally yours,
John C. H. Wu

10. "LAW IS MY IDOL"

After my return to China, I was overwhelmed by the joyful reunions with my dear ones at home. I had a feeling of genuine romance when my two boys, whom I had left as babies, looked suspiciously at me for a long time, as if a stranger had intruded into their home. It was not until my wife told them to greet their "appa" that they jumped into my arms. Later I brought my family to Shanghai and taught at the Comparative Law School of China. For a few months I was too busily occupied to write to Holmes. Sometime in the winter, my good friend Dr. George Sellett, then Dean of the Law School, wrote a letter to Holmes, asking his consent to our dedication of the first volume of the *China Law Review* to him, and requesting a cable from him. The cable came. When Dr. Sellett read it, he could not help chuckling. I said, "What is it?" He read it to me: "Consent Love to Wu." I said, "What is so laughable about it?" He said, "Don't you see that Justice Holmes is playing on your name? 'Love

to Wu' is 'Love to woo'!" How playful the old boy was! And
he was eighty-four then! I suspect that humor was one of
the secrets of his longevity.

Well, after receiving the cable, I wrote him for the first
time from China. The letter will tell what I had been doing;
it will also show that I was tending somewhat toward pan-
theism at that time, speaking, as I did, of the "Vital Energy
of the Universe."

This is Christmas! I wish it were the Christmas of 1923!
No year will bring to me a happier Christmas than that!

Your cable to Dr. Sellett gives me assurance that you are
enjoying perfect health,—I am happy beyond description.
Long live the king of Jurists!

Your cable contains such loving words to me. I *know* that
you love me; I know it not from the cable, but from my love
of you. Other contracts may require expression, but a spiritual contract can exist *even* without expression, because it
does not take a court to enforce it and, *d'ailleurs*, there is no
possibility of a breach.

I have been teaching law for one term. I teach Property
(with Warren's Cases as text), Roman Law (with Sohm's
Institutes), International Law (with Evan's Cases), and
Jurisprudence (with Salmond). I can assure you that teaching
is a creative process. Often a whole class is set on fire by a
new problem. The students naturally divide themselves into
two (sometimes more) groups according to their philosophical tendencies. One day we were discussing the case of
Chapin v. Freeland, in which you so aptly remarked that "a
title which will not sustain a declaration will not sustain a
plea." About two thirds of the students were in favor of
your opinion, while the rest defended Justice Field. One of
the former group observed that you were using logic as a
hand-maid of public policy.

My knowledge of the law has, I believe, become a little
more solid through teaching. I am trying to collect and
closely investigate enough cases in different branches of law

to serve as the data of a work on "Human Nature in Law: Studies in Psychological Jurisprudence." I find that there is no short-cut way to scholarship, and that it is only by way of patient and painstaking labor that one can hope to reach the promised land of knowledge. Study alone can "correct the ignoble excess of a noble feeling."

My most beloved friend! nothing could be more joyful than intellectual creation! I sometimes caught myself in such an ecstasy that I forgot that I was living in this most miserable part of this miserable world. I am thankful to the great Vital Energy of the Universe for having imparted to me a spark of fire and a capacity for worshipping heroes of the intellect. (Dated Dec. 25, 1924)

His answer came promptly as usual, and we resumed our correspondence. That letter of his contains a most beautiful passage, which I want to quote:

It was a great pleasure and relief to get your letter. You had been silent so long that I had begun to fear that you were suffering from the troubles in China. I am so ignorant about them that I know not how far or in what way things affect you. The request for a cable and the mention of you gave me a chance to poke a message at you in the hope of evoking a return shot. I am much interested and a little surprised at the subjects of your teaching. I don't doubt you do more than half in setting your class on fire. When you do that you do the best and the rarest thing that a teacher can do. I used to say that Emerson's great gift was that of imparting a ferment. Of course teaching is a great way to learn. As you say, there is no short cut to scholarship, nor is there to anything else in the way of achievement. I wish that I might know more of your circumstances if discretion does not require you to be silent. Your "this miserable world" makes me anxious. I imagine that you are at the time of life when the staying power of your enthusiasm will be most tried. For me at least there came moments when faith wavered. But there is the great lesson and the great triumph if you keep the fire burning until, by and by, out of the mass of sordid details there comes some result, be it some new generalization or be it a transcending spiritual repose. (Dated Jan. 27, 1925)

For me the "transcending spiritual repose" was not to come until the winter of 1937, when I embraced the Catholic Church. In the meantime I remained as restless as ever. I tried to find one substitute for God after another, but found no peace. Without his knowing it, it was partly due to his influence that my faith in Christianity had been diluted. I still retained some faint belief in God and the immortality of the soul. As Holmes was getting so old, naturally I wished to settle the point with him once for all. In a letter dated March 29, 1926, I added a significant postscript. It reads: "I am re-reading Taylor's version of Faust, pleased with note 126 of the Second Part. This note has reference to future life. Please read it and tell me what you think about it." The note contains a quotation from Goethe: "I do not doubt our permanent existence, for nature cannot do without *entelechie*. But we are not all immortal in the same fashion, and in order to manifest one's self in the future life as a great *entelechie*, one must also become one." Wilhelm von Humboldt said something to the same effect. Now, this may be called a pantheistic theory of individual immortality. As Holmes was a pantheist, I thought he might accept it without much difficulty.

Holmes' answer to my query is this:

As to Taylor's note 126, *Faust* Part II, of course you refer to Goethe's suggestion concerning our permanent existence and W. von Humboldt *ad idem*. I hesitate a little to speak freely because of my impression as to your beliefs or hopes, but I will say a few words. I think men even now, and probably more in Goethe's day, retain the theological attitude with regard to themselves even when they have given it up for the cosmos. That is, they think of themselves as little gods over against the universe, whether there is a big one or not. I see no warrant for it. I believe that we are in the universe, not it in us, that we are part of an unimaginable, which I will call a whole, in order to name it, that our personality is a cosmic ganglion, that just as when certain rays meet and cross there is white light at the meeting point, but the rays go on after the meeting as they did before, so, when certain other streams of energy cross, the meeting point can frame a syllogism or wag its tail. I never forget that the cosmos has the power to produce consciousness, intelligence, ideals, out of a like course of its energy, but I see no reason to assume that these ultimates for me are cosmic ultimates. I frame no predicates about the cosmos. I suspect that all my ultimates have the mark of the finite upon them, but as they are the best I know I give them practical respect, love, etc., but inwardly doubt whether they have any importance except for us and as something that with or without reasons the universe has produced and therefore for the moment has sanctioned. We must be serious in order to get work done, but when the usual Saturday half holiday comes I see no reason why we should not smile at the trick by which nature keeps us at our job. It makes me enormously happy when I am encouraged to believe that I have done something of what I should have liked to do, but in the subterranean misgivings I think, I believe that I think sincerely, that it does not matter much. (Dated May 5, 1926)

This was certainly a crushing answer to me. Holmes was a pantheist, to whom the Cosmos is God, and there is no God beyond the Cosmos. As he wrote me in a later letter dated July 1, 1929: "I bow my head, I think serenely, and say as I told someone the other day, O Cosmos, now lettest thou thy ganglion dissolve in peace." His pantheistic philosophy was even more clearly presented in another letter:

"I send you all the possible good wishes, and hope and expect that you will get satisfaction out of life, in spite of your speaking of it as if it were a miserable business. One sometimes feels so, but we know nothing of its ultimate significance, if the cosmos know the significance. If it doesn't, it is because it is bigger than that. For it has significance in its belly." (Dated March 26, 1925)

I was not convinced at all by his views. To my mind, if the cosmos does not know the significance of life, then it is not God; and if there were no God beyond the cosmos, then all human history would be like dancing to the blind and singing to the deaf; and all noble thought and action would be like kissing a cold statue. I believed in a personal God, not because I wanted to project my personality upon God, but because to deprive Him of this attribute would be making the effect greater than the cause. Later in a paper, I wrote: "In my humble opinion, God is more than a person, and for that very reason He is capable of assuming Personality. Those who think otherwise seem to place themselves above God. They presume that they alone can possess personalities, but not God."

In C. J. Eustace's *An Infinity of Questions*, I have come across a most illuminating passage: "For, in all things in Heaven and earth, there are two obscurities for us mortals. One is the obscurity from on high, that of the spirit, which is so great that its clarity blinds us; the other is the obscurity of matter, to which alas—so many artists succumb." I am afraid that Holmes wobbled between the two obscurities.

But the discovery of our differences in faith did not affect our friendship in the least, although it did disturb my mind.

That I remained persistently a theist in spite of certain pantheistic leanings can be gathered from the following letter which I wrote on January 1, 1927, when I was appointed a judge:

I have some happy news to communicate to my great friend, for happier news could hardly be conceived of. This morning, when I was still in bed, a friend came to me, addressing me in terms of "Your Honor," and showering congratulations upon me. I was astonished and I thought the friend either mad or malicious. But he was neither, for he had seen in the newspapers that I was appointed by the Provincial Government of Kiangsu to be Judge in the newly born "Shanghai Provisional Court," born on the same day as my Judgeship, to wit, the First of January in the Year of our Lord 1927.

I would not trouble you by telling you the nature of the Court, and moreover I am not in a mood to dwell upon minute things. But I can give you some conclusions. This court has jurisdiction over all controversies in the International Settlement of Shanghai, except those cases where the defendants are citizens of the treaty nations, that is, nations enjoying extraterritorial rights. In other words, it will have jurisdiction over cases where both parties are Chinese residents, and over cases where the plaintiffs are aliens and defendants Chinese. I am a *praetor peregrini!* I shall have much opportunity of doing creative work in the law! I shall try to Holmesianize the Law of China!

This Court, while inferior in rank to the Supreme Court, is even superior to it in interest and importance. In fact, two of the greatest Judges have quit the Supreme Court to join this Court.

I just wonder how one could doubt the Providence of God our Heavenly Father. My life (I can hardly call it life, as I have hardly begun to live, being only two years older than a Roman *pubes minor*) would be inexplicable without the love and guidance of God. He has strengthened me with one disillusionment after another. He blew into me a spark of fire, and has now given me a chance to transfigure therewith the hard facts. *Let me always walk in His presence, and*

*may each and every decision that I shall render be an echo
of His still, small voice! Even as your decisions are the articu-
lations of the Inarticulate!*

My newly assumed judicial duties absorbed me; 1927 was
the happiest year of my public life. My decisions were com-
mented upon favorably by the foreign papers as well as by
the Chinese papers. I felt that I was moulding the law of
China by my judicial opinions. In one case involving a point
in International Law, I took the opportunity for laying down
an important principle: "The Law of Nations is a part of
the municipal law of China." In another case, involving the
art of tailoring, an American paper reported the judicial proceedings under the headline of "Solomon Sits in Judgment!"
One Chinese paper dubbed me "Wu Ching T'ien," which
means "Wu the Clear Sky." In one year, I had become so
famous in Shanghai that my wife told me that all the shops
into which she had gone to buy things would gladly give
credit to her. They said to her, "Oh, are you the wife of Judge
Wu? Then you can take away anything without cash pay-
ment. You can pay later."

I was frightened, and asked her, "Did you accept their
politeness?"

"Oh, no," she said, "how can I utilize your prestige?"

This reminds me of a terrible scene I had one day with
my dear sister. She was five years my senior. Our relations
were among the most unpleasant and the most pleasant. As I
am subjectively sure that she is now in Heaven, I think a
naked presentation of our relations would not do her any
harm. She was married to a banker, a good-natured fat boy.
Their economic conditions were fairly good; whenever I was
in need, they never hesitated to give a helping hand. They
were not only generous to me, but to all their friends and

relatives in need of help. Materially speaking, they were all that a sister and a brother-in-law should be. But their philosophy of life was rather materialistic. When I was a judge they used to call me a fool because of my uncompromising attitude against bribery!

One day I visited my sister in an exceptionally cheerful mood, and I found her playing ma-jonng with three relatives, as a pastime. Upon seeing me, one of them was so courteous as to yield his seat to me, and I sat in. Everything seemed to bid fair. My sister, seeing me in such a nice mood, began to expound to me her philosophy of a judge accepting gifts from the litigants. "To receive gifts for doing justice is not bribery," she began her sermon. "It would be different if you distorted justice on account of money. If you do justice, and a litigant make a present to you in appreciation of your fairness, where is the wrong in accepting it? On the contrary, to refuse it would only offend people; and after all one must be sociable."

I do not remember the exact words, but this is the purport of what she said. At first I listened silently, trying to fix my attention on the cards. But she continued to harp upon the same theme to such an extent that the others also joined in to support her argument. I was so fed up with all their words that I could no longer control my anger. I lost my temper and acted like a mad person. I overturned the table and threw all the cards on the ground. I hurled the harshest words at her; I said, "It is indeed a disgrace that our parents should have borne a daughter like you! 'To accept money for doing justice!' Such a thing is unheard of. Do you want me to prostitute my judicial office?"

My sister was also angry, convinced as she was of the reasonableness of her philosophy. She said, "If you do not listen to my well-meaning advice, some day you will regret it. If you are in need, don't expect anybody to help you."

I went away, saying, "Let us each go his way. If no one will help me, God will. Someday you may need my help."

Upon my return home, which was just the next door to the house of my sister, I could not speak a word, brooding over what had happened. My wife, who had heard the noise, asked, "What is it?" I told her all about it. She said, "Your liver must be inflamed. What you said was right, and your sister was wrong. But your manners were awful. Bad manners are no better than receiving bribery! What you should have done was to win her patiently to your way of thinking instead of hurling such harsh words at her. Do you not remember how good she has been to us?"

"Am I not a judge?" I said. "A judge is like a virgin who must guard her chastity with the utmost jealousy."

"You are a judge when you are in court," she said, "but when you are at home you are just a husband and a father. To your sister, you are a younger brother; but you certainly did not act like one."

"Anyway, you agree with my point of view, don't you?" I asked.

"Certainly," she replied, "I would rather be starved with you than expect you to accept bribes." I wept immediately, partly for joy and partly out of gratitude.

Later, my brother-in-law fell on bad days, and whenever my sister came to me for help, I always did what I could, but was mean enough to say to her that the more one desires money the less money one gets, such being the way of Heaven. So long was my memory! But spite does not win any souls to God. As St. Francis of Sales said, "An ounce of sugar catches more flies than a ton of vinegar." Before anyone can imitate the just indignation of Christ, it would be well for him to steep himself in His meekness and humility of heart. If God had been as unforgiving to me as I was to my sister, I should have been in Hell long ago.

In the meantime, I was neglecting my correspondence with Holmes. My silence worried him. One day in early 1928, a friend of mine, Mr. Whitamore of the British Consulate in Shanghai, caught me by the shoulder, and said, "Now I have found the culprit! Here is a telegram from England, communicating to us that Mr. Justice Holmes of the Supreme Court of the United States desires to know whether you are still living." The fact is that Holmes had written to Professor Laski in London, telling him of his anxiety about me, and Laski had started the inquiry. In fact, I had written to Holmes on the New Year's Day of 1928, but the letter was not received before the whole inquiry started.

But the strange thing is that, successful as I was as a judge, I was still feeling restless. In a letter dated February 12, 1928, after describing my popularity in Shanghai, I concluded with this: "But popularity begins to worry me; for a really great man could not possibly be as popular as I am, at least, when he is still living. I have had too much of the Old Testament blessing; I covet the blessing of the New Testament, the blessing of adversity. This thought has reinforced my desire to escape from the prosperity that enshrouds me, by coming to America for further study and self-culture. My great friend, help me to realize this dream." As I look back upon it, I really cannot understand all this restlessness and curvetting. Was it because the Hound of Heaven was chasing after me, so that He did not want to see me rest in anything short of Himself? Or did it come from my Faustian spirit of adventure? Or was it due to an unconscious desire to see Holmes once more? I wonder.

Anyway, Holmes did not approve it. He wrote: "You are

beginning to run a long race, and restlessness and curvetting seem like a waste of precious energy. . . . Brandeis who agreed with me as to what was wisest for you to do sent me the extract from Pliny's letters. It is the advice of some older man to Pliny: 'To be engaged in the service of the public, to hear and determine causes, to explain the laws and administer justice, is a part and the noblest part of philosophy, as it is reducing to practice what the professors teach in speculation.' "

When two Supreme Court Justices decided against my going to America, I was pacified for a period and continued to be a judge. I was promoted to be Chief Justice and later President of the Court. In the summer of 1929, I tried the famous "Roulette Case" which stirred the whole population of Shanghai. I need not enter into the details of the proceedings, because I am not writing an autobiography but only the story of my spiritual pilgrimage. I will only reproduce an editorial from the British paper, the *North China Daily News*, on one of my remarks during the proceedings. The attorney for the defence, Dr. Fischer, had said that if I should be too severe with the foreigners, it would delay or impede the rendition of extraterritoriality. This argument sounded a bit too political to my judicial ears. My answer is embodied in the editorial:

JUDGE JOHN WU ON LAW THE IDOL

Without at all referring to the Garcia case, which must be regarded as sub-judice for the present, one cannot ignore a remark of Judge John Wu, before whom the case is being tried in the Provisional Court. Commenting upon certain remarks of Dr. Fischer, Judge Wu said: "However, the facts you have outlined in your application may be taken into consideration as mitigating circumstances when the second charge is tried, but in my opinion your arguments, political arguments, if I may say so, are neither appropriate nor relevant. Law is the only idol of this court, not the rendition or abolition of extraterritoriality. I would rather do justice and by so doing constitute an obstacle to the rendition or abolition of extraterritoriality than perpetrate a miscarriage of justice which might expedite or favour the abolition of extraterritoriality.'

Hidden away at the end of a long day in Court, Judge Wu's statement may be overlooked, but it is of such importance that it must be isolated from the remainder of the minutes of the case, because it represents an advance in Chinese judicial independence.

The foreign distrust of the abolition of extraterritoriality has been based upon objections more to the administration of China's courts than to the codes, which Dr. C. T. Wang believes will shortly be completed. Codes of law can be enacted without much difficulty but if the enforcement of the law by the Courts represents the practical group or is utilized by political agencies to foster a political cause, then foreigners naturally wonder what would become of their rights and interests, of their lives and property in the event of such courts exercising jurisdiction over them. If then, Judge Wu is laying down the exact status of the administration of the law in Chinese courts, he has done more benefit to his country than reams of manifestoes and interviews on the abolition of extraterritoriality.

The administration of the law in any country involves certain specific protections for the judiciary and the courts. The law becomes an idol. Whether it is a good law or a bad one, it remains the law and as long as it is on the statute books, it may not be transgressed. Persons of high estate and low must be subject to it impartially and the judge must know no friendships or outside obligations. He must have no political, religious or racial affiliations, while he is actually seated on the bench. This is a high ideal, but in many Western countries, this ideal is achieved.

In olden days, such was not the conception of the law and the Courts in China. The magistrates were administrative officers who performed numerous services in addition to their judicial responsibilities. They were guided more by reason than by the law which was rather a philosophic treatise than a legal code. This tradition naturally continues to the present day. The various modern judicial agencies will, in due course, break away from the dangers of personal reasoning and from whimsical resorts to esoteric considerations. But genuine progress in this direction will take time. Making the law an idol has not been achieved in Great Britain or the United States in one century. It will not be achieved in China in one year. If only this sense of time, this need for training, could be emphasized by the more realistic Chinese, who must know that deeds and not propaganda will win the day for them, then their aspirations will be reached with greater rapidity. Judge Wu is to be congratulated on a wise statement of the functions that his court should fulfil.

In the autumn of the same year, I received two invitations from America, one from the Harvard Law School to join its faculty as a Research Fellow for the spring term of 1930, the other from the Northwestern University Law School to be the Rosenthal Lecturer for the winter of 1929. I resigned from the Court to prepare myself for the trip.

An interesting thing happened when I went to the office of Thomas Cook to book my steamship ticket. An English employee of the company, seeing me sign myself as John Wu, waxed warm and said to me, "So you are the son of the famous Judge Wu! You have a great father. We all admire his decisions." Apparently, he took me for John Wu, Jr. I was thirty then, but I looked like a boy of twenty. Well, I answered the gentleman, "My dear friend, you take me for my son, but the fact is that I am my father!" You can imagine how tantalized he was.

In December I found myself in Chicago. I saw my great friend John Henry Wigmore for the first time, and we had a happy time together. Wigmore was one of the outstanding jurists of the world. Besides being the greatest American authority on the Law of Evidence, he was a past-master in comparative jurisprudence. As a man he was most charming and generous to his friends. It was he who first "discovered" Roscoe Pound. When I was with him, I found him studying Arabic. By that time, he must have been around seventy. His love of learning reminded me of Confucius, who was so eager in the pursuit of wisdom that he forgot his age.

I owe to Wigmore a laurel which I regard as one of the chief rewards of my juristic life. The laurel will fade, but the love never. In a lengthy review of my book, *Juridical Essays and Studies*, which was published in 1928, he was so generous as to say among other things:

The Chinese nature—not unlike the American—includes the two marked but opposite forces of idealism and realism. In China, but not in our own country (whose idealism is rather of an emotional type), this idealism takes the form of abstract thinking. China has had its long line of philosophers, as well as its long line of merchant princes. At more than one period, indeed, it would seem that the ideal political status which Socrates described ("when philosophers are kings, or kings are philosophers") was realized in history.

However, when philosophers become judges (and capable judges), and these opposite traits of idealism and realism are thus united in full force in one person, it is an extraordinary combination. (Confucius, by the way, was once chief justice of his province.) And this extraordinary combination is found in John C. H. Wu, the author whose essays are here collected.

As a legal philosopher, the author now stands in the front rank. To the reviewer the most entertaining, original and stimulating parts of the book are the footnotes to each essay.

Here the author comments candidly as if chatting with his friends and readers. There is nothing like it in ordinary books by philosophers or lawyers. These notes read like the frank, intimate, mental play of a Chesterton. A pity that some of our legal authors do not have the easy self-confidence to do likewise!

Another stimulating feature is that the author has read everything—yes, everything, from Spinoza and Bertrand Russell and William James and Benedetto Croce to the Supreme Court of Indiana. Just to glance over the eighty footnotes to the essay on Stammler is to make one wish for more time to read; and in the seventy-seven footnotes to the "Readings from Ancient Chinese Codes," the reviewer is free to confess that he found some bibliographical information that he had sought in vain in more pretentious works.[1]

Another laurel I owe to Roscoe Pound, who, in a review of my *The Art of Law*, was so kind as to write:

By "art of law" Dr. Wu means the art of achieving the ends of legal order through the application of the authoritative technique and the interpretation and application of the authoritative precepts. Thus he means more than the judicial process. His art would include along with that the administrative process. But his is not, any more than was Mr. Justice Holmes's, a realism that would leave us nothing but administrative orders, each on its own basis of individual psychology or prejudice or unguided intuition, masked behind a pretense of laws or law. He understands the role of intuition and that of analysis and does not seek an easy retreat from the hard work of the judicial office in a theory of psychologically inevitable judicial impotence to reach an impersonal result.

Dr. Wu's experience in a cosmopolitan court in which a new body of law had to be applied to an exceptional diversity of cases and men and conditions, joined with a clear insight into men and things, a subtle mind, and very human

[1] *Illinois Law Review*, 1929.

feeling for those who come before him, give his sayings and aphorisms a universal quality which it would be impossible to match in the writings of a common-law judge.[2]

I have introduced these words from the two great masters because I treasure them, and because they are relevant to my present purpose in that they help me to know more clearly my spiritual physiognomy. As I think of it, the dominant characteristic of my mental make-up seems to be a persistent tendency to bring into harmony things which are apparently contradictory to each other. This tendency is a source at once of joy and of pain: of joy, because by every harmonization one transcends the world of discords; of pain, because not all things are reconcilable. I have often felt like one who has lost all the battles of life; as to whether I shall ultimately win the war, only God knows and only God can help. Now let me resume the story of my juristic pilgrimage.

After I had finished my lectures at the Northwestern Law School, I proceeded in January 1930 to Harvard, where I spent a semester making research in juristic thought. But I was not very happy there, because Pound was on leave of absence. He was working with the Wickersham Commission. I got along with Joseph Beal fairly well, but he could not help me much, as he was more a legal technician than a legal philosopher. My spirits were very low, and my mind was blank. Somehow I felt I had made a mistake in leaving my work in China. And I was homesick. So contradictory was my mind! When I was at home, I was sick of my home; but when I was away from home, I was homesick! Although I was near Holmes now, I did not go to see him until some time in April. We were of course very happy in seeing each other again. But I was not all myself, because in the back of my

[2] *Harvard Law Review*, 1937.

mind was the uncomfortable thought that I should have accepted his advice by sticking to my job in China, but I could not bring myself to admit it to him. On his part, I could observe that while he was in good health his cheerfulness had ebbed with age, although his friendship had grown even deeper. Someone was missing. The charming lady was no more!

How low my religious faith had sunk can be gauged by the words I wrote him from Cambridge on April 30:

I was certainly overjoyed to find you in such good shape. You looked no older than a man of sixty, and were more iconoclastic than ever. It takes great mental vigor to be a sceptic, and your scepticism did not show any signs of decay! You cannot be bribed even by the subtle influences of circumstances and age!

At the end of the term, Beal gave me an invitation to be a Lecturer on Comparative Law. On asking what branch of law he wanted me to teach, I learned that it was to be the law of sales! Nothing could be farther from my interest. I arranged with the Law School to let me go back to China in order to collect more materials on the Chinese law of sales, and to bring my family with me.

Before I took the trip, I went to Beverly Farms to see Holmes and to tell him about my arrangement with the Law School for the next year and about my trip to China. He was happy. I showed him also the beginning parts of an article on "The Mind of Justice Holmes." He was extremely pleased with some of my remarks about him. He was especially impressed by this:

Anyone who sees in him only the dissenter is deceived; his very dissent springs from a desire to seek harmony in the cosmos, to catch "a gale confederate with the current of the soul." He is a nonconformist because he is a conformist in the higher sense.

When he came upon this, he read aloud "a gale confederate with the current of the soul." "What a happy quotation!" he said. "It is from Wordsworth," I said, "But the idea is akin to what The Professor at the Breakfast Table said: 'Faith always implies the disbelief of a lesser fact in favor of a greater. A little mind often sees the unbelief, without seeing the belief of larger ones.' " He expressed his delight. When I was saying this, I frequently lifted my eyes to the little portrait of his father under which he was sitting. We enjoyed a few hours of quiet conversation. As I took leave of him, I said, "I will see you again when I come back from China." But actually this was the last time I saw him, because I did not come back from China as planned. Fifteen years later I visited his and Mrs. Holmes' tomb at Allinton.

On June 16, 1930, he wrote me some words which I regard as among the greatest consolations of my life: "As I told you, so far as I can judge from a rapid glance I was deeply pleased with what you had written about me, and thought it showed an insight that I hardly expected from any one."

On my return home, I found my wife in ill health and not in a position to travel, and I would not think of coming back to Cambridge without bringing my family. So I had to resign from my lectureship and think of something else to do in Shanghai. I decided to practise law. That was the beginning of the best and the worst period of my life, best materially but worst spiritually. But of this more later.

I wrote to Holmes that I had resigned from the Harvard Law School and gone into the practice of law. Instead of blaming me, he wrote to express his delight, as he thought it would bring me into contact with the actualities of life.

The last letter I had from him was dated March 14, 1932:

Thank you for your letter. I have been wondering about you and whether things were going well. I can't give you an adequate answer because writing has become difficult to me. I have no other reason than 91 years. Perhaps you know that shortly before my last birthday I resigned my seat on the Bench. I am well but don't want to do any work at present. My secretary reads to me some philosophy and economics but more modern stories. With a daily drive and long hours in bed, calls made upon me and some necessary letters, I find my hands full. Frankfurter was quoted the other day for a suggestion that I might write a book about the law. I can think of a first sentence, but after that I should like to study and I doubt if I shall study any more. At all events I mean to take life easy for a time.

Since I began this I have had a call from Cardozo. I think you would love him as I do and have from the first moment I saw him—a beautiful spirit.

Affectionately yours,

O. W. Holmes

Thanks also for the article which seems to me good.

Holmes died on March 6, 1935. On March 7, his successor, Justice Benjamin N. Cardozo, who was another dear friend of mine, wrote me: "Your letter reached me yesterday, the day on which Holmes died. You will feel as I do that a great light has gone out of the world. There is no one to take his place. He will be buried tomorrow—his birthday. He would be ninety-four if he had lived."

For me, the friendship has not ended. I often remember him in my prayers.

It may be asked how his friendship has influenced my spiritual life. My answer is that I profited by it as I have by

the study of Shakespeare. In fact, in an article which I wrote
in 1935, I compared him with Shakespeare. I said:

Their minds belong to the same order. Their greatness lies
in the combination of the mastery of details with a perennial
yearning after the infinite. With both, this yearning after
the infinite permeates, enlivens, and transfigures all the sordid
questions of the earth they may happen to handle. With
both, an irresistible vision of the whole surged up through
the smallest chink of opportunity. With both, there is an
inveterate habit of seeing things in relation to the stars and
the general scheme of things, and hence, a continual escape
to universal considerations. Like Shakespeare, Holmes is a
philosophic contemplator of the world, to whom the universe
seems infinite, and himself nothing, and whose mind dwells
in the unseen essences of things. It may with equal appro-
priateness be said of both that they see the familiar as if it
were strange, and the strange as if it were familiar; that they
find a deep meaning in what is trivial, and a trifling one in
what appears to be serious; that they have divided so deeply
that they can unite, and united so deeply that they can
divide; that they can move swiftly from point to point, and
be present at the focus where the greatest number of vital
forces unite in their purest energy; that they are so original
that they can borrow, and borrow so well that their origin-
ality is thereby enhanced; that they are otherworldly, and
therefore they can be worldly in a grand manner; and, finally,
that they look at life with a spice of humor, and therefore their works have attained a high seriousness.

It will be noted that this whole "series of counterpoints,"
as my friend Russell Cades calls them, does not really move
beyond the sphere of nature to the realm of grace. But grace
fulfills nature rather than destroys it. If, therefore, this whole
series of counterpoints can be lifted to the sphere of grace,
it would enrich one's spiritual life rather than impede it in
any way. Holmes' catholicity has broadened my mind and

thus prepared me indirectly to embrace Catholicism, the house with many mansions.

Holmes wrote in 1896 a remarkable passage which seems to me to be the key of his mental outlook:

George Herbert's

"Who sweeps a room as for Thy laws,
Makes that and th' action fine,"

has an intellectual as well as a moral meaning. If the world is a subject for rational thought it is all of one piece; the same laws are found everywhere, and if this is so, there is nothing mean, and nothing in which may not be seen the universal law.

Now, Herbert's couplet is one of the most *spiritual* insights that I have come across in the religious poetry of England. Its meaning is higher than merely moral or intellectual. But Holmes applied this highly spiritual insight to a lower sphere, the sphere of intellectual speculation. By a reverse process, one may apply some of Holmes' flashes of insight in the lower sphere of nature and genius to the higher sphere of grace and spirit. For instance, he said, "The mode in which the inevitable comes to pass is through effort." This suggests to me a very practical solution of the problem of free will and predestination. Many people waste their precious time in speculating about whether they are predestined to Heaven or to hell; while all that they need to know is that the will of God is their sanctification, and that they must exert their utmost in cooperating with the grace of God, which is open to all. We may say therefore that the mode in which predestination is fulfilled is through the exercise of your free will.

Take another instance. Holmes used to advise me "to tackle the unromantic with resolution to make it romantic."

Taken on the face value, this moves entirely in the natural sphere. But this does not prevent me from applying it to the sphere of spiritual life so as to transmute, with the indispensable help of grace, the most ordinary things of life into eternal values. Thus uplifted, the attitude of Holmes is clearly akin to the spirit of St. Thérèse. As her sister Marie used to tell her when she was a child, "Look at those who want to become rich, and see how they toil for gold. Now, little Thérèse, with far less trouble and at any hour of the day, we can lay up riches in the Kingdom of God. Heavenly diamonds are so plentiful that we can gather them, so to speak, with a golden rake, and we do this by performing all actions for the love of God." Thérèse herself says, "We must not let slip one single occasion of sacrifice, everything has such value in the religious life . . . *Pick up a pin from a motive of love, and you may thereby convert a soul.*" This is a higher romance than a merely intellectual pursuit. But the fact is, it was Holmes' outlook on life that prepared me to accept the "little way" of St. Thérèse.

The great charm of Holmes to me was that he was old in wisdom but young in spirit.

Our starting points were different. He was a pantheist; I, a theist. His ultimate was the Cosmos; my ultimate, God. His philosophy was more akin to the spirit of Taoism, while mine was fundamentally Christian even when I was not living as a Christian. He seems, in fact, to be more Oriental than I am; although I cannot say that I am more Western than he.

But in spite of our differences in faith and in temperament, our friendship grew up to his very end. He was so good as to keep all my eighty-odd letters except the first few, and after his death his Estate has given all of them back to me. What is the secret of this lasting friendship? So far as I can see,

the most fundamental thing that we have in common is an
ever fresh sense of wonder at the mystery of the universe.
Even when he was in his nineties, he still kept the sense of
wonder as fresh as if he were a child. Although I am a Christian and believe in the revelation, yet I too enjoy the sense of
wonder, for the simple reason that God has not revealed to us
everything, and that His revelation itself is to me a greater
mystery than the existence of the universe. As St. Thomas has
said, "This is the final human knowledge of God: to know
that we do not know God." In the end God is the only Theologian worthy of the name.

We were two old babies. I was a baby who was an old man.
He was an old man who was a baby. And the two old babies
corresponded with each other for fourteen years on questions
belonging more to eternity than to time. We were asking
each other whether life was a dream. Our conclusion was that
we could never prove that we were awake, and that it took
an act of faith to assert that. He never wearied of stressing
the need of faith. He wrote to me, "If I were dying my last
words would be: have faith and pursue the unknown end."
It is ironical that a man who talked so much about faith
should be called a sceptic. Concretely his faith was not mine,
but his philosophy of faith, vague as it was, did encourage
me to embrace what I could not help regarding as the true
Faith. I said to him once, "Beneath your cynicism, Sir, there
pulses a warm heart."

Self-knowledge is proverbially rare. That is why we have
the need of true and wise friends to point out to us candidly
our bad points as well as our good points. Every one of us
needs encouragement; and every one of us needs improvement. A good friend goes a long way towards supplying those
needs. I cannot thank God enough for having given me in
my youth a friend like Holmes who was as frank as he was

kind. I appreciated his kindness because he was frank; and I appreciated his frankness because he was kind. In this respect, he was an unconscious Christian, as so many good Americans are. As my friend Judge Frank McLaughlin would put it, America is essentially Christian, and many people breathe the atmosphere of Christianity without even being aware of it.

In spite of my apparent buoyancy of spirit, Holmes discovered a streak of pessimism in me. So he encouraged me by saying that I bore the fire in my belly, that I could write well, that he expected fine things from me in the field of abstract thought, that what I needed was self-confidence, that I should cultivate faith in faith, that my soul had generous ardors which should be fed with fuel to keep burning, that he agreed with me on this and that and many other points. On the other hand, he saw a tendency in me to forget the particular for the universal, the near for the far, the tree for the wood, the human for the divine. And his advice has stood me in good stead.

In one of his last letters to me, dated June 16, 1930, he made a keen observation of my nature: *"My inference was that you alternated violently between exaltation and discouragement."* Concerning this violent alternation between discouragement and exaltation, I have written in an article called "Thoughts and Fancies" (published in *T'ien Hsia Monthly*, January, 1940) a passage which represents my later state. It is a comment on Pascal, but it indicates what changes had been wrought in my soul by that time. I wrote:

No lay philosopher has understood the spirit of the Christian religion more profoundly than he has. He has taken his time to live into it, and therefore he knows what he is talking about. He tells us, for instance, that the Christian religion makes those tremble whom it justifies, and consoles those whom it condemns; that "it humbles infinitely more than reason alone can do, but without despair," and "exalts infinitely more than natural pride, but without inflating." No one could have written these words, unless he had felt in his very bones this mysterious compound of humble exaltation. Left alone to himself, a man swings back and forth ceaselessly like a pendulum between depression and exhilaration. But with the help of Jesus, the swinging becomes so powerful that it describes a complete circle, in which each point is at once exaltation and humility. It is more than a compromise between the two; it is a mysterious Identification. But a thing is no less real because it is mysterious. Nay more, were it not a mystery, it would not be Reality.

11. DE PROFUNDIS

It was in the fall of 1930 that I started the practice of law in Shanghai. Now, the Shanghai people had known me as a judge well versed in the law; so, as soon as they heard that I was practising, many of them flocked to me as clients. Within the very first month I received so many retainerships and cases that my income amounted to no less than forty thousand taels—almost equivalent to forty thousand American dollars! I had earned in one month more than all the salaries I had got as a judge and as a professor put together. Money, or at least too much money, is the root of all evils. I had an offer from the Supreme Court to join its Bench. My friend Judge Lin Hsi-chih came down specially from Nanking to press me to accept it. But by that time I was already too entangled in the practice to quit it. I continued to earn handsome fees. Gradually my clients began to invite me to attend their parties in the "flowery houses," and I offered parties in the same places in return. Before I realized it I had become

a regular play-boy. For two and one half years I was out
practically every night. Even to think of those days smells
hell. All the time I was utterly unhappy and dissatisfied with
myself, but I was not able to pull my feet out of the mud.
The more unhappy I was the more eagerly I sought after
pleasures; and the more I indulged in the pleasures, the more
unhappy I was. It was a terrible whirlpool that I was in. I
became a prey to the sense of despair. Whenever anybody
talked religion to me, I would get into a temper and call him
down, "Don't be a hypocrite!" I remember one day Mr.
Charles W. Rankin came to my office, trying to restore my
faith in Christianity. We had a long argument, and I
remained unconvinced. I shot harsh words at him, "You are
a bigot. Can you show me the proofs of your faith?" He was
so deeply hurt that he would not even accept my contributions to his institution in Chi-nan, called the Bible University,
saying that he would not take money from such a sinner and
blasphemer. But at heart I knew that he was a good man, to
whom I had owed my first conversion and the rudiments of
my legal education. So I resorted to a ruse in making him
accept my money. I gave the money to one of my classmates,
Dr. T. K. Loh (God bless his memory!), who, although not
a Christian, was not *persona non grata* to Rankin, and
requested him to present it to him in his own name. The
good man accepted it without ever suspecting that the money
came from me.

Another friend of mine, Mr. Yuan Chia-yuan, who was a
Catholic, often came to my office. He made several attempts
at introducing the topic of religion, but I always brushed it
aside by saying, "Let us talk about something more interesting!"

In those days I was also addicted to all sorts of fortune-
telling. A relative of mine was an expert physiognomist. I had

my face examined by him every day, to forecast my luck. I
consulted practically all the famous horoscopists in Shanghai.
I myself learned their art, and used to cast fortunes for others.

One of the reasons why I was so unhappy and restless in
those days was my dissatisfaction with the chaotic conditions
of the country. Another, and perhaps a deeper, cause was
that I had somehow absorbed a worldly philosophy of life.
I regretted that I was married to such an uneducated wife,
a wife who could not help me at all in my intellectual,
social, and political activities. I had made several attempts
to teach her how to read; but every time she said that as soon
as her eyes were fixed on the characters, her head began to
swim. Once or twice I went to the extent of proposing a
divorce so that I might marry an educated wife, as many
others had done. But as soon as she consented, I relented,
for my conscience told me it was wrong. In the meantime,
having nothing in common between us, I felt an utter loneli-
ness at home. I loathed the very sight of my wife, and as for
my children I did not think of them at all, except when any
one of them was sick.

I am deeply ashamed when I recall how I treated my
brother at this time. Equipped (largely through his goodness)
with modern education, I have been more successful in the
world than he; and, materially speaking, I have not been
stingy in helping him. But in terms of affection, I have not
been half as devoted to him as he has been to me. Whenever
I visited him in Ningpo at our old home, he always reserved
the best bed for me and kept me company day and night.
But when he came to visit us in Shanghai, I was never able
to show such a singlehearted devotion. In the daytime I was
surrounded by a group of friends and at night I went to the
flowery houses.

That I am not painting myself blacker than I actually was

can be gathered by some incidents that happened in those days. Once I happened to pick up an exercise book of my eldest daughter, Chin-an (later baptized Agnes), and noticed therein was a diary that she wrote for her teachers. She wrote something to this effect: "Our family life is simply miserable. For the last few weeks, I have not had a glimpse of my father. When I come to school in the morning, they tell me that Father has just gone to bed; and when I return home in the afternoon, they tell me that Father has just gone out to seek for pleasures. My mother is weeping everyday. O heaven, why should I be born in such a family?" On reading these words, my heart was pierced with indescribable grief. However I did not mend my life.

(By the way, just lately I have received a most affectionate letter from the same daughter Agnes, who is now residing in Ecuador with her husband, Henry Sun, telling me, "I cannot imagine a better father in the whole world!" I wonder if she remembers what she had written about me in her diary. It is not without reason that I have written recently: "With Christ, the home is a prelude to Heaven. Without Christ, it is a prelude to Hell.")

On one of those days, my eldest son Tsu-ling (later baptized Thomas), who had just returned from his school in Soochow, took me to task. With a forced smile on his face, he approached me in the tactful way characteristic of him, saying, "Daddy, I wish to speak with you, but I am afraid that Daddy will be offended."

"Speak," I said, sensing something ominous.

"Daddy," he said, "I have heard so many rumors about you even in Soochow that I do not believe that they could be true."

I was deeply impressed by the lad's tactful frankness. I interrupted him by saying, "My dear boy, I know what those rumors are. They are quite true! I promise you that I will reform." But I did not carry out the promise.

Even to recall those days makes me shudder. But the climax was yet to come. In 1934, when I had quit the practice of law and joined the Legislature, drafting the Constitution of China, I took a fancy to a singing girl, and asked my wife's permission to take her to be my concubine. My wife (God bless her!) did not consent. She said, however, "When you reach forty, you make take one."

I jumped at it, and said, "Do you really mean it?"

"I do," she said.

"Let us shake hands to mark this solemn promise," I said, "so that there may be no repentance when the time comes." We shook hands.

In 1938 I was to be forty, according to the Chinese way of reckoning age. I had only four years to wait before I could have a concubine with the authorization of my wife! The promised land was in sight, but the all-merciful Father had better plans. Just a few days before 1938, He snatched me from the grip of the Devil and saved me from myself. I was received into the Holy Catholic Church on December 18, 1937; and the nightmare which had lasted for more than seven long years came to an end.

But even before my reception into the Church, I had begun to react from that extreme point of degradation. My view of marriage was developing. There were two conceptions of marriage striving for mastery in China: the old and the new. The old conception was fatalistic; the new conception, which was supposed to be imported from the "West," was entirely based upon the free will of the parties. As could be expected, the old was steadily losing ground before the onsets of the revolutionary torrents. But the new ideology went beyond the bounds of reason. Some of its war-cries were: "Free marriage, free divorce." "Marriage is the grave of love." For a time I myself fell a prey to this ultra-romantic ideal. In my twenties I wrote: "Philosophical system is to insight what marriage is to love." That is to say, just as marriage is the grave of love, so philosophical system is the grave of insight. In fact, I announced an important principle of legal evolution: Legal institutions progress *from chance to choice.*

Some of the free-willists went so far as to exchange their wives or their husbands with one another—for a change! That kind of thing repelled my esthetic sense. It seemed to me that the free-willists, in emancipating themselves from the tyranny of the will of parents, became slaves to their own free will. Poor flounders, they leaped from the frying-pan to the fire!

In my middle thirties, I had begun to react strongly against the hegemony of sheer individualism, which had spelled the ruin of so many families. Sociologically, I was tending toward a kind of solidarism which, while admitting the importance of individual liberty, would keep it within the bounds of reason so as to secure social stability. On November 5, 1936, midway between my asking my wife's permission to take a concubine and my entering the Church, I made this entry in my diary:

With us old-timers in China, marriage is not the grave of love, but a little garden in which to cultivate the tree of love. As the tree grows, it bears flowers and yields fruits. And we regard our girls as flowers and boys as fruits.

Once I had a quarrel with my wife, and I threw angry words at her. I said, "Look here, a wife is supposed to be a helpmate. What help have you ever rendered to me this many years? You cannot even read my letters to you. . . ."

"Stop!" she cried through sobs, "I know all this myself. But anyway I have borne you children, have I not?"

I wept immediately, and ever since then I have not had another quarrel with my sweetheart.

I have often said to my eldest son, who is already at marriageable age, "Young man! I didn't choose your mother, your grandpa did it for me. But you will have to choose your own wife. Be careful in making your choice. But one thing you must bear in mind: whomsoever you may marry, do not expect her to be an angel all at once. She will become one in the course of time."

Thus, I was groping toward a working synthesis of individual liberty and family stability, by introducing the interests of the children. I had started as a fatalist, became a free-willist, and ended by being a solidarist. In a spirit of self-irony, I wrote the following:

The Circle

I have undergone two recapitulations: once in my mother's womb, and the second time after my birth. In less than forty years I have lived at least for ten centuries. I began as a member of my clan, worshipping my ancestors: by this time I have become a citizen of the world, looking forward to the future of man. My parents chose my wife for me: now I find two of my sons choosing their own wives. I was born under the flickering light of colzaoil lamp; when some of my children saw the light, it was the electrical light. I passed my childhood in the Medieval Age; in my teens and twenties, I went through the Renaissance, the Reformation, The French Revolution and Nineteenth Century Liberalism: from thirty up to now, I have returned to a kind of Solidarism very much akin to my starting point. I am just like a donkey tied to an old-fashioned millstone, that walks round and round for a whole day, but never walks out of a house. Every step seems to be an advance over the last, but in the long run I am just as far from the mill as when I started. I hate geometry, because I am personally insulted by the definition of a circle.

Had I not reached some kind of a synthesis? How was it then that I was still writing as one who had not found his

resting place? The truth is that no merely pragmatic or naturalistic solution could satisfy the deeper needs of my soul. A
true synthesis could only be attained when one is elevated
by grace from the conflicting opposites to a sphere higher
than both of them.

Whenever I think of the infinite mercies of God, I cannot
help exclaiming with St. Paul: "Oh the depth of the riches
of the wisdom and of the knowledge of God! How incomprehensible are his judgments, and how unsearchable his
ways. For who has known the mind of the Lord? Or who has
been his counsellor?"

While reserving the story of my conversion to another
chapter, I want to give the reader a glimpse of what Christ
has done to our family. Since I became a Catholic, my family
has followed me into the Church, and Christ the King has
been enthroned in our house. My wife and I have found our
rest in the Sacred Heart of Christ. We are bound together
by a common Love. As we progress in the love of God, we
progress in the love of each other. For the past few years, my
wife and I have been receiving Holy Communion practically
every day. This has become more or less a habit. Even when
I miss it once in a while, my wife still goes to the church,
saying, "You are tired this morning, you need a rest. I will
go to receive Holy Communion myself. I will pray for you.
It is just like receiving it together." But this is exceptional.
Usually we go together. Every time I find myself kneeling
before the Communion rail by the side of my wife, I feel a
thrill of joy and wonder. It is as though the ceremony of
drinking the love-wine were renewed in a transfigured form
from day to day. We feel as though our marriage itself were
being renewed every morning and each renewal has deepened
our love. O Christ, I say inwardly, how could this be possible?
Am I dreaming or is this a real experience? You have made

our life a continual honeymoon of which our life on earth is only the prelude. O Christ, our hearts are united in the love of You, and how can we ever be separated so long as neither of us is separated from You? In Your Sacred Heart we have found our Home; who says that we are exiles? O God, Your will is our destiny, and to do Your will is our freedom!

God has opened my eyes gradually to the interior qualities of my wife, to such a degree that, whereas I formerly thought she was not worthy of me, now I realize that I am not worthy of her. Christ has become the living bond between us. We have become "two hands folded in eternal adoration." Although, politically and materially speaking, we are much worse off than before we were Catholics, our life for the past decade has really been a perpetual feast. We do not "adore" each other. No, for man and wife to "adore" each other would be sheer idolatry, egoism multiplied by two. We only adore the Christ that we have in common, and it is He who binds us together. As each of us comes closer to Christ, we find that we are coming closer to each other.

Many a time, of course, the old Adam and old Eve have come back again—the old Adam especially. They die pretty hard; and whenever they are alive and kicking, they bring discords with them. But the Divine Composer is always waiting for us at the Confessional, and every time we bring our little discords to Him, He resolves them into a sweeter harmony than ever. Indeed, it was not for nothing that my wife was born at the foot of "the Bridge of Celestial Harmony"! One evening in 1944, when we were in Chungking, I quarreled with my wife in the very midst of our family Rosary. A shame on me! I lost my temper and, quitting the Rosary halfway, went into my room to sulk, closing the door with a bang. I thought my wife would follow me immediately into the room and pat me as a fond mother would pat a spoiled child. But she did nothing of the sort; she continued the Rosary calmly with our children, as if nothing had happened. Suddenly I heard the voice of my second son Edward, who was now leading the Rosary in my stead, calling out to the rest of the kids, "Let us all kneel and pray to Our Blessed Mother for Daddy!" I felt as though the poisonous dragon within me was trampled under foot by Our Lady. Before the Rosary ended I had slipped back quietly, and found myself kneeling humbly behind my little ones. The first had become the last! I learned a salutary lesson. One who is not humble will end by being abject. Ever since then I have not dared to lose temper at the Rosary time. Or do you want to test the power of the Queen of Heaven?

Recently I came across a passage in the writings of one of our dearest friends, Dr. Paul K. T. Sih, who was converted in Rome about two years ago and who has become a most devout Catholic. The passage gives a description of our family, which seems to me overgenerous; but it traces our happiness to the ultimate Source with such a wonderful insight that I cannot resist the temptation of quoting it:

Personally, whenever I had time I liked to go to Dr. Wu's house which I looked upon more as a home than a school or a library. Truly it shed an atmosphere of fragrance and Christian virtues. Under other circumstances, in a large family such as Dr. Wu's, there is usually some germ that tends to breed discord and confusion, but in the healthy atmosphere of the Wu family the bond between themselves must have been warmed by a genuine fondness and the germ could not prosper.

In fact, the Church is the outer wall of the castle; the home is the citadel, the sacred shrine, the inner sanctuary, where His love is best reflected. When men love one another and live together without fuss, willing to see things in the same light, to sacrifice their limited pleasures and to give up their own interests out of love for one another—then the Spirit of God is working among them and His Presence is most vividly felt in the mutual love, domestic peace and real unity. I found this spirit and phenomenon in Dr. Wu's home. It is incomparable; it is beyond the reach of human nature alone. *Congregavit nos in unum Christi amor* (the love of Christ has brought us together).

At the family Rosary, I have often spoken to our children something to the following effect: "There is only one true Father, that is our Father in Heaven. There is only one true Mother, that is the Mother of God. Your Mommy and your Daddy are only the temporary representatives of the true Father and the true Mother. I appreciate the wonderful filial piety you have shown toward us, but always remember there is a higher filial piety, that towards God. Don't depend on us, depend on Him. For we shall be taken from you sooner or later, but God will never leave you. Do not think that we have a big family, for however big the family may be, sooner or later we shall be scattered. In this world, there is no feast that does not come to an end. If, therefore, you want to see this family united forever, there is only one way to attain this end, and that is for every one of us to be united with Christ. Whether we are together, whether we are separated, so long as we are united with Christ, we are united in Christ. There is only one separation that is real, the separation between Heaven and hell. If all of us belong to Heaven, then we are united in life and in death. If one of us belong to Heaven, and another to hell, then we are separated even in life. Physical togetherness means nothing; what is of value is spiritual togetherness."

Usually, my words do not strike root in the minds of my children immediately. But when they are away from home, they often write to me that what I said at the Rosary has come to their minds like a sudden awakening. Just the other day, I received a letter from Francis, whom we have left in Rome, in which he says, "I have realized the truth of what you once said: '*Our only rendez-vous is in Holy Com-munion!*'" Did I put it so poetically?

On the natural plane, there is no pathos like the pathos of a big family. The dialectical process of time carries every-thing along with it. To be big is to shrink in the end. To be together is to be separated ultimately. "Woe to you that laugh now: for you shall mourn and weep." This sums up the pathos of life in the natural sphere.

The great mission of Christ is to lift us from the natural sphere to the supernatural sphere, to free us from our bond-age to the dialectical process of time. What is more, by His grace we are enabled to reach the Beyond by riding the chariot of mutability. For, Christ has also declared: "Blessed are ye that weep now: for you shall laugh." Here we are no longer in the natural sphere, but in the sphere of grace. We can sail safely across the ocean of time and reach the shore of Eternity, because we have welcomed Jesus into our boat.

Before concluding this chapter, I cannot help saying that God has been so good to me that He even drew some good out of the wild life I was leading. Grace has transformed me, and God forbid that I should ever return to my vomit! But my association with those girls whom respectable society looked down upon opened my eyes to the fact that there is a potential saint in every soul. I have not met a single human being in my life who is essentially bad. Given proper environ-ment and education, and given timely response to the stir-rings of grace, there was not a single girl I knew who could not have turned out to be a saint. I know very well that I am offering no new theory, but I *feel* it in my very bones. One girl confided to me that she had an old mother to support and a younger brother to help through school. Whenever I think of her, I feel deeply ashamed of myself, for by nature I am not half as devoted as she was. I can understand why Christ said from the Cross, "I thirst." I think He thirsts especially for those souls who are victims of social institutions.

Part Two

12. THE RELIGIONS OF CHINA

Now that I am approaching the end of my spiritual wanderings, I must speak in some detail of the religions of China. They constitute my moral and religious background, and hence they form an integral part of the development of my spiritual life. They are an important portion of the natural dowry with which God had endowed me in preparation for my marriage with Christ. I often think of myself as a Magus from China who lays before the Divine Infant in the arms of the Blessed Virgin the gold of Confucianism, the musk of Taoism, and the frankincense of Buddhism. At a single touch by His hands, whatever is false in them is purified, and whatever is genuine is transmuted into supernatural values.

In this connection, Monsignor Fulton Sheen has written something about me which is as kind as it is keen: "Although in his generosity he was ready to give up his pagan cultural heritage, he found out that none of it that was good was lost to him now that he was a Catholic. On the contrary, it was uplifted and complemented. Indebtedness to life became indebtedness to God for His graces, filial piety was made stronger because it had its source in filial piety to God and His Mother. Confucian moralism and Taoist contemplativeness were marvellously balanced and he could be even more Chinese because he was a Catholic. His thirst for Love was satisfied and he realized that true spirituality has its basis in moral life, which in turn is based on contemplation; and that the Love of God transformed action into prayer and made the latter overflow into action. He also realized that all the great minds he had followed were as nothing before God, Who alone is; and his intuition that love and not science is supreme became a joyous certitude."

What a wonderful privilege it is to have been born in China in my generation! I was brought up as a child entirely in the atmosphere of the old tradition. To be steeped in the old tradition and later to come into contact with the spirit of Christianity makes one feel like a contemporary of the first Disciples of Christ, who had more or less fully lived their lives under the dominion of Law and were suddenly introduced into the Reign of Grace. Far be it from me to assert that my cultural and spiritual heritage was on a par with the Old Testament. What I do assert is that, in an analogical way, the three religions of China served as my tutors, bringing me to Christ, so that I might find justification in faith (Gal. 3.24). Of course, every conversion is due to the grace of God; but there is no denying that in my case God used parts of the teachings of Confucius, Lao Tzu and Buddha as instruments to open my eyes to the Light of the world.

To begin with, to have lived under the moral tradition of old China has proved to me the absolute necessity of sanctifying and actual grace in order to live up, even imperfectly, to the lofty ideals of life. Speaking of the Mosaic Law, St. Paul said, "Is the Law sin? By no means! Yet I did not know sin save through the Law. For I had not known lust unless the Law had said, 'Thou shalt not lust.' But sin, having found an occasion, worked in me by means of the commandment all manner of lust, for without the Law sin was dead" (Rom. 7.7–8). Now this was *exactly* what happened to me when I had read some of the moral books current in my childhood. They warned young folks against doing this and doing that. I do not know how they worked on others; as for me, they only served to stir up my curiosity and my passions, with the result that the more resolutions I made the more often I broke them. I honestly believe that few persons are as bad as I am by nature; but speaking for myself, the Confessional has proved to me the only effective channel of medicinal grace, so effective as many a time to surprise myself. I am no longer surprised, knowing as I do the absolute veracity and power of the Divine Physician Who said, "It is not the healthy who need a physician, but they who are sick" (Matt. 9.13).

With this preface, I want to proceed to give a sketch of the three religions, paying particular attention to those aspects which in one way or another prepared my mind to recognize the True Lord and the Holy Trinity. The reader may skip the rest of this chapter if he chooses; but I hope he will not. For it bears not only on my own conversion, but on the whole relation of China to Christ.

1

CONFUCIANISM

Confucius has been called an agnostic. This seems to me hardly fair. When a disciple of his asked him about death, he replied, "When one does not know about life, how can one know about death?" When he was asked how to serve the ghosts, he answered, "When one does not know how to serve men, how can one serve ghosts?" This has been taken as a flat denial of the existence of ghosts. I do not think it can be taken to mean that; for if he did not believe in their existence, he would have said it in so many words. What he was saying was simply that before one knew how to serve the ghosts, one must learn how to serve fellow-men; thus the existence of the ghosts was implicitly taken for granted. However, this is not an important point. Whether one is religious does not depend upon one's belief in ghosts. The important question is whether Confucius believed in God, and what was his conception of God.

Confucius did not use the word "God"; he spoke only of "Heaven." I will let him speak for himself:

The Master said: "At fifteen I set my mind upon the pursuit of wisdom. At thirty I stood firm. At forty I was free from perplexities. At fifty I knew the biddings of Heaven. At sixty I heard them with docile ear. At seventy I could follow the desires of my heart without overstepping the boundaries of right" (Analects, II, 4).

When the Master was very ill, Tzu Lu caused some of the disciples to prepare themselves to act as official retainers. Coming to himself for a short while, the Master said, "For what a long time has Yu been inured to the art of deception! In pretending to have retainers when I have none, whom do I deceive? Do I deceive Heaven?" (IX, 11).

The Master said, "Heaven begat virtue in me; what have I to fear from such a one as Huan T'ui?" (VII, 22).

When the Master was in jeopardy in Ku'ang, he said,

"Since King Wen died has not the mantle of culture rested here on me? If Heaven had intended to destroy culture, a latter-day mortal like me would not have been able to link himself to it. But if Heaven does not intend to destroy culture, what have I to fear from the people of Ku'ang?" (IX, 5).

The Master said, "Alas, no one knows me!" Thereupon Tzu Kung asked, "Why do you say, Master, that no one knows you?" The Master replied, "I make no complaint against Heaven. I lay blame upon men. I study from below, but my mind soars above. Heaven alone knows me."

These passages which I have chosen from the *Analects* should suffice to show what Confucius conceived of Heaven. To his mind, Heaven has will, intelligence, creative power, and protective love. In fact, his attitude toward Heaven is that of a docile child toward its parent. In another book, *Li Chi*, he is reported as saying to a Duke, "The man of true humanity serves Heaven as his parent, and serves his parents as Heaven."

I cannot help thinking that Confucius was a theist. His childlike attitude towards Heaven, which was for him but another name for God, was the source of his greatness. It was only in the hands of his disciple Tseng Tzu that Confucianism became almost purely humanistic, laying exclusive emphasis on the moral duties involved in the ethical relations of man, especially the duty of filial piety. Tseng Tzu himself being noted as a filial son, it is little wonder that his emphasis should have taken that direction. In his hands, filial piety became the fountain of all other virtues, the bond of perfection. He extolled this virtue to the skies:

Set up filial piety, and it will fill the space from earth to heaven; spread it out, and it will extend over all the ground to the four seas; hand it down to future ages, and from morning to evening it will be observed; push it on to the eastern sea, the western sea, the southern sea, and the northern sea, and it will be everywhere the law for men, and their obedience to it will be uniform. There will be a fulfilment of the words of the ode:

"From east to west, from south to north,
There was no unsubmissive thought" (*Li Chi*, XXI).

The reason that Tseng Tzu gave for filial piety is that we inherit our very body from our parents, so that it would be the height of ingratitude on our part if we should fail to make good use of it. In his own words, "The body is that which has been transmitted to us by our parents; dare any one allow himself to be irreverent in the employment of their legacy? If a man in his own house and privacy be not grave, he is not filial; if in serving his ruler, he be not loyal, he is not filial; if in discharging the duties of office, he be not careful, he is not filial; if with friends he be not sincere, he is not filial; if on the field of battle he be not brave, he is not filial. If he fail in these five things, the evil of the disgrace will reach his parents;—dare he but reverently attend to them?" (*Ibid.*)

During the Sung Dynasty (A.D. 960–1279) there arose a group of Neo-Confucianists, who broadened the idea of filial piety by transporting it to our relations with the Heaven-and-Earth, which is the Chinese expression for the Cosmos. I can only give here a specimen of their philosophy, which as the reader will see, is pantheistic rather than theistic. When Confucius used the word "Heaven" he meant God; but when the Neo-Confucianists used "Heaven-and-Earth" they meant the Cosmos. The following little essay by Chang Tsai (11th century), represents the peak of that school of thought:

Heaven and Earth as Father and Mother

Heaven is called Father, Earth is called Mother. Little as I
am, I dwell harmoniously (like an innocent baby) in their
bosom. Therefore, what fills the heaven and earth constitutes
my body; and what directs their movements constitutes my
nature. All men are my brothers of the same womb; and all
things, my fellows. The great ruler is the eldest son of our
Parents, and the ministers are his stewards. To pay respect
to the men of old age is to perform our duty towards the
elder children of our Parents; to be tenderly kind to the
young and weak is to perform our duty toward their little
ones. The sages are men who are completely united in virtue
with them; the worthy ones are their tender sprouts. All the
lame and crippled, the lonely and needy, the widowers and
widows are those of my brothers who are hapless and helpless.
To give them seasonable aid and protection is to offer filial
cooperation to the Parents. To be joyful and unworried is
the purest form of filial piety towards them.

To act contrary to the laws of heaven and earth is to be
a disobedient child. To injure one's humanity is to be an
unfilial son. He who indulges in wickedness is a good-for-
nothing son of the Parents; but he who embodies goodness
in his person resembles the Parents. To know their orderly
ways of change and transformation is to be able to carry on
the family tradition. To penetrate into their Spirit is to be
able to carry out their wishes. To have no cause for blushing
when alone in a room is to prove worthy of them. To keep
intact one's heart and to foster one's nature is to serve them
without negligence. To loathe sweet wine (to practise mod-
eration) is to serve them as Emperor Yu served his father; to
bring up men of talents is to hand one's filial piety to others
as Yin K'ao-shu did. Let us work tirelessly in order to please
our Parents just as Emperor Yu did so well with his father;
let us submit ourselves entirely to their will unto the very
sacrifice of our lives, just as Shen Sheng did to the will of his
father.

If we realize what we have received from our Parents and
return to them whole and intact, we may be called *their*

Tseng-sun. If we are heroic in obeying and following their decrees, we may be called *their Po Ch'i.* Riches and honours, blessings and comforts are given to enrich our life. Poverty and oblivion, sorrows and griefs are sent us to bring us to perfection. To live is to serve; to die is peace.

The idea of filial piety is so deep-rooted in the Chinese mind that when a Chinese becomes a Christian he naturally would apply it to his relations with God. To him the imitation of Christ means the imitation of His supreme filial piety toward His Father Who is also our Father. It is significant that the great Chinese Benedictine Dom Lou Tseng-Tsiang should have written: "If Providence permits me, I hope one day, in the light of filial piety, to approach with very profound reverence the most considerable fact in the history of mankind. I shall attempt to describe to my compatriots and my friends how the revelation and the redemption of Jesus Christ have seemed to me. That redemption is the great meeting-place of the ways, the unique point where the filial piety of children and men is opened upon a divine filial piety which Jesus Christ has shown us, and to which He gives us the right, and which reunites the human creatures with our Father who is in Heaven."[1]

The idea is not new, but the feeling-tone is typically Chinese. I regard Dom Lou's philosophy as the logical development of the original idea of Confucius that the virtuous man serves Heaven as his parent. Jesus has redeemed us from the slavish bondage to "Heaven-and-Earth" which is but the creation, and has empowered us to become filial children of the Creator Himself. Thus Dom Lou has contributed a great deal toward the realization of the ideal set forth by Monsignor Celso Contantini: *To conserve and deepen the ancient*

[1] *The Ways of Confucius and of Christ*, Burns, Oates and Washbourne (London, 1948), p. 114.

national Chinese culture, by giving it the rejuvenation of Christianity.

2

TAOISM

So long as we are dealing with Confucianism, we feel our feet on solid ground. Everything appears so neat and distinct. All virtues have their appropriate names and proper scopes of application. Confucianism is essentially a science of ethical relations. But as soon as we pass beyond Confucianism to Taoism, we are plunged into the sea of mystery. By the word "Tao" is meant Ultimate Reality which cannot be expressed in words. Tao is the undifferentiated, indefinable Source of all things and virtues. It is the Simple, the One. If we embrace the One, we embrace all. On the other hand, if we ignore the One, we are lost in the many.

In short, Confucianism deals with moral life, while Taoism is chiefly interested in contemplative life.

Let us try to see more closely what the Taoists mean by "Tao." Lao Tzu, the founder of Taoism, describes Tao in the following terms:

Look at it but you cannot see it,—
It is called the Invisible.

Listen to it but you cannot hear it,—
It is called the Inaudible.

Grasp at it but you cannot touch it,—
It is called the Intangible.

These three cannot be fathomed;
Therefore they blend into one.

Its upper part is not bright,
Its lower part not dark.

Endless like an infinite series, there is no name for it.
It returns again to the realm of thinglessness.
This is what is called the formless Form, the thing-
    less Image.
This is what is called the Indeterminate and Incom-
    prehensible.

Confront it and you do not see its head.
Follow it and you do not see its back.
Yet, equipped with the Tao of old,
You can ride on the things of the present.
To be able to know the first beginnings
Is to have a clue to the Tao.

Thus, Tao is invisible, inaudible, indefinable, indeterminate, and incomprehensible. It is the formless Form and
the imageless Image. It is at once transcendent and immanent. Its transcendental aspect is not bright, nor is its immanent aspect dark. It is everywhere and nowhere; it is the
same throughout all ages, because it is eternal. It is the very
origin of the Cosmos.

Concerning the transcendency and immanence of the Tao,
no one has written better than Chuang Tzu. On the one
hand, Tao must not be identified with any thing or phenomenon in the universe, because it is the very origin of the
universe. "It produces fulness and emptiness, but it is neither
fulness nor emptiness; it produces growth and decay, but it is
neither growth nor decay. It produces the root and branches,
but is neither root nor branch; it produces accumulation and
dispersion, but is itself neither accumulated nor dispersed." [2]
Even the dialectical process of the universe is not to be identified with the Tao, because it is only an operation of the Tao,
not the Tao in its essence. It exists, but it exists in the pre-

___

[2] Legge's translation of the writings of Chuang Tzu in *The Texts of
Taoism*, Oxford University Press (London, 1929), Bk. 22, p. 67.

eminent sense, not in the sense that things exist. In the sense
that things are things, it is *Nothing*.

On the other hand, while the Tao is nothing in particular,
it subsists in all things. To illustrate this point, we will give
an interesting passage from *Chuang Tzu*:

Tung-Kuo Tzu asked Chuang Tzu, saying, "Where is what
you call the Tao to be found?" Chuang Tzu replied, "Everywhere." The other said, "Specify an instance of it. That will
be more satisfactory." "It is here in the ant." "So low?" "It
is in this panic grass." "Lower still!" "It is in this earth tile."
"Certainly that is the lowest?" "It is in that excrement." To
this Tung-Kuo Tzu gave no reply (Bk. 22).

That Tao is at once so transcendental and so immanent
constitutes for the Taoists its chief mystery, the Mystery of
Mysteries. It is in this light that we can understand the opening chapter of the *Tao Teh Ching*:

If Tao could be expressed in words, it would not be
    the unchanging Tao.
Any name that we could give to it would not be the
    the unchanging name.
It is nameless, being the origin of the heaven-and-
    earth (the Cosmos).
It may be named, being the "Mother of all things."
Nothing in particular, yet we should see in it the
    hidden source of all things.
Present in all things, yet we should see in it their
    ultimate end.
Both belong to the same Unity, though differently
    named, and this Unity is called the Mystery.
Oh, Mystery of mysteries!
The Door of all wonders!

Tao, then, is nothing and everything, the Source and the

End of all things, beyond names and no-names. It is precisely because the Tao is unnamable that Lao Tzu has called it by so many names. He calls it "the Mysterious Feminine," "the Mother," "the Origin," "the Great," "the Small," "the Subtle Essence," "the Ultimate End," "the Hidden Reservoir," "the Dark," "the Treasure," "the One," "the Ancestor of the Realm of Images," "the Spirit of the Valley," "the Uncarved Block," "the Father of All Things." Indeed, as Léon Bloy has put it, "when one speaks lovingly of God, all human words are like so many blind lions seeking a spring in the desert."

It is the persistent attempt to evoke by means of words what lies beyond all words and all thoughts that has made Lao Tzu utter so many paradoxes. He says:

> The bright Way looks dark.
> The progressive Way looks like retrogression.
> The smooth Way looks rugged.
> High Virtue looks like an abyss.
> Perfect whiteness looks like blackness.
> Abounding Virtue looks deficient.
> Solid Virtue looks like a thief.
> Integral Virtue looks like disintegration.
> Great squareness has no corners.
> Great talents ripen late.
> Great sound is silent.
> Great Form is shapeless.
>
> Tao is hidden and nameless;
> But it alone can render help and fulfill (41).

Again, he says:

> The greatest perfection seems imperfect,
> Yet its use is inexhaustible.

The greatest fulness seems empty,
Yet its use is endless.

The greatest straightness looks like a curve.
The greatest skill seems clumsy.
The greatest eloquence sounds like stuttering (45).

All these paradoxes are but sober statements of the truth, because Tao is so far above man that its ways are not man's ways nor its ideas man's ideas. As Lao Tzu put it, "All the world tells me, 'The Tao is great, but queer, being like nothing in the world.' But it is precisely because it is so great that it is like nothing in the world. If it were like anything in the world, it would have been extremely limited indeed from the very beginning!" (67).

But the important question is: How did Lao Tzu himself arrive at his vision of the Tao? By turning his eyes inward! For, "the force of words is soon spent. Far better is it to keep what is within your heart" (5). The truth is that although Tao is transcendental, it dwells also in the innermost centre of our heart. We can find it within us, if only we would cultivate our interior spirit. Lao Tzu says:

Can you keep the restless soul from straying, hold
fast to the Unity, and never quit it?
Can you, when concentrating your vital breath,
make it soft like that of a little child?
Can you wipe and cleanse your inner vision till it
is rid of all dross? (10).

As soon as this is done, then you can truly love your people and govern your nation without resorting to cleverness, you can play the feminine part to the opening and shutting of the door of heaven, that is, you can respond with perfect docility and spontaneity to the rhythms of the cosmos. Moreover, your mind will be so clear as to see everything, but at the same time remain non-attached to anything (10).

This is why Lao Tzu never wearied of pointing out the importance of recollection and quiet. He says:

> Without going out of your door,
> You can know the world.
> Without peeping through your window,
> You can see the Way of Heaven.
> The farther you go,
> The less you know.
>
> Thus, the Sage knows without travelling,
> Sees without looking,
> And achieves without fussing (47).

Lao Tzu would have agreed with À Kempis who said: "In thy chamber shalt thou find what abroad thou shalt too often lose."

The Taoistic doctrine of Wu Wei does not mean doing nothing, but rather doing everything in accordance with the inner light, which is the Tao, and being unattached to the fruits of your action. In this respect, Taoism is most akin to the teaching of the Bhagavad-Gita: "The self-possessed knower of Truth should think: 'I do nothing at all,' though seeing, hearing, touching, smelling, eating, walking, sleeping, breathing, speaking, letting go and holding, opening and closing the eyes, firmly convinced that senses alone move among sense-objects. He who performs actions, surrendering them to Brahman and abandoning all attachment, is not polluted by sin, as a lotus-leaf by water." [3] However, the spirit of the Gita seems to be more positive than that of Taoism.

---

[3] Translated by Swami Paramananda. See Lin Yutang, The Wisdom of China and India, Random House (New York), p. 74.

For instance, the *Gita* says: "Renunciation (of action) and performance of action both lead to liberation. But of the two, performance of action is superior to renunciation of action."[4] Lao Tzu, on the other hand, would have said that, all things being equal, renunciation of action is superior to performance of it. Chuang Tzu, likewise, would advise people to remain inactive unless they are compelled by objective circumstances to act. *Wu Wei*, therefore, besides signifying non-attachment to the fruits of your action, means also the reduction of activity to what is essential and necessary. To warn his readers of the danger of unnecessary activity and dexterity, Chuang Tzu told an interesting story about a monkey:

The prince of Wu took a boat and went to the Monkey Mountain, which he ascended. When the monkeys saw him, they scampered off in terror, and hid themselves among the thick hazels. One monkey, however, was not afraid, but swung about on the branches, displaying its cleverness to the prince, who took a shot at it. With a nimble motion, it caught the swift arrow. So the prince ordered his attendants to hurry forward and shoot it; and the monkey was seized and killed. The prince then, looking round, said to his friend Yen Pu-i, "This monkey made a display of its artfulness, and trusted in its agility, to show me its arrogance. This was what brought it to this fate. Beware! Do not flaunt your superiority in the faces of others."

The Taoists never wearied of extolling purposelessness, uselessness, and complete detachment from the world. At the first sight, therefore, their theories and speculations might seem to be utterly impractical in the sense that they have nothing to do with life, being merely transcendental roamings in the clouds. And yet, if they talk about purposelessness,

[4] *Loc. cit.*

they have in mind a higher purpose; if they talk about uselessness, they have in mind a higher usefulness; and if they talk
about a complete detachment from the world, it is only
because they want to show how one should conduct oneself
in the world. In the last analysis, Tao is nothing but a way
of life. In this sense, the Taoists are eminently practical.

Perhaps the best way to see the practicalness of the Taoists is to study their ideas about the perfect man—what they
were driving at, what kind of man they wanted to become.
Whether they themselves actually realized their own ideals
is immaterial to our present purpose; what we want to know
is their aspirations.

One of the recurring themes in the Taoistic writings is the
importance of self-effacement. Lao Tzu says:

> Heaven and Earth last long.
> What is the secret of their long abidingness?
> Is it not because they do not live for themselves
> That they can live so long?

> Therefore, the Sage wants to remain behind,
> But finds himself ahead of others;
> Reckons himself out,
> But finds himself secure.
> Is it not because he is selfless
> That his Self is realized? (7).

Self-realization through self-effacement—this is the teaching of Lao Tzu. But here we must add a little explanation.
One's self can only be realized through self-effacement; but
in the practice of self-effacement, one must sincerely forget
oneself and must not think consciously of realizing oneself.
In other words, all that one is required to do is to efface himself; as to the realization of his self, he should leave it entirely

to the operations of the Tao. If he tried to efface himself with a view to realizing himself, he would not be really detached from himself, with the result that he would never be able to realize himself. He would not be practising the doctrine of *wu wei*, which means passivity; he would be practising *yu wei*, which means activeness or self-assertiveness. Many later Chinese have practised *wu wei* in the spirit of *yu wei*, and this is why in their hands Taoistic philosophy has degenerated into a kind of strategy of living.

One does not practise self-effacement for an ulterior motive, but because one wishes to follow the Way of Heaven. As Lao Tzu says:

> This is the Way of Heaven:
> *When you have done your work, retire!*

It is in this light that we should read the following quotations:

> Bend and you will be whole.
> Curl and you will be straight.
> Be empty and you will be filled.
> Grow old and you will be renewed.
> Have little and you will gain.
> Have much and you will be lost.
>
> Therefore, the Sage embraces the One,
> And becomes the Model of all under Heaven.
> He does not make a show of himself,
> Hence he shines;
> Does not justify himself,
> Hence he is glorified;
> Does not boast of his ability,
> Hence he gets his credit;
> Does not brandish his success,
> Hence he endures;

Does not compete with anyone,
Hence no one can compete with him (22).

From the above passage, it is clear that Lao Tzu's method
is not entirely negative. It is because of your positive embracement of the One that you can detach your heart and mind
from the many; and "the One" is but another name for the
Tao.

The One is to be looked for within ourselves, whereas the
many are external to us. The former is the only thing essential, and the latter are non-essentials. This is why the Sage prefers what is within to what is without. Lao Tzu expresses this
idea by means of a beautiful figure. "The Sage," he says,
"wears coarse clothes, but keeps the jade in his bosom" (70).
This is probably what Chuang Tzu had in mind when he said
that "the true Sage discards the light that dazzles and takes
refuge in the common and ordinary," [5] and that "when virtue
excels, the outward form is forgotten." [6]

For Chuang Tzu as for Lao Tzu, the Sage is one who values the Tao above all things. As Chuang Tzu put it, "To
him who has what is most noble, all the dignities of a state
are as nothing; to him who has what is the greatest riches,
all the wealth of a state is as nothing; to him who has all that
he could wish, fame and praises are as nothing. It is true that
the Tao admits of no substitute." [7] It is because the Sage
embraces the Tao that he can afford to be self-effacing vis-à-
vis the world and to be detached from all things.

Even in the practice of virtues, the Sage does not feel virtuous. The reason is that he realizes that the virtues are but
streamlets flowing from the living fountain of Tao; and as
he drinks directly at the fountain, the virtues flow out from

[5] Lin, *op. cit.*, p. 638.
[6] *Ibid.*, p. 656.
[7] Legge, *op. cit.*, Bk. 14, p. 348.

him spontaneously, without any effort or merit on his part. This is why Lao Tzu said:

> High Virtue is non-virtuous;
> Therefore, it has virtue.
> Low virtue never frees itself from virtuousness;
> Therefore it has no virtue.

Chuang Tzu expounded this point more fully:

Therefore, while the truly great man does not injure others, he does not credit himself with charity and mercy. While he seeks for no gain, he does not despise the servants who do. While he struggles not for wealth, he does not lay great value on his modesty. While he asks for help from no man, he is not proud of his self-reliance, neither does he despise the greedy. While he acts differently from the vulgar crowd, he does not plume himself on being eccentric (17).[8]

Thus, the Sage, because he has embraced the Tao, transcends the material world and the sphere of morality. But he has yet a stage further to go in his spiritual pilgrimage. The fact is that the Tao is so transcendental that no human being can really be said to understand it. This realization of one's final ignorance of the Tao seems, according to both Lao Tzu and Chuang Tzu, to constitute the highest stage of sagehood. Lao Tzu says:

> To know, and yet not to know,—this is the highest.
> Not to know, and yet to know,—this is sickness.
> Only when you are sick of sickness will you cease
>   to be sick.
> The Sage is never sick, because he is sick of sickness;
> This is why he is not sick.

That is to say, the Sage does not pretend to know what he

[8] See also Legge, Bk. 2, pp. 305-6, 356, 369.

really does not know; he knows that in his knowing there is unknowing; and that keeps him from mental sickness.

In an allegory, Chuang Tzu explains the point:

Grand Purity asked Infinitude, saying, "Do you know the Tao?" "I do not know it," was the reply. He then asked Do-nothing, who replied "I know it." "Is your knowledge of it determined by various points?" "It is." "What are they?" Do-nothing said, "I know that the Tao may be considered noble, and may be considered mean, that it may be bound and compressed, and may be dispersed and diffused. These are the marks by which I know it." Grand Purity took the words of those two, and asked No-beginning, saying, "Such were their replies; which was right? and which was wrong? Infinitude's saying that he did not know it? or Do-nothing's saying that he knew it?" No-beginning said, "The 'I do not know it' was profound, and the 'I know it' was shallow. The former had reference to its internal nature; the latter to its external conditions." [9]

My own interpretation of this interesting passage is that those who practise the doctrine of non-assertion, as represented by Do-nothing, have only realized the immanence of the Tao, while those who are true contemplatives, as represented by Infinitude, have got some glimpse of the transcendence of the Tao. The former realize that Tao is everywhere, while the latter realize that it is nowhere.

To sum up, the Sage undergoes three awakenings. In the first awakening, he sees the worthlessness of all external things. Therefore, "he lets the gold lie hid in the hill, and the pearls in the deep; he considers not poverty or money to be any gain, he keeps aloof from riches and honours, he rejoices not in long life, and grieves not for early death; he does not consider prosperity a glory, nor is ashamed of indigence; he would not grasp at the gain of the whole world to be held

[9] Legge, op. cit., Bk. 22, pp. 68–9.

as his own private portion; he would not desire to rule over the whole world as his own private distinction. His distinction is in understanding that all things belong to the one treasury, and that death and life should be viewed in the same way." [10]

In the second awakening, he sees clearly that all his virtues come not from himself, but from the Tao, and that in governing others he should practise the doctrine of non-assertiveness. As Chuang Tzu said: "In the governing of the intelligent kings, their services overspread all under the sky, but they did not consider it as proceeding from themselves; their transforming influence reached to all things, but the people did not refer it to them with hope. No one could tell the name of their agency, but they made men and things be joyful in themselves." [11] In this state, the Sage "sees where there is the deepest obscurity, and hears where there is no sound." [12]

In the third awakening, the Sage realizes that his understanding of the Tao is no understanding after all. For the Tao is of Heaven, and therefore infinite and beyond the comprehension of man. He therefore becomes a little child, depending entirely upon Heaven as a baby upon its mother. The following passage, as translated by Legge, seems to represent this stage:

He whose mind is at peace emits a Heavenly light. In him who emits this heavenly light men see the True man. When a man has cultivated himself to this point, thenceforth he remains constant in himself. When he is thus constant in himself, what is merely the human element will leave him, but Heaven will help him. Those whom their human element has left we call the people of Heaven. Those whom Heaven helps we call the Sons of Heaven. Those who would by learning attain to this seek for what they cannot learn.

[10] *Ibid.*, Bk. 12, p. 310.
[11] *Ibid.*, Bk. 7, p. 262.
[12] *Ibid.*, Bk. 12, p. 311.

Those who would by effort attain to this, attempt what effort cannot effect. Those who aim by reasoning to reach it reason where reasoning has no place. To know to stop where they cannot arrive by means of knowledge is the highest attainment.[18]

Perhaps, it was to such a man that Lao Tzu addressed such cryptic words as the following:

> Know the masculine,
> Cling to the feminine,
> And be the Brook of the world.
> To be the Brook of the world is
> To move constantly in the path of Virtue
> Without swerving from it,
> And to return again to infancy.

> Know the white,
> Cling to the black,
> And be the Pattern of the world.
> To be the Pattern of the world is
> To move constantly in the path of Virtue
> Without erring a single step,
> And to return again to the Infinite.
> Know the glorious,
> Keep in disgrace,
> And be the Fountain of the world.
> To be the Fountain of the world is
> To live the abundant life of Virtue,
> And to return again to Primal Simplicity (28).

I have summed up the practical lessons in Taoism in these words: "The significance of time is to evoke Eternity; that of voyaging is to evoke the Home; that of knowledge is to evoke Ignorance; that of science and art is to evoke Mystery; that of longevity is to evoke the Evanescence of life; that of

[18] *Ibid.*, Bk. 23, pp. 82–3. See also *Ibid.*, Bk. 24, pp. 112–13, on Heaven.

all human greatness is to evoke Humility; that of complexities and subtilities is to evoke Simplicity; that of the many is to evoke the One; that of war is to evoke Peace; that of the cosmos is to evoke the Beyond. It is not the voyage that causes harm; but to lose oneself in the voyage so as to forget one's destination is a tragedy indeed."

Father John Monsterleet, S. J., writing on the influence of Confucianism and Taoism on my spiritual life, says: "A disciple of Confucius for moral truth, he turns more to Lao Tzu for mystic truth, and the mystic in him surpasses the moralist." This seems to me a keen insight into my soul. Not that I do not practise moral virtues, but that I do not want to be entangled in them. I agree entirely with Reverend Edward Leen that even one's own holiness "is not to be pursued as an end," but "must remain simply as a means to God." [14]

3

BUDDHISM

Every Chinese, up to my generation, was an implicit Buddhist. So widespread and deep-rooted was its influence in China! In social relations, the Chinese acted according to the canons of Confucianism, as balanced by the Taoistic philosophy of detachment, but in their interior life they followed Buddhism. In my own case, its influence has sunk so deep in my mind that it is not easy to render an account of it. But I shall try my best.

The original teachings of Buddha are simple and easy to understand. First of all, he preached the doctrine of the Middle Path, steering between the Charybdis of sensual indulgence and the Scylla of excessive asceticism. In this respect

[14] *Progress Through Mental Prayer*, Sheed & Ward (New York), p. 89.

he is as matter-of-fact as Confucius. According to the *Buddha-Carica* or "The Acts of Buddha" written by Asvaghosha Boddhisattva, after giving himself up to the greatest austerities for a period of six years, he came to realize that wisdom was not to be found in that way, and the very first sermon he preached after his sudden enlightenment under the Bodhi tree contains these significant words:

The emaciated devotee by suffering produces in himself confused and sickly thoughts, not conducive even to worldly knowledge, how much less to triumph over sense! For he who tries to light a lamp with water, will not succeed in scattering the darkness, and so the man who tries with worn-out body to trim the lamp of wisdom shall not succeed, nor yet destroy his ignorance or folly. Who seeks with rotten wood to evoke the fire will waste his labor and get nothing for it; but boring hard wood into hard, the man of skill forthwith gets fire for his use. In seeking wisdom then it is not by these austerities a man may reach the law of life. But to indulge in pleasure is opposed to right; this is the fool's barrier against wisdom's light. The sensualist cannot comprehend the Sutras or the Sastras, how much less the way of over-coming all desire! As some man grievously afflicted eats food not fit to eat and in ignorance aggravates his sickness, so can he get rid of lust who pampers lust? Scatter the fire amid the desert grass, dried by the sun, fanned by the wind—the raging flames who can extinguish? Such is the fire of covetousness and lust. I, then, reject both these extremes: my heart keeps in the middle way.[15]

The kernel of his teachings lies in the "Four Noble Truths" and the "Eightfold Noble Path." What are the four noble truths? They are the truth concerning misery, the truth concerning the origin of misery, the truth concerning the cessation of misery, and the truth concerning the path leading to the cessation of misery. As to the first truth, Buddha said,

[15] Translation of Samuel Beal.

"Birth is misery; old age is misery; disease is misery; sorrow, lamentation, suffering, grief, and despair are misery; to wish for what one cannot have is misery; in short, all the five attachment-groups are misery." [16]

As to the origin of misery, Buddha found it in the desire for sensual pleasure, for permanent and transitory existence. In other words, the will to life lies at the source of all misery. As to the truth about the cessation of misery, Buddha held that since we know the cause of misery, only the destruction of the cause can really destroy the effect. Therefore he preached the complete fading out of the desire for sensual pleasure and for life, a giving up, a loosing hold, a relinquishment, and a perfect detachment.

As to the noble path leading to the cessation of misery, this is what Buddha called "the noble eightfold path," which consists of right belief, right resolve, right speech, right behavior, right occupation, right effort, right contemplation, and right concentration. "Right belief" consists in the knowledge of the four noble truths we have already sketched. "Right resolve" is the resolve to renounce sensual pleasures, to have malice towards none, and to harm no living creature. "Right speech" consists in abstaining from falsehood, backbiting, harsh language, and frivolous talk. "Right behavior" consists in abstaining from destroying life, from taking that which is not given one, from immorality. "Right occupation" consists in quitting a wrong occupation and getting one's livelihood by a proper occupation. "Right effort" means to make a heroic and persistent endeavor to the end that evil and demeritorious qualities not yet arisen may not arise, that those already arisen may be abandoned, that meritorious qualities not yet arisen may arise, and that those already arisen may be preserved, developed and perfected.

[16] Henry Clarke Warren, *Buddhism in Translations*, Harvard University Press (Cambridge, 1947), p. 368.

On "right contemplation," Buddha said, "Whenever, O
priests, a priest lives, as respects the body, observant of the
body, strenuous, conscious, contemplative, and has rid himself of lust and grief; as respects sensations, observant of the
sensations, strenuous, conscious, contemplative, has rid himself of lust and grief; as respects the mind, observant of the
mind, strenuous, conscious, contemplative, and has rid himself of lust and grief; as respects the elements of being, observant of the elements of being, strenuous, conscious, contemplative, and has rid himself of lust and grief, this, O priests,
is 'right contemplation.'" [17]

As to the "right concentration" Buddha pointed out four
successive trances. "Whenever, O priests, a priest, having
isolated himself from demeritorious traits, and still exercising
reasoning, still exercising reflection, enters upon the first
trance which is produced by isolation and characterized by
joy and happiness; when, through the subsidence of reasoning
and reflection, and still retaining joy and happiness, he enters
upon the second trance, which is an interior tranquilization
and intentness of the thoughts, and is produced by concentration; when, through the paling of joy, indifferent, contemplative, conscious, and in the experience of bodily happiness
—that state which eminent men describe when they say,
'indifferent, contemplative, and living happily'—he enters
upon the third trance; when through the abandonment of
happiness, through the abandonment of misery, through the
disappearance of all antecedent gladness and grief, he enters
upon the fourth trance, which has neither misery nor happiness, but is contemplation as refined by indifference, this,
O priests, is called 'right concentration.'" [18]

[17] *Ibid.*, p. 374.
[18] *Loc. cit.*

From the above quotations it is as clear as daylight that Buddha was really more a moral teacher than a religious teacher. He had a most sensitive and generous heart; perceiving as he did the misery of life, he made heroic efforts to achieve an emancipation for himself and for others. But he had no knowledge whatever of divine grace, with the result that the contemplation and concentration he preached moved entirely in the natural and physical sphere. He attempted to achieve recollection, quiet and self-unconsciousness by means of reflection and self-hypnosis. Thus, he was a quietist like Molinos, because the means he used for the attainment of quiet were really active.

What I admire about Buddha is his personality. Born a prince, he had the magnanimity to sacrifice all the luxuries and comforts that life could furnish to a human being in order to search for the Truth which would set himself and others free. Whether he actually found the Truth is quite another question. To my mind, he did not. But his was a glorious failure. A prince willingly becoming a beggar for the sake of finding the right path to lead all sentient beings to freedom! I often think of him as a foreshadowing of Christ, the eternal Son of God, Who "descended from the kingdom of imperishable glory to our earth, in order here amid brambles and stones to seek the lost, weary, wounded sheep and lead them back to eternal bliss." [19]

I cannot dismiss Buddhism without mentioning the tremendous influence that its later development exercised upon my mind when I was a child through the popular Sutra called "The Prajna-Paramita-Hridaya Sutra" (The Sutra of the Kernel of Transcendental Wisdom). It is as follows:

[19] Nikolaus Gihr, *The Holy Sacrifice of the Mass*, Herder, p. 63.

THE PRAJNA-PARAMITA-HRIDAYA SUTRA

(The Sutra of the Kernel of Transcendental Wisdom)

When the Boddhisattva Avalokitesvara was engaged in the practice of the deep Prajnaparamita, he perceived the emptiness of all the five Skandhas, and was delivered from all suffering and misery. (Addressing himself to Sariputra, he said):

"O Sariputra, form is not different from emptiness, nor is emptiness different from form. Form *is* emptiness; emptiness *is* form. The same can be said of sensation, thought, confection, and consciousness.

"O Sariputra, when things are seen in the light of emptiness, they are neither born nor extinguished, they are neither tainted nor immaculate, they neither increase nor decrease. Therefore, in the realm of emptiness there is no form, no sensation, no thought, no confection, no consciousness; no eye, ear, nose, tongue, body, mind; no form, sound, odor, taste, objects. There is no Dhatu of vision, nor of consciousness. There is no ignorance, nor extinction of ignorance. There is no old age and death, nor extinction of old age and death. There is no suffering, no accumulation of suffering, no annihilation of suffering, no path leading to the annihilation of suffering. There is no knowledge and no attainment, as there is nothing to be attained.

"The mind of the Bodhisattva who relies on the Prajnaparamita is free of all obstacles; and because there are no obstacles in his mind, he has no fear, and, going beyond all perverted views, reaches final Nirvana. All the Buddhas of the past, present, and future, depending on the Prajnaparamita, attain to the highest perfect enlightenment.

"Hence, we know that the Prajnaparamita is the great Mantram, the Mantram of great wisdom, the highest Mantram, the peerless Mantram, which can truly and effectively heal all sufferings."

Therefore, he recited the Mantram of the *Prajnaparamita,* as follows:

Gate, gate, paragate, parasamgate, bodhi, svaha!
(O Bodhi, gone, gone, gone to the other shore,
landed at the other shore, Hail!)

Some explanation is necessary before we can understand
this Sutra in the proper light. The Buddhistic notion of
"emptiness" (Sunyata) is not easy to comprehend. It is
important to keep in mind that "emptiness" does not mean
"non-existence." On this point, I agree perfectly with Dr.
D. T. Suzuki, who said: "When Buddhists declare all things
to be empty, they are not advocating a nihilistic view; on the
contrary, an ultimate reality is hinted at, which cannot be
subsumed under the categories of logic. With them, to pro-
claim the conditionality of things is to point to the existence
of something altogether unconditioned and transcendent of
all determination. Sunyata may thus often be most appropri-
ately rendered by the Absolute." [20] While the Absolute "is
immanent in all concrete and particular objects, it is in itself
not at all definable." [21]

Thus explained, it is easy to understand why this Sutra has
been so popular among the Buddhists in China and Japan,
for to them it is like a ferry-boat to go from this shore to the
Other Shore, from the world of contingency to the world
of the Absolute, from time to Eternity, from appearance to
Reality, from the empty to Emptiness.[22]

[20] Essays in Zen Buddhism (Third Series), Luzac and Company (London, 1927), I, p. 194.
[21] Loc. cit.
[22] I do not know how many times I heard my big mother chant this
Sutra. Whenever she was not otherwise occupied, she did it from morning to night with a rosary in hand. The Buddhist rosary has a hundred
and eight beads on it; and oftentimes my mother managed to finish
twenty rounds in a single day! She was illiterate, as practically all ladies
of her generation were; but by dint of repetition, she seemed to have
an inkling of its meaning. Even to my childish mind, it conveyed some
vague idea of the unreality and transiency of life in this world, and
evoked a nameless longing for the Other Shore.

In my thirties, I was deeply influenced by a particular school of Buddhism, called the school of Zen (*Dhyana*). The mystical tendencies that I had imbibed from Taoism were reinforced tremendously by the study of the Zen masters.

There is something very charming about Zen Buddhism, which has been described as one of the most beautiful flowers of the Chinese mind. Let me begin with an anecdote about the Zen master Hsuan Sha, which has impressed me as truly Franciscan. Hsuan Sha had ascended to the platform and was ready to preach a sermon, when he heard the twitter of a swallow. Quite abruptly he remarked to his audience, "What a wonderful sermon on Reality!" Thereupon he came down from the platform and retired.

The Zen masters are head over heels in love with Reality, they are intoxicated with the Paramitaprajna, which may be translated as "Transcending Wisdom." Reading their writings and recorded words and actions often makes you feel as though you were suddenly transported into a strange land, into the Peach-Blossom Fountain, as it were. The landscape is so strange and yet so familiar! In the words of one of the Zen masters, Yuan Wu, "You gain an illuminating insight into the very nature of things, which now appear to you as so many fairy flowers having no graspable realities. Here is manifested the unsophisticated Self which is the original face of your being; here is shown all bare the most beautiful landscape of your birthplace." [28] The prose of daily life has become poetry. Things that you have taken for granted look as fresh as if they had just come from the hands of God, so that you are able to say with the Sung philosopher Shao K'ang-chi, "Although my body is posterior to the universe, my mind is anterior to it." Zen enables you to "live Eternity

---

[28] D. T. Suzuki, *An Introduction to Zen Buddhism*, Philosophical Library (New York), p. 47.

in the hour," and to turn the business of living into a thrilling romance.

I like one of the remarks that the Zen master Chin-yuan Wei-hsin made on his platform: "Thirty years ago, before Old Monk (that is, himself) had studied Zen, he saw the mountains as mountains, waters as waters. Later when he came to know a good master and was first initiated into Zen, he no longer saw mountains as mountains or waters as waters. Now that he has got a resting-place, he again sees that mountains are only mountains and waters only waters. My friends, are these three preceptions the same or different? If anyone can put it in black and white, he will be allowed to see for himself Old Monk." No answer is recorded; nor do I know what to say, except that the second view is more interesting than the first, but the third is the most interesting of all. You see mountains as mountains and waters as waters. There is nothing extraordinary about it, and that is why it is so extraordinary. To call anything ordinary is to blaspheme the Absolute. All things, as they are, are wonderful enough; this seems to be the central tenet of Zen. It was Einstein who said, "The most beautiful thing we can experience is the mysterious. It is the source of all true art and science." It is exactly the function of Zen to awaken in you the sense of the Mysterious in everything. This gives us a clue to the enchanting quality of Zen and its masters.

Every one of us bears the Mysterious within himself; and yet he often seeks it outside. This is perhaps why the Zen masters so often answered the apparently reasonable questions of their pupils with the obviously unreasonable kickings and beatings. To the logically minded, such actions are mystifying; but to the mystics, they open their eyes to the mysterious. As Suzuki puts it, "The inner eye is to be opened under a shower of thirty blows." [24]

[24] *Ibid.*, p. 68.

An apparent fiasco happened between a monk and the Zen master Ching Tung. The monk asked Ching Tung, "Who is Buddha?" Ching Tung instead of answering him with words, struck him; and the monk struck back. The master said, "There is a reason in your striking me, but there is no such in my striking you." The fact is that Buddha was no longer looked upon as a particular person, but identified with Reality, which is above all reason and logic and language. The master, in saying "there is no reason in my striking you," was hinting at this truth.

But it must not be imagined that the Zen masters were always beating their pupils. If the Reality cannot be talked about, it cannot be knocked about either. All words and all actions should be taken as "a finger pointing at the moon"; and so long as they are so taken, there is no danger of confusing the Real with the unreal. Hui Neng, the Sixth Patriarch of the School of Zen, and certainly the greatest Zen master that China has produced, preached long sermons at once understandable and pointing to the mysterious.

When Lung T'an was a disciple of Tao Wu, he served him as a personal attendant for a long period of time. During all this time, Tao Wu did not speak a single word to him concerning Zen. Lung T'an became impatient, and said to the master, "Ever since I came, I have not received any instruction on the Essence of Mind." Tao Wu replied, "Ever since you came, I have been continuously pointing out to you the Essence of Mind." Lung T'ang was nonplussed and asked, "Where is the instruction?" Tao Wu answered, "When you brought me tea, I accepted it from you. When you served me with food, I received it from you. When you made bows at me, I lowered my head. On what occasion have I ever neglected pointing at the Essence of Mind?" Lung T'an lowered his head and meditated for a long time. Tao

Wu said, "You have to catch it by direct insight; to reflect upon it is to miss it." Lung T'an was suddenly enlightened; then he asked how to keep this insight, to which Tao Wu replied, "Let your inner nature have full freedom; adapt yourself to all circumstances without being attached to any. Use fully your ordinary mind; besides this, there is no extraordinary view." [25]

All this reminds me of some of the flashes of insight thrown out by the Neo-Confucianist, Chen Hao. Take this for instance: "The Tao is in the ordinary activities of your daily life, such as sweeping the floor and conversation with your friends." Here is another: "To look at the sky from within a well does not actually make the sky small. It is only because you are in the well that your vision is bounded by its mouth. However, there is nothing wrong with the well, nor can it be dispensed with. The important thing is for you to get out of it, that you may see how big the sky is. After your vision is enlarged, being no longer bounded by the well, it will do no harm for you to re-enter the well." [26]

It is well known that Chen Hao spent several decades of his life in the study of Buddhism and Taoism before he returned to Confucianism. There can be no question that his vision was broadened immensely by getting "out of the well" and enjoying the sight of the unbounded sky together with Chuang Tzu and the Zen masters. I cannot help thinking that all the great Neo-Confucianists were deeply influenced by Taoism and Zenism; but none of them was big enough to acknowledge the debt.

Let me give a poem by Shao Yung, which is full of the spirit of Zen:

[25] *Transmission of the Lamp*, Bk. 14, p. 117.
[26] *Sung Yuan Hsueh An*, I, p. 330.

Beyond Silence and Speech

If you speak when you ought to keep silence,
    Your speech is dirt.
If you keep silence when you ought to speak,
    Your silence is dust.
If you speak and keep silence according to the
    occasions,
    Without being attached to either,
Then neither dirt nor dust has any way
    Of coming to your person.[27]

C. G. Jung says, "Zen is one of the most wonderful blossoms of the Chinese spirit, which was readily impregnated by the immense thought-world of Buddhism." Now, what is the most fundamental characteristic of the Chinese spirit? To my mind, it is the union of the abstract with the concrete, of the universal with the particular, of utmost unearthliness with complete earthliness, of transcendental idealism with a matter-of-fact practicalness. This union is not a matter of theoretical synthesis, but a matter of *personal experience*. As Confucius put it, "All people eat and drink, but few know the taste." Wisdom is something to be relished, and no one can do it for you; you have to relish it for yourself. In the parlance of Zen, only he who drinks the water knows how warm or how cold it tastes. Yuan Wu expressed the same thing by a romantic poem:

    She waits behind the brocade screens,—
    The incense in the Gold Duck is burning out.
    In the midst of flute-playing and songs,
    He returns intoxicated, supported by friends.

[27] See *Yi Ch'uan Chi Hsiang Chi*, Bk. 4.

The happy adventure of the romantic youth,—
The lady alone knows its sweetness.[28]

It is the innermost personal experience of Wisdom, which
you find within you, but which you cannot share with
others, that the Zen masters set their hearts upon. They have
not the slightest care for external things. One of them went
to the extent of using some wooden statues of the Buddha
as fuel for his stove. It happened this way. Tan Hsia was a
guest at the Hui Lin Temple. As the weather was very cold,
he made a fire with a wooden Buddha. The Abbot of the
Temple reproached him, saying, "How dare you burn my
wooden Buddha?" Tan Hsia digged at the ashes with a stick,
saying, "I am trying to find a relic of the Buddha." The
Abbot said, "How can you find a relic in a wooden Buddha?"
Tan Hsia answered, "Since there is no relic, let us burn two
more statues!" [29]

The lesson that Tan Hsia wanted to point out was that
Buddha is within and not without. Later, one of his disciples,
Ts'ui Wei Wu Hsueh, was found by a monk making offerings
before the image of an Arhat. The monk took him to task,
saying, "Tan Hsia burned a wooden Buddha; why are you
making offerings to a wooden Arhat?" Ts'ui Wei said, "Even
when it was burned, it could not be burned up; and as to my
offerings, just leave me to do as I please." The monk again
asked, "When these offerings are made to the Arhat, does
he come to receive them?" Ts'ui Hsia said, "Do you eat
everyday?" The monk remained silent; thereupon the master
remarked, "How few are the intelligent ones!" [30]

The point that Ts'ui Wei was driving at was that one

[28] *Chih Yueh Lu*, Bk. 29, p. 12.
[29] *Ibid.*, Bk. 9, p. 40.
[30] *Transmission*, 14, p. 117.

should keep his mind entirely free, being detached from all things, whether images or no-images. If anything, the iconoclast is a worse slave than the idolater. As Buddha himself said in *The Diamond Sutra*, "Even the Dharma should be abandoned; how much more no-Dharma!"

The famous Zen layman, Pang Yun, wrote a poem, which seems to put the spirit of Zen in a nutshell:

> In my daily life there are no affairs
> Except those I casually meet.
> None I choose, none I refuse;
> I just do whatever I am called to do.
> What is the true glory?
> Hills and mountains without a speck of dust!
> What is supernatural power and wondrous work?
> Drawing water, and carrying fuel!

The idea that the ordinary duties of one's daily life are charged with spiritual significance is typically Chinese. Suzuki has written something very appropriate on this point:

No doubt the idea was greatly enforced by the characteristic industry and practicalness of the Chinese people by whom Zen was mainly elaborated. The fact is that if there is any one thing that is most emphatically insisted upon by the Zen masters as the practical expression of their faith, it is serving others, doing work for others, not ostentatiously indeed but secretly, without making others know of it. Says Eckhart, 'What a man takes in by contemplation he must pour out in love.' Zen would say, 'pour it out in work,' meaning by work the active and concrete realization of love. Tauler made spinning and shoe-making and other homely duties gifts of the Holy Ghost; Brother Lawrence made cooking sacramental; George Herbert wrote:

> "Who sweeps a room as for thy laws
> Makes that and the action fine."

These are all expressions of the spirit of Zen, as far as its practical side is concerned. Mystics are thus all practical men, they are far from being visionaries whose souls are too absorbed in things unearthly or of the other world to be concerned with this life.[31]

Now that I think of it, I have inherited from Buddhism an intense longing for the "Other Shore," which is but another name and a faint foreshadowing of the Kingdom of God which is within us. Furthermore, Buddhism had disposed my mind for the appreciation of such Biblical passages as:

Vanity of vanities, said Ecclesiastes, vanity of vanities, and all is vanity. What has a man more of his labor, that he taketh under the sun?

Make known to me, O Lord, my end, and what is
the measure of my days,
That I may know how frail I am.
Behold Thou hast made my days but a short span,
And my life as nothing before Thee:
Every man is nothing but a breath.

It has also taught me the importance of direct personal experience in the matters of spiritual life. As Frank Sheed puts it, "If you want to know how wet the rain is, do not judge by someone who went out into it with an umbrella." He advises us to go *stripped* into the shower of truth and life. The spirit of Zen is nothing else than this.

Since I became a Catholic, all the wisdom of the East is grist to my mill. The Psalmist put it very well, "In Thy light shall we see light." I suppose it primarily means that in the light of the Father we shall recognize the Son, Light of the

[31] *Essays in Zen Buddhism* (First Series), Harper & Brothers (New York, 1949), I, p. 305.

World. But in a secondary sense, it may also be taken to mean that in the light of God, we can perceive all lights, whether natural or moral. To illustrate, when I read in a Buddhist Classic: "Avoid all evil, cherish all good, and keep the mind pure. This is the teaching of all the Buddhas"; I said to myself, "How similar this is to three ways of the Christian spiritual life: the purgative, illuminative and unitive!" When I read Confucius' program of education of his pupils: "First arouse their interest in wisdom by means of poetry; then establish their character by making them practise the moral rules; finally, harmonize their personality by means of music"; it reminded me of the Psalm of the Good Shepherd. The spheres are wide apart as heaven and earth, but the stages of progress are quite similar, for the simple reason that even grace has to work upon the natural and psychological apparatus of man. With regard to the wisdom of the East and Christian wisdom, God has given to my mind an organic unity of transparent differences.

Vis-à-vis the three religions of China and, for that matter, all other religions, I am in full accord with the sentiments expressed by Evelyn Underhill in the following passage:

The greatest mystics have not been heretics but Catholic saints. In them "natural mysticism" which, like "natural religion," is latent in humanity, and at the certain point of development breaks out in every race, came to itself; and attributing for the first time true and distinct personality to its Object, brought into focus the confused and unconditioned God which Neoplatonism had constructed from the abstract concepts of philosophy blended with the intuitions of Indian ecstatics, and made the basis of its meditations on the Real. It is a truism that the chief claim of Christian philosophy on our respect does not lie in its exclusiveness but in its Catholicity: in the fact that it finds truth in a hundred different systems, accepts and elucidates Greek, Jewish, and

Indian thought, fuses them in a coherent theology, and says to speculative thinkers of every time and place, "Whom therefore ye ignorantly worship, Him declare I unto you." [32]

While the three religions were distinct from one another, the syncretic disposition of the Chinese mind fused them into a unity of diversities. While Confucius, Lao Tzu and Buddha were worshipped by the Chinese people, they were never regarded as more than sages and deified men. In the Chinese mind, they never took the place of Shang Ti, that is, God the Supreme Sovereign of Heaven and the Ruler over all the universe. When a Chinese worshipped the deities, whether Confucian, Taoist, or Buddhist, he worshipped them only as the representatives and favored children of God, but never as God himself. [33]

But the question naturally arises: Why did not the Chinese worship God directly? The answer is that they regarded God as too high for them, and that, just as an ordinary subject did not deal with the Emperor directly but had to obey the orders of his immediate superiors, so the ordinary man, in his religious life, had just to pay his homage to the minor deities who were appointed by the Supreme Deity to supervise his daily life. As a child I used to worship the kitchen god, the deities of the village shrines and the city temples. But on the back of my mind was always God, whose ministers the minor deities were. In doing homage to them, I felt as natural as in honoring the tutors to whose hands my father had entrusted me. God was so high and heaven so far away that it would take the minor deities some days to go to report to Him their duties. For instance, we

[32] *Mysticism*, E. P. Dutton and Company (New York) pp. 105–6.
[33] It was in this homogeneous atmosphere of the Religion of the unknown God that both my wife and I were brought up. This is the ocean we swam in, while the "three religions" were but waves on the ocean.

used to burn the paper image of the kitchen god on the 23rd of the twelfth month, and wait for his return from heaven on the New Year's Eve, when a brand new image of the same deity was installed. The mission of his trip to heaven was to report to God all our doings and sayings throughout the year. But we were not too anxious, because we knew that he was our friend.

Our conception of the Court of Heaven was really an idealized version of feudalistic officialdom. W. E. Soothill, in his interesting book *The Three Religions of China*, gives a very accurate picture of the popular religion, which constituted an amalgamation of the three:

What, then, is, or was, the official religion? Its centre was the worship of Shang Ti, the Ruler over all, the Supreme Being. Its circumference was the worship and control of demons. Between center and circumference were concentric circles of nature deities, sages, ancestors, and deified men.

The highest act of national worship was the imperial sacrifice to Shang Ti. Only the emperor, the High Priest of "the world," the Son of Heaven, might perform this great sacrifice, which existed from all antiquity until the fall of the empire.[34]

When I became a Christian in 1917, I felt as though I had become an emperor overnight, because now I could worship God directly, having been empowered to be a son of God. My embracement of Christianity was a tremendous spiritual revolution on a par with the political revolution which had changed an absolute monarchy into a republic.

[34] Oxford University Press (London, 1929), p. 229.

John Wu.

Mrs. John Wu.

John C. H. Wu and Teresa Li Wu.

His Holiness, Pius XII, with the Wu family.

The author writing a scroll in the presence of Bishop James E. Walsh, M.M., Bishop Lefebre of Ningpo, and missionary priests.

13. THE LOTUS AND THE MUD

On January 1, 1933, I joined the Legislative Yuan together
with Dr. Sun Fo. He immediately organized the Constitu-
tion-Drafting Committee, with himself as Chairman, and
me as Vice-Chairman. The Committee appointed me to
make a preliminary draft to serve as the basis for later
discussions. In one month I completed the draft, which I
submitted to Dr. Sun. He agreed with it on general lines,
and suggested that in order to interest the public in the
making of the Constitution and to feel its reactions towards
the contents of the draft, I should release it for publication
in my own name and solicit constructive criticisms from
all quarters. These criticisms, he said, might serve as a useful
reference in our Committee discussions. I knew that my
draft would inevitably become a target for attacks, but
yielded to his suggestion. After all, in such an important
matter as the making of the Constitution, the whole nation
should be given a chance to participate in some way. So I

released it for publication in all papers and periodicals in my own name. Immediately there came an avalanche of critiques. On the whole they were more favorable than I had expected. It was bad enough, but it could have been worse.

This is, of course, no place for writing a history of the Chinese Constitution. What I am supposed to show here is how my active participation in practical politics reacted upon my interior life. Happily, my diary of November 17, 1936, contains a passage which records quite faithfully what I thought and felt in those days:

The much mooted question of idealism and materialism I have solved with some satisfaction to my own mind. Ideals, like lotus flowers, can only grow from the mud of matter. A sculptor cannot dispense with the plastic material. Without it no bust can be made, whether that of Hsishih or that of her ugly mimicker Tungshih. On the other hand, I believe with equal conviction that matter alone does not constitute beauty. Othewise all busts or even living persons would be equally beautiful—which, unfortunately, does not seem to be true. Only through a fit arrangement of material things can ideals be created, or at least be made to emerge. Even justice depends upon a harmonious distribution of material wealth. Similar to this problem of idealism and materialism, but more fundamental still, is the problem of worldliness and otherworldliness. Is life a dream? Or is it real and earnest, as Longfellow would have it? Formerly I used to swing like a pendulum between the two extremes as most of my countrymen seem to do. But now I have gradually come to realize that life is a dream, but that something real and earnest may come out from a dream. And I have learned this from experience. It is thanks to my intensive participation in practical life that although I am by nature a star-gazer, yet I seldom fall into wells. For life, especially in politics, is like tightrope-walking. You have always to maintain your balance. A little slip may cause you to fall. Your superiors, your subordinates, your colleagues, your friends and finally jobseekers are all to be dealt with tactfully and yet with sincerity: with such tactfulness as to satisfy them, and with such sincerity as to satisfy yourself. You will often find yourself between the devil and the deep sea.

So far, so good! Although several years ago when I was drafting the Constitution, I used to be a target for many a sling, I can now console myself by calling to mind the fact that many of the ideas bodied forth in that rough Draft, which now bears my name, have been incorporated into the Final Draft to be submitted to the forthcoming people's Congress for adoption. It is most interesting to study the meandering course of public opinion. In 1933, the current was strongly against me; in the Spring of 1934, it began to turn, and by the fall of the same year, it was on the whole for me! During these four trying years, one person has remained my constant friend, and that is my political superior, Dr. Sun Fo. He is one of those leaders who never fail to defend their associates against unreasonable attacks. He is also a man from whom you can really learn something. His intellectual interests are so wide that my contact with him had broadened my mental horizon. While in the daytime we might be arguing about some insignificant bills in the Legislative Yuan, in the evening, especially when the stars were sparkling over our heads, we used to meditate together on the evanescence of life. His favorite astronomer seems to be Sir James Jeans; but my favorite astronomer is Shakespeare. Ultimately, Sir James and Shakespeare have the same message for us—only Shakespeare has expressed it more beautifully and directly:

> . . . Man, proud man,
> Drest in a little brief authority,
> Most ignorant of what he is most assur'd
> His glassy essence, like an angry ape,
> Plays such fantastic tricks before high heaven
> As make the angels weep.

But all this more or less Taoistic philosophy of life has not prevented us from taking our workaday duties seriously.

On the contrary, both he and I agree heartily with Alfred Austin that life is worth living "So long as there is wrong to right." Isn't it possible to try the best we can to right the wrong in the humble spirit and without playing "such fantastic tricks before high heaven as make the angels weep" or, maybe, even laugh their heads off? Political power as an end in itself is an empty illusion; but it may be something when used as a means to an end. The end always is to transform ugly illusions into beautiful ones, to lead ourselves and our fellow travellers in dreamland out of a nightmare into a regular dream. In Buddhist parlance, it's only by friction between illusions that you can get fire out of flint, and the little spark, transient as it is, is what brings us to the Samadhi, for it is "a thing of beauty" and "a joy for ever."

As will be noted, the above passage shows a marked influence of Buddhism. The fact is that the average Chinese, up to my generation at least, was at bottom a Buddhist. In his soul, Confucianism constituted the positive element, and Taoism the negative element. The former represents tension, the latter relaxation. But both of them have to do with his world, whereas Buddhism aspires to a transcendence from this world to a sphere beyond the rhythm of life.

Although Taoism is more subtle and ethereal than Confucianism, yet, compared with Buddhism, it is still earthbound. Confucianism is ethical, Taoism is philosophical, but Buddhism is spiritual. If Taoism, according to a happy phrase of John Dewey, colors the way in which Confucianism is received, Buddhism is the atmosphere in which both of them are bathed. Such was the physiognomy of the Chinese soul before the Western influence had taken root.

In order to make this comparison more clear, I will give some concrete illustrations from Chinese poetry.

Confucianism deals primarily with the affections between human relations. When it enters into poetry, it can be extremely touching. Here is the famous "Song of a Wandering Son" composed by Meng Chiao (A.D. 761–814):

> Thread in the hand of a tender mother:
> Clothes on the body of a wandering son.
> Before I left, she added one stitch after another,
> Lest I might be tarrying in my journey.
> Ah me! How could the heart of an inch-long grass
> Requite the sunshine of a whole Spring?

This is one of the best poems on motherly love. It makes you see that filial piety is not a duty, but a spontaneous expression of human nature. Here is a poem not so well-known but just as touching, written by Sun Chia-shu of the seventeenth century:

My Little Boy

> When I left home, my little boy did not speak a
>   word:
> Clinging to my knees, he sobbed for a long time.
> On my return, he gives me a warm welcome;
> Holding my skirts, he cries out, "Mother, come
>   quick!"

In this again the poet drew his inspiration from the Confucianism in him.

Now let me present some pieces of Taoistic inspiration:

Old Age

By Chu Tun-ju (circa 1080–1175)

> Old age is not without its delight for me:
> Having gone through a variegated life,
> I have come to sense the Beyond.
> I have seen through the bubble of life,

15-12-18 Annihilating the oceans of regret and mountains of
        sorrow.

> Flowers no longer keep me in a maze;
> The wine no longer holds me in the leash;
> Everywhere I find myself sober and free.
>
> When my stomach is filled, I go to sleep.
> When I get up, I play my role in conformity with
>   the changing scenes of the stage.
>
> Talk not to me about the past and the future,—
> Your old man's heart has no room for such gossips.
> I neither cultivate the Tao, nor curry the favor of
>   the Buddha,
> Nor follow the foot-steps of the restless Master
>   K'ung.
> I am too lazy to argue with you, Sir!
> Let others laugh!
> I am like this because I am like this!
>
> When the play is over.
> I just doff my costume and give it to the fool.

It was because he was a radical Taoist that he could say
that he neither cultivated the Tao, nor curried the favor of
the Buddha, nor emulated the restless Confucius. He just
wanted to take life easy. Although he spoke of "the Beyond,"
he was really not very far from the realm of things. The
Beyond, with him, is just the finer breath of the cosmos, the
overtone of the music of life.

Another poem of the same nature is the following piece
by Hsin Ch'i-chin (1140–1207):

The Philosophy of the Fool

> How much longer can I live, being ill and old?
> Every particle of time is worth a thousand pieces of
>   gold.

In my life, I have paid up my dues to the hills and
    brooks;
But there is no remedy against the lust of books.

I may be wise! I may be otherwise!
What if I fall? What if I rise?
Each of us has his unique face,
So each may keep his peculiar pace.
Were I to write an autobiography,
What a perennial fountain of laughter it would be!

All this reminds me of the mental landscape of Holmes,
who said: "We must be serious in order to get work done,
but when the usual Saturday half-holiday comes I see no
reason why we should not smile at the trick by which nature
keeps us at our job. It makes me enormously happy when
I am encouraged to believe that I have done something of
what I should have liked to do, but in the subterranean
misgivings I think, I believe that I think sincerely, that it
does not matter much."

But whereas the Taoistic poets stop at the subterranean
misgivings about the ultimate worth of our human values,
the Buddhists introduce us into a region which is at once
deeper and higher, where we begin to doubt our doubts, to
have misgivings about our misgivings, and to divine that
there may after all be a Mind beyond the cosmos. Mahayana
Buddhism is more negative than Taoism and more positive
than Confucianism.

Take the following poem by a Buddhist monk, Hsuan-
chueh (A.D. 665–713):

Let them slander, let them abuse!
Who tries to burn the sky only wearies himself out.
When I hear their words, I feel like drinking the
    sweet dew.
They purge me! I suddenly enter into the Ineffable!

If you are able to regard gossip as charity,
The slanderer may serve as your spiritual guide.
Let no bad words provoke hatred in you.
Otherwise how can one reveal the supernatural
    power of loving patience?

I cannot imagine either a Taoist or a Confucian writing in this vein. This is what I call "more positive than Confucianism."

When my baby Hsiu-sze died in October of 1936, Dr. Sun Fo sent me a note of condolence as follows:

I am shocked to hear the sad news from you. I hasten to write you to offer my deep sympathy in your great loss. But I think you should take it more taoistically. Such things will happen to any and all of us sometime: it is the law of nature, and we can't do much about it. We must be brave and ready to face it philosophically.

The reader can easily see how the two strains of Confucianism and Taoism were working in him and checking each other. But I write a poem in memory of my little baby:

Sweetly you smiled when you were alive.
Bitterly I cried when I saw you die.
Now that I have tasted the fruit of the Bodhi,
You are gone,—and so am I!

This is more radically negative than Taoism, and yet it gave me a greater consolation than any amount of philosophical rationalization could. As to the question of "Gone where?" I just left it open.

I realize now that the influence of Buddhism on me has been much greater than I was aware of at the time. To begin with, I am endowed with a speculative cast of mind. I remember when I was in my early 'teens, I was laid to bed on account of some slight fever. When the evening came, a thought came to my mind that the courtyard in which I was in the habit of playing might no longer be existing now! I got up from the bed and ran to the window and peeped through the lattice at the courtyard. Seeing that it was still there, I went back to bed. But no sooner had I lain down than the doubt came again: "It was indeed there when you saw it, but how do you know that it is still there?" I got up again and again and ran between the bed and the window about half a dozen times, till I was utterly worn out. My mother thought I was mad, and so did I. When, in my late twenties, I studied *The Surangama Sutra* and other Buddhist classics under the direction of Abbot Ti Hsien, I was amused to find that the same kind of problem was discussed there which had puzzled my infantile mind. When, still later, I came to read the writings of Berkeley and Wang Yang-Ming, I found with great consolation that I was not the only madman in the world.

In the second place, the generous compassion of the Buddha for all sentient beings has impressed me very profoundly. When I read William Oldy's wonderful little poem *On a Fly Drinking Out of a Cup of Ale*, I said, "Here is a Buddhist!" When I read Robert Burns' *To a Mouse* and *To a Mountain Daisy*, I said, "Here is a Buddhist!" When I came across somewhere in Shakespeare's plays the most touching lines—I cannot locate them now—where he spoke about sparing the little fly because it might have a mother and a father to weep over its premature death,[1] I jumped and said, "Dear William, you have the heart of a Buddha! No matter how many deer you may have killed, this sentiment alone covers them all!" I used to be scandalized at

[1] My friends Jean Charlot and Marigold Hunt made a thorough search for this little fly in the works of Shakespeare, and after two weeks they found it in *Titus Andronicus*, Act III, Scene II.

seeing some Catholic missionaries in China going to hunt. But later I found how wonderfully kind the saints were to the animals; I began to see that those missionaries do not represent the best of Catholicism.

Last but not least, the Buddhistic saying: *As soon as a butcher lays down his knife, he becomes a Buddha on the spot,* was a tremendous encouragement to me in my attempts to reform my life.

The fatal mistake of Buddhism lies in its denial of God. Its belief that the flow of the world has no other cause besides itself, that there is no divine author of our being, that a man is born from his own deeds, fails to solve the mystery of existence. If a man is born from his own deeds, how do you explain his first existence and all the events of that existence? In this respect, Hinduism, as represented by the Bhagavad-Gita, is much nearer to the truths of Christianity than Buddhism. God is the proper object of contemplation. When contemplation is practised aside from God, it is bound to degenerate into hypnotism: and this is exactly what has happened in the case of Buddhism. Buddhism I regard as a magnificent adjective without a substantive.

What fascinated me in Buddha was not his teaching upon the nature of reality but his great personality, his generous love for all creation, his heroic renunciation of the world, his singlehearted search after the Truth. He did not succeed in finding the Truth, for it has to be revealed from above; but he is to be judged by his aspirations rather than his accomplishments. It was these aspirations that jerked me into a kind of spiritual wakefulness which prepared me remotely to return to God like the prodigal son. Buddha was one of the pedagogues to lead me to Christ.

Anyway, I owed to the Mahayana Buddhism *the ideal of being in the world but not of it.* I did not succeed in living up to it, but that I tried to do so can be gathered from my talk with an intelligent girl who called on me in Nanking. I quote from my diary for January 28, 1937:

A very intelligent girl called and we had a good chat. She wanted to be my pupil, and I presented her with a copy of *T'ien Hsia* containing my "Beyond East and West." I said that the next time she comes here, she will be required to tell me in her own words what the article is about. I also hinted to her something of my philosophy of life. "Did you know," I asked her, "that I was such a bookworm the first time you saw me at the party?" "No," she said. "You see then," I philosophized, "how hard it is to build up a real personality. At the social parties I try to appear as cheerful and carefree as a butterfly. But when I am alone, or at home with some friends talking about life and letters, I show my real self. In other words, I am a serious-minded man putting up a happy-go-lucky appearance in parties where one is supposed to be cheerful. You see life is a very difficult art, just like painting a picture,—both bright colors and sombre shades are to be used and harmonized with each other." She gave a hearty approval, and seemed inspired.

14. MENTAL ROAMINGS [1]

May 6, 1935, was a red-letter day for my literary career. It was the day on which the editorial board of the *T'ien Hsia Monthly*, which I had organized, met for the first time in its office in Shanghai. The birth of *T'ien Hsia* was as casual as any of the good things that have happened to me. I had met at one of the *China Critic* dinners Wen Yuan-ning, a former Professor of English Literature at the Peking University. I was deeply impressed by this man's erudition and personality. We took to each other, and became friends. One day, we were talking about the possibility of starting a cultural and literary periodical in English, for the sake of interpreting Chinese culture to the West. That was only wishful thinking. Such a periodical would be too high-brow to have a circulation that would make it self-supporting. And who would finance it? So we left the matter at that.

[1] These thoughts are taken from my diary and published writings. In the selection and arrangement of them, Mrs. Richard H. Kavanagh has given valuable advice.

Now it happened that I was the head of the Publicity Department of the Sun Yat-sen Institute for the Advancement of Culture and Education, concurrently with my legislative job. One morning, as I was walking with Dr. Sun Fo in a park, I mentioned to him my conversation with Wen. To my great surprise, he was more enthusiastic about the idea than I was. He said immediately, "Give me a project. Maybe the Institute can subsidize it." So we made up a project and submitted it to him. He approved of it right away in his capacity as the President of the Institute. Yuan-ning and I consulted together on the personnel of the editorial board, and we decided to approach Lin Yutang and Chuan Tseng-ku. Both of them accepted our invitation without any hesitation. With Yu Ming as our Advertising Manager, we set the ball rolling. Our office was situated on Yuyuen Road, "Yuyuen" literally meaning "the garden of fools," which fitted us like a glove.

The name "T'ien Hsia" was my suggestion. I had seen in Dr. Sun Fo's study a large horizontal scroll on which were inscribed four words: *T'ien Hsia Wei Kung*, which means "everything under heaven should be shared with all people." I thought that, as our magazine had to do with everything under heaven, which was to be shared with others, "T'ien Hsia" would not be a bad name. My suggestion was adopted at the first meeting of the board.

Now it happened that on the day I was giving birth to *T'ien Hsia*, my wife gave birth to our tenth child, a boy. I called him "Chi Wen," which means "the commencement of culture."

My association with Dr. Sun and the *T'ien Hsia* friends broadened my intellectual interests considerably. It also intensified my love of learning. I tended toward a new, broadened Humanism. How earnestly I was trying to acquire

knowledge and to cultivate my mind may be gathered from
the following passage of my diary published in *T'ien Hsia*:

I have just written a reply to my eldest son Chu-ling, who
had asked me in a letter how to acquire interest in studies.
I said that interest in studies has to be acquired by a special
effort in the beginning. For instance, I wept a whole day
when I first went to school. Writing and reading seemed so
artificial and uncalled-for to my childish mind. It seemed
ridiculous that people should have to resort to such clumsy
ways of communicating their thoughts when they could
speak with their mouths. And I thought to myself, "What is
the grand idea of tethering me to a post, when I should be
roaming the fields and flying kites?" Every day, I crept like a
snail unwillingly to school, and upon proper occasions I
played hookey. But when I was twelve, as a teacher was
lecturing on that part of the *Analects* which contained the
sentence: "When I was fifteen, I was resolved to dedicate
my life to learning," I was inspired and wrote down on the
upper margin: "I am resolved to dedicate my life to learning
when I am twelve." I felt as though I had beaten Confucius
by three years! From that time on, I made a special effort to
study; gradually a habit was formed; and by this time, I
would rather die than live a single day without enjoying
books and conversations with learned and interesting friends.

Nowadays, young folks are apt to be too sophisticated.
They dare not entertain, much less talk about, their ambitions. They have no courage to face ridicule. I used to be
called a bookworm; I am afraid I still am one. But the irony
is that some of my early sneerers are now pestering me for
jobs. "Rather be an idealistic bookworm when you are young
than become a practical job-seeker when you are old." That
is the conclusion of my letter. I admit this sentiment is not
absolutely honest, for I have seen more learned men than
myself unemployed.

I am not a learned man, but a learning man. I only hope
I shall not cease learning until I cease breathing. I have a big
library, and I have also a nice collection of friends whom I

regard as walking books of reference. Each of your friends must be superior to you in some respect, and it's up to you to make the best of them for your own edification. In these years, I have profited by my friends very much. I go to Dr. Sun Fo for economics and other social sciences except jurisprudence; to Pingsheung for memoirs and biographies; to Yuan-ning for English literature; to Dubosc for French literature; to Hsin-nung for current Chinese novels and dramas; to Ferguson for Chinese paintings; to Tseng-ku for Greek philosophy; to Ju-ao and Ching-ling for current affairs and international relations; to Yutang for books on humor and the nuns. I would have gone to Yu-wen if only I were more interested in the T'aip'ing Rebellion. Fortunately, none of them seems to be interested in my specialty, namely, the law of torts, which I have been teaching for more than ten years. Otherwise, I should also have to give for what I have taken so liberally from them.

As I read over all the writings I contributed to the *T'ien Hsia* from August, 1935, up to the winter of 1937, when I embraced the Catholic Faith, and as I follow my diary of the same period, I cannot help marvelling at the infinite goodness, wisdom and patience of God in preparing me, without my suspecting it, for my forthcoming conversion. He was playing hide-and-seek with me, just as a fond father would do with his little boy. Sometimes He led me on a wild-goose chase, until I cried and said, "Daddy, where are you?" At other times He visited me, but no sooner had I recognized him than He was gone again. He kept me guessing at His qualities and His ways. Occasionally I hit, but most of the time I missed. It seems to me that He wanted to broaden my mind, to lift up my heart, to season my zeal with humor, and finally to make me rely upon His grace by driving me to my wits' end. All my attempts at synthesis by rising from one pair of opposites after another were but a tuning up for the great harmony which He Himself was to infuse into my

soul. He unchurched me in order to lead me into the true
Church. No matter how high I jumped, how far I ran and
how deep I dived, and in spite of all my somersaults, I found
that I could never escape from Him. I cannot think of those
years without recalling the first stanza of Francis Thompson's
The Hound of Heaven:

> I fled Him, down the nights and down the days;
>   I fled Him, down the arches of the years;
> I fled Him, down the labyrinthine ways
>   Of my own mind; and in the midst of tears
> I hid from Him, and under running laughter.
>   Up vistaed hopes, I sped;
>   And shot, precipitated,
> Adown Titanic glooms of chasmed fears,
>   From those strong Feet that followed, followed
>   after.
>   But with unhurrying chase,
>   And unperturbèd pace,
> Deliberate speed, majestic instancy,
>   They beat—and a Voice beat
>   More instant than the Feet—
> "All things betray thee, who betrayest Me."

One of the most spontaneous descriptions of my spiritual
state in the middle 1930's is found in a book review that I
wrote on Pearl Buck's *The Exile.* That book tells the story
of a missionary in China called Andrew, and his wife Carie.
The husband was a Puritan, while the wife was a lover of the
fine things of life. The author's sympathy was with the wife,
and so was mine. But at the end of my review, I introduced
a paragraph which tells more of myself than of the book:

The only serious criticism I have to make of the book is
that at places the author is a bit too hard on Andrew. To
understand all is to pardon all, as the French say, and Andrew

deserves a great deal more sympathy than she seems willing to give. No one understands the psychology of a religious fanatic better than I do, for the simple reason that I used to be one myself. Twenty years ago, when I was newly converted from Confucianism to Christianity, I felt so cocksure of my religious beliefs that whenever I was introduced to a new friend, my first question invariably was, May I ask whether you are a Christian? If the answer was yes, I felt as though I had got one more companion in Heaven. But if the answer was in the negative, I felt as though I saw before my eyes a man on the point of drowning—and of course eternal drowning was an infinitely more serious case than simply drowning in the river. What could be more logical under such an emergency than to raise an alarm? "So, you are not a Christian!" I would exclaim: "It is too bad! You must read the Bible and be converted!" When I was in the United States, I was a missionary in my own way. I remember once I asked an American schoolmate whether he was a Christian, and I was simply scandalized when he answered, "No, and I don't want to be saved!"

I even tried to convert Mr. Justice Holmes, and the irony of it is that I was converted by him! I shed my religiosity, and became humbly religious. I no longer pretended to know more about God than Jesus did.

But the thing is that with the advent of doubt, I have lost my peace forever. I have never been so happy as when I was trying to save people's souls. I did not care what they said about me—some of them even suspected I was mad, but I was sure of their madness as they were of mine. I was never afraid of hurting the feelings of others. I don't think my legs would have trembled or my teeth chattered if I were to be sent to the guillotine on account of my religious belief. I didn't mind dying without leaving a posthumous fame, which I regarded as the merest husk of true Immortality. I used to despise Confucius for saying a gentleman hates to die unknown. I could even bear with equanimity the death of my dearest ones—for in this world of God's, no harm could really happen to anyone. How happy I was then! And maybe I was right too! Who knows, after all?

Now the melody of life is lost, and the harmony is yet to be achieved. I, too, have tried dancing, chewing gum, drinking wine, reading stories, studying philosophy, playing mah-jong, and other desperate remedies, but so far they have not given me any real happiness. I am no longer God-intoxicated, nor yet entirely sophisticated. Indeed, I feel like a fallen angel! I wish to be Andrew, but I am Carie! Eloi, Eloi, lama sabachthani?

Sometimes, it is true, I did think of God. For instance, my diary of October 13, 1936, contains a striking confession:

I have tried one substitute for religion after another; all of them have failed to satisfy me. Friendship? Well, I have found my friends wanting in perfection. Books? Well, the more learned you are, the more you are vexed by the insipidity of the wisdom of man. Science? It is only a part of Religion, that part which makes us as cunning as a serpent. Official life? The higher you climb, the emptier your life becomes. Money? I used to earn lots of money, but that didn't make me any happier. Health? It is good, but only as a foundation to build your temple of life. Fame? I have had my share of it, but the only advantage is that my wife can go shopping without bringing cash. Girls? I have had enough of them. Children? Yes, they are charming, but they take me to be a toy capable of making grimaces and provoking laughter. Animals? They make good company and remind me of my origin. But they can give little more. Gardens? They are beautiful, but I hear echoes of the miseries of life outside. Self-reliance? But I am a slender reed.

After a long period of mental wandering, I have finally come back to God. God includes all pleasures of life and heightens their meaning. He is the ideal friend who knows your heart better than you do yourself; He is the meaning of all books worthy of the name, the overtone of music, and the very subject-matter of all science and philosophy. He teaches you how to execute your official duties; He teaches you how to make use of money and other material things;

He transforms fame into a vessel of love; He sanctifies girls to be your mothers and sisters; He teaches you how to learn from children and animals; He inspires you to make a garden of the world; He strengthens moral and intellectual fibre and leads you to shed the cocoon of self.

This seems to be a noble conception of God; but did I really return to Him? No, there was no real change of heart, nor was there a true peace of soul. God can only be found in His Way, that is, through Christ, and by walking in His commandments, but not merely by speculating about Him. The proof of the pudding is in the eating; and the proof of religion is in the living. The truth is that you cannot shed the cocoon of self, unless you allow the seed of spiritual life, sanctifying grace, to grow gradually until the Christ is formed in you. Spiritual life is not a matter of jets and spurts; it is a continuous stream of living water springing up unto life everlasting. Sometimes, it bubbles; at other times, it flows on quietly; but there must be a continual flow, which presupposes the reception of the Sacraments that God Himself has established through His Christ. But in those days, I was indulging in mental roamings, and jotted down in my diary many thoughts as they occurred to me. I have gathered together here a few specimens of my thought, which constituted, as it were, some of the rough bricks that the Divine Architect was later to transmute into materials for erecting in me the temple of the Holy Ghost. For grace does not destroy nature, but purifies it and builds upon it. The following thoughts date mostly from 1936 and 1937.

ON GOD AS A MOTHER

God is not only our father, who is supposed to be as fearful as the summer sun, but also our *mother*, who is as tender and kind as the winter sun, or the autumn moon, or the

spring breeze. Unless you recognize this and can play inno-
cently on the knees of your Mother and prattle to her your
childish inconsequences, she will not love you but will regard
you as unnecessarily timid and worry for your future. She
would say, "I wonder what is wrong with my little Ah-pao.
Whenever he sees me, he feels shy and becomes stiff in his
manners. What have I done to estrange him thus?"

How do you know that God is masculine, and not also feminine? To me, God is my Mother. And my whole life is a
search after my Mother.

ON LUKEWARMNESS

Unless you love God with joy singing in your heart, it
would be better not to love Him at all. For your time is not
yet come.

It seems to me that the wise men of all countries and of all
ages are unanimous in their denunciation of the comfortable
worldlings. They have given them different names. Christ
called them Pharisees, Confucius called them country smugs,
Thackeray called them snobs, and modern Americans call
them Babbitts. Dante found them in a secret place just inside
of the gate of Hell. I suspect that even Minos the Infernal
Judge does not want them near him. They seem to drag along
their festering existence like parasites on Hell. They "lived
without praise or blame," they were neither rebellious nor
true to God, they displeased both God and His foes. No one
has given a better description of the miserable tribe than
Shelley:

They who, deluded by no generous error, instigated by no
sacred thirst of doubtful knowledge, duped by no illustrious
superstition, loving nothing on this earth, and cherishing no
hopes beyond, yet keep aloof from sympathies with their
kind, rejoicing neither in human joy nor mourning with

human grief; these and such as they, have their appointed curse. They are morally dead. They are neither friends, nor lovers, nor fathers, nor citizens of the world, nor benefactors of their country.

ON THE SPIRIT OF THE MORNING

Good day to Thee, Spirit of the Morning! Once more I feel like a boy looking forward to a full day—not a day of leisurely pleasure, but a day full of absorbing tasks and thrilling enterprises. There is within me a spontaneous call for effort, a surging willingness to meet Life halfway, to shake him warmly by the hand.

"Have done with brooding over your past!" says the Spirit of the Morning. "Your past is something to be excreted from time to time, if you are not to suffer from spiritual constipation. Yesterday's bread does not satisfy the hunger of today. Yesterday's water does not satisfy your present thirst. Yesterday's inspiration is turned into ashes overnight. Yesterday's optimism does not help you from falling again into the Slough of Despond. You can die only once, but life must be renewed every moment, and everything that is of value to you must be kept constantly in repair."

"O sweet Spirit of the Morning!" I answer, "there is tonic in your words; they are like the rays of the sun that give health and strength to me. O sweet invigorating Spirit, let me imbibe more of thee, let me kiss and embrace thee, let me praise and worship thee. Teach me, like a gentle nurse, the songs of childhood. Help me gird up my loins and live like a man. Drive away my fears that were nursed in darkness. I had entrusted my life to the whims of Fate; now let me take it into my own hands once more, and make of it what I like and what thou wouldst like to see. Let me wear my life like a ring on my finger, ever ready to give it up, not for all the wealth of the world, but for a song, the song of love and sacrifice, of innocence and perfection. To give it not to the first person I meet on the street, but to an ideal lady conceived and begotten of thee, O mighty Spirit of the Morning!"

THE SPIRIT OF YOUTH

I may grow old in years, but my heart will remain young forever. Every morning I am born anew. And I sing:

> And ah for a man to arise in me,
> That the man I am may cease to be!

THE SENSE OF WONDER

Science has turned the universe into a wonderland, but at the same time it has destroyed our sense of wonder. We are living in an age when not only our bodies but also our souls are starving in the midst of abundance. Ah, when will man become a child again?

THE WONDERS OF ORDINARY LIFE

Happiness, like the boiling point, is relative. The same circumstances would pass even unnoticed if worse circumstances hadn't been experienced. In passing through bad circumstances to better ones, one feels the external pressure lightened, while the mind still retains the power of resistance appropriate to the former situation: and there arises the boiling point of happiness. In order to be happy in all conditions of life, you must always remember the blackest days. Otherwise you will find that happiness will always linger coyly just over the horizon. When a man is on the point of drowning, all he cares for is his life. But as soon as he gets on shore, he asks, "Where is my umbrella?" Wisdom of life consists in not asking for the umbrella.

Only when you have tasted sickness can you realize with all the muscles of your body what a great joy it is just to be in normal health. To breathe freely, to enjoy your food, to sleep soundly, to crack jokes, to sun-bathe yourself, to listen to the birds in the morning, to listen to the radio in the evening, to have nothing in the secret corners of your mind to make you blush, to have no enemy, to have no friend who has betrayed you, to read and sing over the typewriter, to attend to your daily duties, to write your diary, even though it is not the dial of the world, to cultivate your own garden and to enjoy the garden of your neighbor,—each and every one of these little things of life we have by a special grace of God. Oh, the wonders of ordinary life!

A COMMENT ON CHESTERTON

Chesterton says, "The only way to enjoy even a weed is to feel unworthy even of a weed." The same is true of your friends, books, wife, children, everything that God has allotted to you. You are unworthy of them, and even of your own achievements, humble as they may be. The sum of the wisdom of life, I agree with Chesterton, consists in "having a great deal of gratitude even for a very little good."

THE FEAST OF LIFE

Life is a feast which you can only enjoy when nobody else is crying in the hall with his face to the wall. No matter how rich the feast may be, my appetite is spoiled if I find the host quarrelling with his wife, or even kicking the dog for stealing a pitiful morsel of food from under the table.

A good life is a great bundle of little kindnesses. But the

tragedy is that even little kindnesses are so costly. O God! forgive me the lukewarmness of my gratitude to Thee for feeding me and my family. Until all Thy children be well fed as I am, my spirit will remain hungry although my body is satisfied. My body thanks Thee, but my spirit is pulling at my legs.

ON THE ART OF LIFE

Living is the greatest of all arts, and it is also the most difficult art to master. As Goethe says, "Life is a quarry, out of which we have to mould and complete a character." The art of life is harder than swimming, harder than tightrope-walking, flying and boxing, harder than sculpture, painting, poetry and music. And yet people seem to think they can practise this great art without assiduous self-discipline and self-cultivation. That's why there are so many half-baked amateurs in life.

LIFE AS A PLAY

So many strange things have happened during these few years of my life that I should not be surprised if the sun should arise in the west tomorrow. On the contrary, I should be somewhat surprised if no more strange things will happen, for that would be strange indeed. What's the use of going to the theatre when you have so many dramas and melodramas to see outside? The only excuse seems to be that there are better actors and actresses in the theatre than on the stage of the world, where you too often meet

> . . . a poor player,
> That struts and frets his hour upon the stage
> And then is heard no more.

THE RÔLE OF A JUDGE

When I was a judge, I used to take my duties seriously, as in fact I always do. But somewhere in the corners of my mind there lurked an awareness that I was only playing the rôle of a judge on the stage of life. Whenever I had to sentence a man to death, I secretly prayed to his soul to forgive me for doing it, as it was my rôle and not my will that consented to the judgment. I felt like Pilate and wished to wash my hands of shedding anybody's blood, however guilty he might be. Only a perfect man is qualified to cast a stone at a guilty one, and there is no perfect man.

PLAY YOUR RÔLE WELL

Life is a play. It may be a comedy or a tragedy—that makes no difference. The thing is to play your rôle well, whatever your rôle may be. So far, I have laid the blame on the rôles that have been assigned to me by God the Great Playwright and Theatre-Manager. I have found now that the chief trouble with me does not lie in the rôles I have been playing, but in the lack of spirit with which I have played them. In my ignorance, I had imagined that to be a great actor one must needs act the rôle of a man of power. As a matter of fact, you can powerfully act the rôle of a man without power.

ON SUICIDE

The root of all evil is attachment to life. So long as we don't strike at the root, no use hacking at the branches and leaves. I don't mean that we should commit suicide, but that we should emancipate ourselves in spirit from the thraldom to life in order to treat it objectively as the material of the grand art of living. To commit suicide, on the other hand, is to break the piano into pieces because we despair of learning to play the music well. Indeed, to commit suicide is to take one's life too seriously.

ON SELFISHNESS

Selfishness is a luxury wasted upon the wrong person.

One of the most interesting stories I have ever heard is that a fellow was shaving, but due to some optical illusion he was shaving the wrong face, for it happened to belong to another fellow who was standing near by. But this is not half as ludicrous as when a man takes care only of his own face and will not lift a finger to help another who is struggling in the mire. For in that case, he is indeed shaving the right face, but the right face belongs to the wrong person.

ON FRIENDSHIP

I think it was Emerson who said that the condition which high friendship demands is the ability to do without it. This, however, is only the condition of friendship, not its substance. After the condition has been fulfilled, a considerable degree of warm feeling is required to keep the friendship alive. You ought to be able to do without it, but at the same time you must feel as though you could not do without it. Friendship, in other words, is mutual dependence built upon mutual independence.

THE PHILOSOPHY OF LOVE

How wonderful is love! It is the creator of all things. It is the highest principle of the cosmos; it stands above Yin and Yang, for it brings them together. The commerce between Yin and Yang is holy, when inspired by Love, it is mere lust, when unaccompanied by it. Lust is to Love what talent is to genius, what a politician is to a statesman, what fish's eyes are to pearls. Lust is a forgery and mimicry of Love; it is a mere husk with no living kernel inside; but like all hypocrisies, it pays homage to virtue by imitating its external incidents. Cultivate Love, and everything will be added to you. Joy is perfection, says Spinoza; I may add, joy and pleasure are as wide apart from each other as heaven and earth.

ON CONFUCIANISM AND TAOISM

Lin Yutang says that "when a Chinese scholar is in office he moralizes, and when he is out of office he versifies, and usually it is good Taoistic poetry." Again he says, "For Taoism is the playing mood of the Chinese people, as Confucianism is their working mood. That accounts for the fact that every Chinese is a Confucianist when he is successful and a Taoist when he is a failure. The naturalism of Taoism is the balm that soothes the wounded Chinese soul." In this connection I beg to register a dissent. It has always seemed to me that the greatest statesmen in the history of China have been men who acted like Confucians but felt like Taoists. And they acted like Confucians precisely because they were Taoists at heart. Chang Liang was a regular Taoist. Chu-ko Liang was another, and no one can deny that they were among the greatest of Chinese statesmen. Confucius himself was a man in the Tao.

Dr. Lin seems to stop and tarry just before the door that opens to a living synthesis between Confucianism and Taoism. If life is a play, as indeed it is, it does not follow that one should play playfully. For instance, if one wishes to dance well, one must take care not to trample on the feet of one's partner. And to play well, one must forget that one is playing. There are also rules for the game one has to follow.

ANALYSIS AND SYNTHESIS

Autumn is the season in Nanking. The maples are so very charming. Their leaves are not violently red, but soberly red. The sky is serene and crystalline. The pagodas stand out from the background of the green hills so clearly and distinctly that you feel as though you were looking at a picture fresh from the hands of a master-artist. In autumn everything takes on definite and chiselled contours; things you have been looking at, as it were, through mist and fog, suddenly reveal their clear outlines and naked colors to you. It is as though you had just discovered your nearsightedness and put on a pair of spectacles exactly suiting your eyes. You begin to see the distinctions where you used to see only a block of monotonous sameness, and your heart is captivated by the new-found beauty. I know there is a whole school of philosophy which holds that distinctions falsify Reality. But distinctions are to be distinguished from *tours de force* and violent contrasts. The sense of beauty depends, partly at least, upon an awareness of the subtle distinctions shading off gradually into each other, discernible only to the keen-sighted. To introduce distinctions where there are none is, indeed, to falsify Reality; but not to see distinctions that are glaring at you is to blur Reality. The cosmos itself has enough of fringy and nebulous forms for you to enjoy, and does not need to borrow additional charm from your muddleheadedness. I believe that only a profoundly analytical mind can achieve a vital synthesis.

BETWEEN MELODY AND HARMONY

The evolution of music from melody to harmony is symbolic of the development of human society and of the growth of man's inner life. But the most painful moments are those in which melody is gone and harmony is yet to be achieved; for in those moments we have only discords, which are neither melodious nor harmonic. This explains why in times of transition "tender-minded" philosophers so often wish to return to nature, craving, as it were, after lost melody.

ON THE PATHOS OF MIDDLE AGE

Human life, it has been wittily said by Lichtenberg, is divided into two halves; during the first one looks forward to the second, and during the second one looks backward to the first. But there are years that lie on the borderland between the two, and a man looks both before and after. He rips up the past, he scans the future. The past is gone, and the future is uncertain; so he is driven to retire into himself, and explore the mystery of his own soul. In the meantime, however hard he tries to withdraw from the world, he still hears the tide of time passing over his head and the far off hubbub of the cosmic ocean. He is saturated through and through with the pathos of life.

ON FLASHES OF THOUGHT

Flashes of thought are like children in that, while you may be their father or mother, you have no control over their quality. Some of them are beautiful and much liked by others; others are not so good. Some of them are wiser than yourself; others are below your level. Some of them will survive you and live to an advanced age; others die in their infancy or even stillborn.

ON THE CHOICE OF NIBS

It is quite a job to pick out a new nib when the old one is worn out. Each nib has an individuality of its own; and even

those of the same patent differ from one another in their
degree of manageability. Some of them are too sharp, others
too dull. Some are stubborn, others a bit too pliable. Indeed,
the choice of a nib is like the choice of a wife.

ON THE UNITY OF MANKIND

Humanity is *one* in spite of the national boundaries and
underneath the differences of color. The differences between
races are skin-deep, but the unity of mankind lies in the
innermost heart of hearts.

EAST AND WEST

I think it is within limits to assert that on the whole the
East has more of the feminine, and the West more of the
masculine qualities. The hope of the future depends upon
their mating, and the mating season is on even now!

In spite of the alarms of war that I hear on every side, I
believe that this century will have something to contribute
toward the grand symphony of man, and that out of the
boiling cauldron something beautiful will finally emerge.
We may not enjoy the harvest; we may at least enjoy the
sowing. Don't be disheartened by the depressing environment. Long after all the peace-breakers and trouble-makers
of the world, whom Shakespeare would have called "the
idols of idiot-worshippers," shall have gone to complete
oblivion, this century will be looked upon as the herald of a
New Civilization, the turning point in which men begin to
be transformed into Man.

THE SEARCH FOR HAPPINESS

Both China and the West have been searching for happiness, but their methods are fundamentally different. On

the whole, we try to cut down our desires, while the Occidentals try to amplify the means of satisfying them.

TEA AND COFFEE

The difference between the East and the West is only the difference between tea and coffee. And yet there are not lacking tea enthusiasts among Westerners. "Thank God for tea!" cried Sydney Smith in his *Recipe for Salade.* "What could the world do without tea? I am glad I was not born before tea." But the interesting thing is that even such a great tea lover should talk as though he had just gulped down some cups of coffee. So excited he appeared. This reminds me of John Cowper Powys, who raises a thrilling alarm when he sees philosophy on the point of being brushed aside by the ruthless torrent of modern civilization, crying at high pitch: "We must bring back philosophy! It is philosophy we all need at this juncture." Powys seems to preach quiet wisdom in a rather noisy way, and that is the humor of it.

ON CIVILIZATION

All civilization is a disease; and there are different types of civilization as there are different kinds of disease. Chinese civilization is beriberi; Western civilization is wandering sickness. The former is tuberculosis, the latter typhoid fever.

Chinese civilization is a museum, Western civilization a circus, Indian civilization a graveyard. You go to a museum for curiosity, to a circus for excitement, and to a graveyard for meditations.

The modern Chinese knows only the glittering beauty of the light; but they do not know the glamorous fascination of the twilight. But what is the use of crying over spilt milk?

China is doomed to progress, to follow the brilliant path of the West, to out-west the West in its material civilization; but we should do it with as much reluctance of heart as swiftness of foot. The apple will fall to the ground, although we don't worship the law of gravitation.

ON THE MOON

One difference between the East and the West lies in their different ideas about the moon. To the East, the moon is the symbol of constancy; to the West, she is the embodiment of inconstancy. In the Chinese *Book of Songs*, we find a line which has since become a proverb:

He is as constant as the moon.

On the other hand, Shakespeare made Juliet declare against the moon:

O! swear not by the moon, the inconstant moon,
That monthly changes in her circled orb,
Lest that thy love prove likewise variable.

Whether the moon is constant or inconstant depends upon whether you look at it through the lunar calendar or the solar calendar. In the lunar calendar, the moon is so constant that it always keeps its date. The full moon comes invariably on the middle of the month. True, it waxes and wanes like the diastole and the systole of the heart. But everybody could predict exactly on what days it would be like a goose-feather, and on what other days it would be like a round mirror hanging in the sky. It completes its course each month. Nothing is so dependable as the moon. On the other hand, to one who is familiar only with the Grecian calendar, nothing would appear so irregular and capricious as the moon. The full moon comes every month like a thief.

I was born under the lunar calendar; but in 1911 it was drastically abolished, and the Grecian calendar became the official one. Ever since then I have felt homesick for the Moon Year. When I was a child the year was a living presence. It was like a tree, full of leaves and flowers and fruits. It was studded all over with beautiful festivals which made life interesting and worth living. But the Grecian year is like a bare tree, it is so prosaic and insipid. It has not stretched its roots deep into the Chinese soil. To me the Year looks like a pet dog newly shorn of its beautiful fur. It is clean enough, but there is something strange and pitiful about it.

ON HUMOR

Westerners are seriously humorous, but we are humorously serious. While they are better acquainted with the misery of being funny, we are better acquainted with the fun of being miserable.

CHINESE HUMOR

The staple of Chinese humor is the seeing of the ludicrous in the pathos of life. It is the result of resignation to fate wedded to a blend of self-pity and good temper. Among Western authors, Charles Lamb is the only one that I know who seems to embody this demure type of humor. But you find it very often in the writings of old Chinese authors. I admit it is rapidly dying out at present. For I find our young people, women as well as men, boisterously clamoring for their constitutional right to be happy, when their real trouble is that they are constitutionally unhappy.

TESTS OF HUMOR

One sure test of a person's sense of humor is whether he will be angry when he is accused of lack of humor. If he pleads guilty, he is not guilty. If he pleads not guilty, it would be wiser for you to have no more arguments with him, lest something worse should come from him. You know you hold your body in trust from your parents with your children as the *cestui que trust*; you can't afford to expose it to unnecessary risks.

Another test is whether the person in question delights in gossiping about and laughing over the failings and shortcomings of another. If he does, he is not humorous, no matter how loudly he laughs. If he does not, he has at least a *prima facie* claim to humor. For instance, I am so humorous a man that I find no urge to laugh at others, as I find more than enough in myself to laugh at. I am a multi-millionaire in follies, if I may boast a little. And I take as much delight in counting my own follies as a miser does in counting his riches.

It is significant that with all my mental roamings and literary activities I found neither happiness nor peace. Materially, intellectually, socially, and politically, I was enjoying exceptional prosperity. But spiritually I was pessimistic to the extreme. This was how I wrote about life: "My conception of life is spiral. A man respires, aspires, perspires, inspires and finally expires." Deep down in me, I felt a yawning abyss of nothingness, which only God could fill, and I had not found God. I did not find God, because I had drifted away from Christ, the only Divine Bridge that God had built from Heaven to earth. Having drifted away from Christ, my faith in God was fading rapidly, and with it the belief in the immortal-

ity of the soul. "You little ganglion," I wrote on the eve of the
New Year 1937, addressing myself, "why do you take so
seriously to writing? Do you think that writing will save you
from final dissolution? What if you could write as well as
Shakespeare and Tu Fu, what if you were the author of all
the masterpieces that have been produced by the hands of
men? . . . What if you were Abraham Lincoln, Walt Whitman, Charles Darwin, Karl Marx, Goethe, Heine, Emerson,
Li Po, Tolstoy, Schopenhauer, Carlyle, Lamb, Einstein,
Pasteur, all in one? You little ganglion, are you therefore
pasteurized against the Microbe of Time?" O John, O John,
what was ailing thee?

The more I think of my life, the more I am convinced
of the truth of the words that St. Augustine addressed to
God: *"Thou hast made us for Thyself and our hearts are
restless till they rest in Thee."*

Without God's grace I could never have returned to Him.
But the abyss of my nothingness touched the abyss of His
mercy. Is it not marvellous that I was converted in the very
year in which I had written:

> O God, if You are there,
> I wish to know Your secret will!

15. RETURN OF THE PRODIGAL

In a letter which Léon Bloy wrote to Jacques Maritain before the latter's conversion, I find a most striking passage:

You are *seeking*, you say. O professor of philosophy, O Cartesian, you believe, with Malebranche, that truth is something *one seeks!* You believe that the human mind is capable of something! You believe—in other words—that with a certain degree of effort a person with black eyes could manage to acquire green eyes spangled with gold! You eventually understand that one finds what he desires only on that day when he has most humbly renounced seeking what lay under his hand, unbeknown to him. For my part, I declare that I never sought or found anything unless one wishes to describe as a discovery the fact of tripping blindly over a threshold and being thrown flat on one's stomach into the House of Light.[1]

Now, this is exactly what happened in my conversion:

[1] Léon Bloy, *Pilgrim of the Absolute*; selected by Raissa Maritain; trs., John Coleman and Harry Binsse; Introduction by Jacques Maritain, The Pantheon Press (New York, 1947), p. 278.

tripping blindly over a threshold and being thrown flat on my stomach into the House of Light.

It will be recalled that the incident of the Marco Polo Bridge, which introduced the Sino-Japanese War, occurred on July 7, 1937. The war gradually spread to the south, and on August 13 began the battle of Shanghai. At that time I found myself in Nanking. The regular communications were cut between Nanking and Shanghai. I was sorely homesick. Meanwhile I received a telegram from home, telling me that they had moved from our house at the West End, which was no longer safe, into the French Concession. On August 18 I made a desperate attempt to return to Shanghai by motoring. I succeeded in coming into Shanghai through the British sector. So I was reunited with my family and with the *T'ien Hsia* friends who were still continuing bravely to defend the cause of China, although we were practically bottled up in Shanghai. Besides the regular editorial work, we also did some broadcasting.

The October number of *T'ien Hsia* published an article of mine called "More Pathos and Humor." It contains my diary of September 19. As it presents my philosophy of war, I want to reproduce it here:

By a queer coincidence, last night just as I was reading in Murry's article: "The airman in a bombing plane—that is Man today," our planes were raining incendiary bombs on the Yangtzepoo, Wayside, and Broadway areas, "sending showers of flames and sparks up like Roman candles," as this morning's *North-China Daily News* had it. "Chinese planes proved more daring than they had been up to date, zooming down from the brightly moon-lit skies and dropping their bombs from low altitudes."

In a real sense, I am glad that China has adapted herself so perfectly well to the environment of the present era when Death has veritably become the master of Life. In order to survive, we have to pay our dues to the reigning Power of the day, or rather of the night. If we take a long view, we shall find that this Dynasty of Death is only a temporary phase the Commonwealth of Life has to go through in order to rise to a high level.

> And embryo Good, to reach full stature,
> Absorbs the Evil in its nature.

The Evil is a necessary evil, we have to submit to it as inexorable Fate. We must do it manfully, but with unutterable regret at heart. This regret serves to keep us in touch with the innermost core of Life, and to maintain our continuity with the next phase of Life when the Dynasty of Death shall have fallen, when Death itself shall have died. If we fall in love with Death, being intoxicated with her charms, we shall find ourselves out of place in the Dawn of Life. We shall have become like those fishes which are so accustomed to darkness that they have lost their eyes.

Wars are just to those to whom they are necessary. China is compelled to fight for her existence; therefore her citizens have a duty to fight. But it would be lack of candor to say that the duty is a pleasant one. The duty should be carried out with a firm hand, but also with a sombre heart, as if we are attending a funeral service. This is why Loatze said, "When armies are raised and issues joined, it is he who does not delight in war, who feels sorry for the killing, that will win." This is also what is meant by General Chiang's phrase "To respond to the war with calm sobriety."

In literature as in life, candidness is all. Was Branford candid when he sang:

> I too have drunk delight in weakling's tears,
> The rapture of quick cruelty, and the prize
> Of sudden prey. I too have handled fears
> And filled the air with iron merchandise,
> Like a pitiless falcon nailed upon the skies.[2]

[2] In T'ien Hsia, Vol. V (1937), pp. 126–7.

One feels that he was singing in falsetto. One feels he was making a virtue of a necessity. It is no part of wisdom to drink the hemlock as if it were a fountain of delight. It's all right to take the hemlock as Socrates did, feeling a little tickled by ironic Fate. But to drink it voluptuously and rapturously is no sign of calm sanity, but of pathology—more like Lady Macbeth and Salome than Socrates and Jesus. Jesus took death as a bitter cup. He died in agony, not ecstatically. How much more sorry we should be when we are compelled to walk on the brink of Spiritual Death, as we are doing now in killing others. '

In the meantime, I was missing my library in my own house which we had vacated. One day my wife and I stole into the western section and entered our house quietly. I spent a whole afternoon in my library. As I could not take out too many books, I had a hard time in selecting from thousands of them on my shelves the few which I would bring with me. For one reason or another, I picked out the following books (besides a bundle of Chinese books):

The Holy Bible, "Newly Edited by the American Revision
     Committee, 1901."
William James, The Varieties of Religious Experience.
Carl Van Doren, The World's Best Prose.
Giovanni Papini, Life of Christ.
T. S. Eliot, Selected Essays, 1917–1932.

I would have chosen more, but my wife was impatient because it was already late. She said, "We don't want to be caught in the curfew. You can come another time." So we hastened back to our house in the French Concession.

At that time, I was living all alone in a room which I had rented next to the house where my wife and children were putting up. Being utterly lonely, I meditated on life and death, war and peace, God and men, and a thousand and one other problems. In my pride and ignorance, I murmured against God. I said to myself, "If I were God, the world would have been better off. I would not have permitted the wars. Is He not omnipotent? Could He not have prevented all these sufferings? . . ." My attention was attracted by the Holy Bible lying on my desk, the Bible which had been my companion for a period of twenty years. I opened it at random, and my eyes fell on Psalm 14. I read:

> The fool hath said in his heart, There is no God.
> They are corrupt, they have done abominable works.
> There is none that doeth good.

> Jehovah looked down from heaven upon the chil-
>   dren of men,
> To see if there were any that did understand,
> That did seek after God.

> They are all gone aside; they are together become
>   filthy;
> There is none that doeth good,
> No, not one.

I was not able to finish the Psalm. What an unanswerable answer God had given to my murmurings! "There is none that doeth good, no, not one." That made me look into myself. "Am I the one who does good?" I asked myself. "No!" my conscience answered within me. "Have I not committed abominable actions?" "Yes!" "Have I a right then to murmur against God?" "No, not at all!" "If I were perfect, if I were intelligent, if I had sought after God seriously and earnestly, would I perhaps have disarmed the just wrath of God?" "Maybe," I speculated.

To be converted, one must first know himself to be per-verted. For the first step down in our own estimation is the

first step up towards God. My pride was already crushed, but
it was too painful to continue that condemnation of myself.
Consequently, I closed the Bible like a child whose finger
had been burnt by accident. I wanted to read something
lighter to distract my mind. What was more natural for me
to do than to seek for some amusement in Carl Van Doren's
World's Best Prose? I opened it at random, and found an
essay under the queer title "Infallibility." I did not know
exactly what it meant. It was a selection from Cardinal Newman's *Apologia Pro Vita Sua.* Now I was an admirer of Newman's style of writing. So I entered upon this piece hoping
for some literary enjoyment. Great was my surprise when I
read the opening paragraph:

Starting then with the being of a God, (which, as I have
said, is as certain to me as the certainty of my own existence,
though when I try to put the grounds of that certainty into
logical shape I find a difficulty in doing so in mood and figure
to my satisfaction,) I look out of myself into the world of
men, and there I see a sight which fills me with unspeakable
distress. The world seems to give the lie to that great truth,
of which my whole being is so full; and the effect upon me
is, in consequence, as a matter of necessity, as confusing as
if it denied that I am in existence myself. If I looked into
a mirror, and did not see my face, I should have the sort
of feeling which actually comes upon me, when I look into
this living busy world, and see no reflexion of its Creator.
This is, to me, one of those great difficulties of this absolute
primary truth, to which I referred just now. Were it not for
this voice, speaking so clearly in my conscience and my heart,
I should be an atheist, or a pantheist, or a polytheist when I
looked into the world. I am speaking for myself only; and I
am far from denying the real force of arguments in proof of
a God, drawn from the general facts of human society and
the course of history, but these do not warm me or enlighten
me; they do not take away the winter of my desolation, or
make the buds unfold and the leaves grow within me, and

my moral being rejoice. The sight of the world is nothing else than the prophet's scroll, full of "lamentations, and mourning, and woe."

These words captivated my attention. They were most tantalizing. I said to myself, "Isn't it true that the sight of the world is full of 'lamentations, and mourning, and woe'? Is not the world of the twentieth century much worse than the world that Newman saw? Does it not give the lie to the great truth of the existence of God? Where do I see the reflection of the Creator? O Newman, I fully sympathize with you in your bewilderment. If anything, I am more bewildered than you!" Then I read on, and found the next two paragraphs even more tantalizing than the first:

To consider the world in its length and breadth, its various history, the many races of man, their starts, their fortunes, their mutual alienations, their conflicts; and then their ways, habits, governments, forms of worship; their enterprises, their aimless courses, their random achievements and acquirements, the impotent conclusion of long-standing facts, the tokens so faint and broken of a superintending design, the blind evolution of what turn out to be great powers or truths, the progress of things as if from unreasoning elements, not towards final causes, the greatness and littleness of man, his far-reaching aims, his short duration, the curtain hung over his futurity, the disappointment of life, the defeat of good, the success of evil, physical pain, mental anguish, the prevalence and intensity of sin, the pervading idolatries, the corruptions, the dreary hopeless irreligion, that condition of the whole race, so fearfully yet exactly described in the Apostle's words, "having no hope and without God in the world,"—all this is a vision to dizzy and appall; and inflicts upon the mind the sense of a profound mystery, which is absolutely beyond human solution.

What shall be said to this heart-piercing, reason-bewildering fact? I can only answer, that either there is no Creator, or this living society of men is in a true sense discarded from His presence. Did I see a boy of good make and mind, with tokens on him of a refined nature, cast upon the world without provision, unable to say whence he came, his birth-place or his family connections, I should conclude that there was some mystery connected with his history, and that he was one of whom, from one cause or other, his parents were ashamed. Thus only should I be able to account for the contrast between the promise and the condition of his being. And so I argue about the world;—if there be a God, since there is a God, the human race is implicated in some terrible aboriginal calamity. It is out of joint with the purposes of its Creator. This is a fact, a fact as true as the fact of its existence; and thus the doctrine of what is theologically called original sin becomes to me almost as certain as that the world exists, and as the existence of God.

"Enough, enough, Cardinal Newman!" I said, "I know better than you do that the human race is out of joint with the purpose of its Creator. But tell me what is the remedy?" Then I came across this remarkable sentence: "Since the world is in so abnormal a state, surely it would be no surprise to me, if the interposition were of necessity equally extraordinary—or what is called miraculous." In the margin of the book, I wrote: "An extraordinary disease requires an extraordinary remedy!" As I read on, I came upon the paragraph which interested me for the first time in my life in the Catholic Church:

Supposing then it to be the Will of the Creator to interfere in human affairs, and to make provisions for retaining in the world a knowledge of Himself, so definite and distinct as to be proof against the energy of human scepticism, in such a case,—I am far from saying that there was no other way,—but there is nothing to surprise the mind, if He should think fit to introduce a power into the world, invested with the prerogative of infallibility in religious matters. Such a provision would be a direct, immediate, active, and prompt means of withstanding the difficulty; it would be an instrument suited to the need; and, when I find that this is the very claim of the Catholic Church, not only do I feel no difficulty in admitting the idea, but there is a fitness in it, which recommends it to my mind. And thus I am brought to speak of the Church's infallibility, as a provision, adapted by the mercy of the Creator, to preserve religion in the world, and to restrain that freedom of thought, which of course in itself is one of the greatest natural gifts, and to rescue it from its own suicidal excesses. . . . I say, that a power, possessed of infallibility in religious teaching, is happily adapted to be a working instrument, in the course of human affairs, for smiting hard and throwing back the immense energy of the aggressive, capricious, untrustworthy intellect.

I knew next to nothing about the Catholic Church. On reading these words from one whose integrity and good sense I had learned to admire through his other writings, I promised myself to learn more about the Church.

But what struck me most was this statement: "The Catholic Church holds it better for the sun and moon to drop from heaven, for the earth to fall, and for all the many millions on it to die of starvation in extremest agony, as far as temporal affliction goes, than that one soul, I will not say, should be lost, but should commit one single venial sin, should tell one wilful untruth, or should steal one poor farthing without excuse." This sounded to my worldly ears like the most revolutionary cry that I had ever heard. It jerked my mind into a sphere of which I had no idea. It compelled me to turn my eyes from the external world and its sufferings to the soul within and its sins and miseries. One has to return to oneself before one can return to God. Is it of no significance that the prodigal son "came to himself" before he went back to his father?

In the next few days, I found myself reading *Life of Christ* by Giovanni Papini, translated by Dorothy Canfield Fisher. I liked the style of the book from the very beginning. "It was not by chance that Christ was born in a stable. What is the world but an immense stable where men produce filth and wallow in it? Do they not daily change the most beautiful, the purest, the most divine things into excrements? Then stretching themselves at full length on the piles of manure, they say they are 'enjoying life.'" [3] Was it not true of myself, who had spent one Christmas Eve dancing in the Canidrome? "First to worship Jesus were animals, not men. Among men He sought out the simple-hearted: among the simple-hearted He sought out children. Simpler than children, and milder, the beasts of burden welcomed Him." [4] This appealed to my oriental sense of the lovableness of animals. In fact, there is a current Buddhist saying, "The beasts are worthier of salvation than men!"

Everything that Papini touched became lively and graphic. But the pages that moved me most deeply were those dealing with the anointing of Jesus by the "sinning woman." The story was familiar enough, but the way Papini dealt with it touched me to the core. It is worth quoting at some length:

This sinning woman who silently entered the house of Simon with her box of alabaster was no longer a sinner. She had seen Jesus, had known Him before that day. And she was no longer a woman for hire; she had heard Jesus speak, and was no longer the public woman, flesh on sale for masculine desires. She had heard the voice of Jesus, had listened to His words; His voice had troubled her, His words had shaken her. She who had belonged to everyone had learned that there is a love more beautiful than lust, a poverty richer than clinking coins. When she came to the

[3] Harcourt, Brace and Company (New York, 1923), p. 22.
[4] *Loc. cit.*

house of Simon she was not the woman she had been, the woman whom the men of the countryside had pointed out sneeringly, the woman whom the Pharisee knew and despised. Her soul was changed, all her life was changed. Now her flesh was chaste; her hand was pure; her lips no longer knew the bitter taste of rouge, her eyes had learned to weep. From now on, according to the promise of the King, she was ready to enter into the Kingdom.

Without taking all this for granted it is impossible to understand the story which follows. The sinning woman wished to reward her Saviour with a token of her gratitude. She took one of the most costly things left to her, a sealed box full of nard, perhaps the gift of a chance lover, thinking to anoint her King's head with his costly oil. Hers was an act of public gratitude. The sinning woman wished publicly to thank Him who had cleansed her soul, who had brought her heart to life, who had lifted her up out of shame, who had given her a hope more glorious than all joys.

She went into the house with her box of alabaster clasped to her breast, timid and shrinking as a little girl on her first day of school, as a released prisoner in his first moment outside the prison. She went in silently with her little box of perfume, raising her eyes for only a moment to see at a glance where Jesus was reclining. She went up to the couch her knees trembling under her, her hands shaking, her delicate eyelids quivering, because she felt they were all looking at her, all those men's eyes were fixed on her, staring at her beautiful swaying body, wondering what she was about to do.

She broke the seal of the little alabaster flask, and poured half the oil on the head of Jesus. The large drops shone on His hair like scattered gems. With loving hands she spread the transparent ointment on the curls and did not stay her hand till every hair was softened, silky and shining. The whole room was filled with the fragrance; every eye was fixed on her with astonishment.

The woman, still silent, took up the opened box and knelt by the feet of the Peace-bringer. She poured the remaining oil into her hand and gently, gently rubbed the right foot and the left with the loving care of the young mother who bathes her first child, for the first time. Then she could control herself no longer, she could restrain no longer the great burst of tenderness which filled her heart, made her throat ache and brought tears to her eyes. She would have liked to speak, to say that this was her thanks, her simple, pure, heartfelt thanks for the great help she had received, for the new light which had unsealed her eyes. But in such a moment, with all those men there, how could she find the right words, words worthy of the wonderful grace, worthy of Him? And besides, her lips trembled so that she could not pronounce two words together; her speech would have been only a stammering broken by sobs. Then not being able to speak with her lips, she spoke with her eyes: her tears fell down one by one, swift and hot on the feet of Jesus, like so many silent thank-offerings.

Weeping freed her heart of its oppression; the tears relaxed the tension. She saw and felt nothing now but an inexpressible delight which she had never known on her mother's knees or in men's arms; it ran through all her blood, made her tremble, pierced her with its poignant joy, shook all her being in that supreme ecstasy in which joy is a pain and sorrow a joy, in which pain and joy become one mighty emotion.

She wept over her past life, the miserable life of her vigil. She thought of her poor flesh sullied by men. She had been forced to have a smile for them all, she had been forced to offer her luxurious bed and her perfumed body to them all. With all of them she had been forced to show a smiling face, to those whom she despised, to those whom she hated. She had slept beside the thief who had stolen the money to pay her. She had kissed the lips of the murderer and of the fugitive from justice; she had been forced to endure the acrid breath and the repellent fancies of the drunkard.[5]

Hardly had I finished the last paragraph when I burst into a violent fit of weeping myself. I said, "Jesus, I, too, am a prostitute. God has endowed me with beauties of soul and

[5] *Ibid.*, pp. 224–7.

intellect, and I have wasted them on the search for worldly honors and material riches. In the world of politics and in social life, I too have been forced to pretend a pleasure I did not feel, and to show a smiling face to those whom I despised. And all the time I have been neglecting you, my Redeemer and my Spouse. Forgive me, Jesus, and let me anoint you with my tears! And forgive all my dear sisters, those poor sing-song girls, who are much better than I am. Turn them into your saints!"

When I had uttered this prayer, my soul was inundated with such joy and consolation that tears of gratitude gushed from the bottom of my heart to join the tears of repentance. I felt at that moment that Christ had received me again with His open arms. I experienced such an ecstasy of joy that I can never forget it. As I was a Protestant, and did not even know of the institution of Confession, this return was sufficient for me, for the time being at least. It was after this return to Christ that Christ gave me His Mother to be my Mother as an expression of His love.

Having finished Papini's book, I took up William James' *The Varieties of Religious Experience*. I found that my soul belonged to the category which he called "the sick soul," rather than to what he called "the healthy-minded." He said that "healthy-mindedness is inadequate as a philosophical doctrine, because the evil facts which it refuses positively to account for are a genuine portion of reality; and they may after all be the best key to life's significance, and possibly the only openers of our eyes to the deepest levels of truth." [6] One mark of the sick soul is that it is conscious of the pain of existence, not only of his own but of other beings' as well. James made a very thoughtful remark in this connection: "Even if we suppose a man so packed with healthy-minded-

[6] Longmans, Green and Co. (New York, 1923), p. 163.

ness as never to have experienced in his own person any
of these sobering intervals, still, if he is a reflecting being,
he must generalize and class his lot with that of others; and,
doing so, he must see that his escape is just a lucky chance
and no essential difference. He might just as well have been
born to an entirely different fortune. And then indeed the
hollow security!" [7] Now, this was exactly what my wife had
once told me: "You will never be happy until all others are
as happy as you are!" Being a sick soul, the chords of my
heart responded sympathetically to the following passages
penned by James:

All natural goods perish. Riches take wings; fame is a
breath; love is a cheat; youth and health and pleasure vanish.
Can things whose end is always dust and disappointment be
the real goods which our souls require?

In short, life and its negation are beaten up inextricably
together. But if the life be good, the negation of it must be
bad. Yet the two are equally essential facts of existence; and
all natural happiness thus seems infected with a contradiction. The breath of the sepulchre surrounds it.

The pride of life and glory of the world will shrivel. It is
after all but the standing quarrel of hot youth and hoary eld.
Old age has the last word: the purely naturalistic look at life,
however enthusiastically it may begin, is sure to end in
sadness.

For naturalism, fed on recent cosmological speculations,
mankind is in a position similar to that of a set of people
living on a frozen lake, surrounded by cliffs over which there
is no escape, yet knowing that little by little the ice is melting, and the inevitable day drawing near when the last film
of it will disappear, and to be drowned ignominiously will be
the human creature's portion. The merrier the skating, the
warmer and more sparkling the sun by day, and the ruddier
the bonfires at night, the more poignant the sadness with
which one must take in the meaning of the total situation.

[7] *Ibid.*, p. 136.

Our civilization is founded on the shambles, and every individual existence goes out in a lonely spasm of helpless agony.[8]

James concluded his chapter on "The Sick Soul" with these remarkable words: "the man must die to an unreal life before he can be born into the real." This suited me like a glove, and reminded me of the most consoling promise of Christ: "It is not the healthy who need a physician, but they that are sick." I certainly needed a thorough purgation and a thorough invigoration from the Divine Physician.

It was in William James' book that I first knew the names of the Catholic Saints, such as St. John of the Cross, St. Teresa of Avila, St. Francis Xavier, St. John of God, Margaret Mary Alacoque, St. Elizabeth of Hungary, St. Frances de Chantal, the Curé of Ars, St. Catherine of Genoa, St. Ignatius, and others. They are all to be found in the chapter on "Saintliness." Inadequate as his treatment was, it impressed me profoundly at that time. For instance, when I read his quotations from St. John of the Cross: "To possess all things, resolve to possess nothing"; "To be all things, be willing to be nothing"—I underlined them, and added a word on the margin: "Taoistic!" I thought that the Church that had given birth to all these gigantic personalities, not to mention St. Thomas Aquinas, St. Augustine, and St. Francis of Assisi, whom I had heard of before, must have been a prolific mother of sanctity. I wondered if I should be so fortunate as to be one of her sons.

This book broadened my mental horizons considerably. It gave me many psychological insights such as the following:

But just as our primary wide-awake consciousness throws open our senses to the touch of things material, so it is

[8] *Ibid.*, pp. 139, 140, 141–2, 163.

logically conceivable that if there be higher spiritual agencies that can directly touch us, the psychological condition of their doing so might be our possession of a subconscious region which alone should yield access to them. The hubbub of the waking life might close a door which in the dreamy Subliminal might remain ajar or open.[9]

As soon as I had done with James' book, I took up T. S. Eliot's *Selected Essays*. This time I did not open the book at random. I first examined into the Table of Contents, and found several essays that interested me, such as "Tradition and Individual Talent," "Shakespeare and the Stoicism of Seneca," and "Lancelot Andrews." I read them through, but they made no impression on me. Finally, I came to his essay on Dante, which impressed me profoundly, because some of his observations stirred my mind. For instance, he made such statements as these: "The majority of poems one outgrows and outlives, as one outgrows and outlives the majority of human passions: Dante's is one of those which one can only just hope to grow up to at the end of life. . . . If any one is repelled by the last canto of the *Inferno*, I can only ask him to wait until he has read and lived for years with the last canto of the *Paradiso*, which is to my thinking the highest point that poetry has ever reached or ever can reach. . . . The style of Dante has a peculiar lucidity—a *poetic* as distinguished from an *intellectual* lucidity. The thought may be obscure, but the word is lucid, or rather translucent." [10] But what disturbed me most was this: "Shakespeare gives the greatest width of human passion; Dante the greatest altitude and greatest depth. They complement each other." [11] Now, for me, Shakespeare had no peer in literary genius. As for Dante, he had always repelled me whenever I attempted to

[9] *Ibid.*, p. 242.
[10] Harcourt, Brace and Company (New York, 1932), p. 212.
[11] *Ibid.*, p. 226.

read him. But I trusted Eliot as a literary critic, and his words
made me conclude that I could not afford to die before I
had read the *Divine Comedy*. So I requested some friend to
get a new copy of Cary's version in the Everyman's Library.
I knew very well that there were better translations in my
own library, but that version was the easiest to procure. It
was war-time, and one had to be contented with what one
could get hold of.

When the book came I addressed myself immediately to
it. A most wonderful thing happened: I was held spellbound
right from the beginning:

> In the midway of this our mortal life,
> I found me in a gloomy wood, astray
> Gone from the path direct: and e'en to tell,
> It were no easy task, how savage wild
> That forest, how robust and rough its growth,
> Which to remember only, my dismay
> Renews, in bitterness not far from death.

Was this not a most faithful portraiture of the state of
my own soul? In fact, the agony of my soul was so bitter that
death itself would have been a welcome relief. Not so long
ago I had written in my diary (September 16, 1937) thus:

Darkness is soothing. Silence is sweet. What a pleasure
when lying in bed in the dead of night you feel as though
you were in your grave. Nothing comes to disturb your illusion. You have a foretaste of death. If by some magic, you
can slow down the motion of your heart gradually until it
stops—just as a skilful conductor of a train does with his
engine—you will be in the land of your forefathers before
you know it. To die in imperceptible degrees is the highest
bliss of life. But very few can attain it. Most of us have to
take a leap in the dark.

A man who could write like that, you can easily imagine how low were his spirits! Why did I not commit suicide? Well, I wrote somewhere in my diary: "I am too pessimistic even to commit suicide, because I really do not believe that the next world will be better than this." So far as I know, two principal causes had brought me to this state, one interior and the other exterior. Interiorly, I had desired Paradise but, owing to my own sins, found myself in hell. Exteriorly, I had desired peace and harmony but found nothing but war and discords.

What could be more profitable and uplifting for a man in my state than to be a fellow-pilgrim of Dante, starting from Hell, going through Purgatory, and finally having a nice promenade in Paradise? In a few days I completed the journey and returned to earth a happier man. How I felt then can only be described in Dante's own words:

> As one, who from a dream awaken'd, straight,
> All he hath seen forgets; yet still retains
> Impressions of the feeling in his dream;
> E'en such am I: for all the vision dies,
> As 'twere, away; and yet the sense of sweet,
> That sprang from it, still trickles in my heart.

The influence of the *Divine Comedy* upon me is too deep for me to articulate even now. When the Holy Father, in his speech to me, said, "We welcome your Excellency as a loyal son of the Church, whose journey to the Catholic faith was illumined by Dante's *Divine Comedy*" I was simply astounded that the Holy Father knew my secret.

Some time in November of 1937 my old schoolmate Mr. Yuan Chia-huang came to call on me. By that time, Nanking had fallen, and Shanghai was isolated. As I had been writing and broadcasting against the Japanese militarists, and there

was a rumor that they would try to liquidate all their op-
ponents, Mr. Yuan suggested that I should take refuge in
his house for a few days and slip away quietly to Hongkong.
I was deeply touched by his solicitude over my safety and his
willingness to share my fate in case I should be discovered.
After consulting with my wife, I went to live in his house.
Now both he and Mrs. Yuan were very devout Catholics.
Every night they called together all their children to recite
their family Rosary. It was the first time in my life that I
heard the Rosary recited. The family atmosphere was cordial
and harmonious. They explained to me the fifteen mysteries
of the Rosary, and they told me that they had recommended
my safety to the care of the Blessed Virgin. One night, seeing
a picture of St. Thérèse of Lisieux, I asked Yuan, "Is this
the Blessed Virgin?" He appeared astonished by my ignorance, saying "Oh no, this is St. Thérèse of Lisieux, known
as 'The Little Flower' in the English-speaking world." "I
have never heard anything about her," I said. "What?" he
said, "you are a learned man and yet you do not even know
such a famous Saint!" I remained silent, but I thought in
my mind that Yuan was just like one of those countrymen
who would regard anybody as not well-informed if he did
not happen to know his grandmother!

Then he gave me a French pamphlet on the life and
thoughts of St. Thérèse. I brought it to my room after the
Rosary. On opening it at random, my eyes fell upon a most
remarkable thought: "Ah! I feel it, even if I had on my
conscience all the crimes that could be committed, I would
lose nothing of my confidence; I would throw myself, with
my heart broken with repentance, into the arms of my
Savior. I recall His love for the prodigal son, I have heard
His words to St. Mary Magdalen, to the woman taken in
adultery, to the woman of Samaria. No, there is no one who

can make me afraid, for I knew too well what to believe concerning His Mercy and His Love, and I know that all that multitude of offences would vanish in the twinkling of an eye like a drop of water in a white-hot brazier."

"What a brave girl!" I thought, "Judging by her words, even a man like myself is not so hopeless!" I asked Yuan if there was a bigger book on her. He gave me *Histoire d'une âme*. I ran through the book and was so deeply impressed by it that I said to myself, "If this book represents Catholicism, I don't see why I should not be a Catholic." For there I found the living synthesis between all pairs of opposites, such as humility and audacity, freedom and discipline, joys and sorrows, duty and love, strength and tenderness, grace and nature, folly and wisdom, wealth and poverty, corporateness and individuality. She seemed to me to combine the heart of the Buddha, the virtues of Confucius, and the philosophic detachment of Lao Tse. Here was a young Sister who died at twenty-four, and had attained such perfection. What was the secret? How could she realize her individuality so fully if she were not an integral member of the Mystical Body of Christ?

It was through reading this book that I decided to become a Catholic. Grace had touched my heart.

When I confided my decision to Yuan, he appeared dumbfounded and said, "How wonderful is God's grace! We have been praying for your conversion for the last ten years!" I asked him to introduce me to a priest to instruct me, and he requested Father Germain, the Rector of the Aurore University, to come to see me. I was impressed by the Father's kindness and good sense. On December 18, 1937, he gave me conditional Baptism in the little chapel of Our Lady attached to the University. Everything was done quietly. Only Yuan and my son Thomas were present. On the next morning I received my First Communion in the same chapel. I saw Father Tosten there beaming in smiles. He had been my teacher of French twenty years ago. For all that I know, the good priest must have been praying for me all those years. A few days after my First Communion he passed away.

All my life I had been searching for a Mother, and at last I had her in the Catholic Church, and this in a triple sense. God is my Mother, the Church is my Mother, and the Blessed Virgin is my Mother; and these three Mothers have merged into one Motherhood, in which I live, move and have my being.

Even when I was still a Methodist, I had often wondered why the Mother of Our Lord was so little mentioned. I had a vague but intense yearning for her, but at that time I did not know of her place in the Catholic Church at all. When I came to know of it, I saw in it one of the earmarks of the True Church of Christ. As I wrote then:

Is God a Father or a Mother? To me He is both, but it is especially his Motherliness that endears Him to me. How tenderly He spoke to His children: *Hearken unto me, O house of Jacob, all the remnant of the house of Israel, who are carried up by my bowels, are borne up by my womb* (Isaias 46.3). *As one whom the mother caresseth, so will I comfort you* (Isaias 66.13). And with what maternal anguish Jesus wept over Jerusalem: *How often would I have gathered thy children, as the hen doth gather her chickens under her wings, but thou wouldst not.* Our Lord is no fighting Cock, but a brooding Hen! Who can help succumbing to the love of a mother?

One of the charms of the Catholic Church is that this feminine element in the Character of Jesus is institutionally represented in the person of the Blessed Virgin. It is indeed the True Church, for it embodies the Personality of the Founder in Its fullness.

16. THE KINDERGARTEN OF MY CATHOLIC LIFE

Strange to say, I did not feel any joy either on the day of my Baptism or at my First Communion. My mind was a blank, feeling neither joy nor sorrow. I am always slow to react to any experience. In my childhood my schoolmates used to call me "the Wooden Rooster." In my youth people used to laugh at my slowness in laughing at a joke. Many a time, when I was conversing with a group of friends, and someone happened to tell a funny story, the whole crowd would be aroar with laughter immediately, but I simply could not laugh that quickly, especially if the story was really funny. Very often, after five or ten minutes I suddenly burst into laughter in ruminating upon the joke when everybody else had forgotten about it. A friend of mine, Y. L. Chin, used to say, "I can well imagine Teh-son suddenly laughing on New Year's Eve at a joke he had heard on New Year's Day!" That was an exaggeration; but there is no denying that

245

I am slow to react, not only to jokes, but also to the most momentous experiences of my life.

Anyway, it was not until five days after my Baptism that I found myself writing in my diary (December 23, 1937) as follows:

What a joy I feel in my heart! After long years of aimless wandering, I have come back to Christ, this time to stick to Him forever. My pen is too weak to describe the joy of my heart, or rather my heart is too weak to bear the burden of my joy. I have only tears to offer as a token of my infinite gratitude to my Lord. I would anoint His hair with nard and bathe Him with my tears as that humble woman did in the house of Simon. I too was a prostitute, wasting my body and soul in the pursuit of the things of the world. But I have repented, and Christ has cleansed me in and out. I have committed adultery, and Christ has said to me, "Come back and sin no more." I have coveted money, but now I have found a poverty richer than all the riches of the world. I have thirsted for the praises of men, but now my mouth has tasted living water and my thirst has been quenched once for all by the approval of God. I have hated many people, but as soon as I knelt down to pray for them, even the merest notion of "enemies" disappeared: now I have only one enemy in the world, and that is none other than myself, but Christ has even reconciled me to myself. I have feared death, but now I am already dead and can die no more: I have jumped out of Time and live and move and have my being in Eternity.

I have only one sorrow in my mind, for my joy is dearly bought. It has been bought at the cost of the tons of blood that has been shed during the last few months by my fellow-beings. O merciful God, forgive them and save their souls, for they did not know what they were doing.

From a worldly point of view, I should say my present condition is one of sheer wretchedness. One job after another has dropped off from my hands like the unripe figs blown from the branches by a terrific storm. I do not know what will become of myself and my family in a few months. But I don't care. I believe God will provide for me. And even if He will not, I feel it will be better to be starved to death with a pure soul than to be overfed with filth.

As my *T'ien Hsia* friends had gone to Hongkong, I too slipped away from Shanghai by the middle of January on board a French boat. In this trip I was accompanied by my devoted brother-in-law, Fung Han-hsien. We had a nice trip, but one day we were rather scared. The French boy who took care of our room awoke us roughly from our nap, and without telling us the reason, put lifesavers on us, saying, "*Vite, vite!*" Han-hsien and I looked at each other like fools. Well, it turned out to be just a drill!

In Hongkong I was reunited with the *T'ien Hsia* friends, and we set up our office and continued our publications. In February my family came to Hongkong to join me, and we settled down on the Kowloon side. I continued to write for *T'ien Hsia*. My interest had taken a turn for Chinese poetry. Besides translating many Chinese poems into English, which were published under the pen-name of Teresa Li, I wrote a long article on "The Four Seasons of the T'ang Poetry." In addition to these, I contributed my translation of the Taoistic classic, the *Tao Teh Ching*. From the standpoint of literary output, that was perhaps the most active period of my life. Of particular significance for my spiritual life was "A Birthday Song" which I wrote in the spring of 1938:

A Birthday Song

(1)

Forty years are gone! Where can they be?
A drop of water lost in a boundless sea!
Time is a flower that fades in your hand,

And happiness a light that never was on sea or land.
But as I look to my past, I have more cause
For joy than for remorse.
Even in my wildest wanderings, my soul
Has been homesick for God, my ultimate Goal.
And what blessings He has showered on me!
He has blessed me with a good family;
He has blessed me with many a good friend;
He has blessed me with a wondrous Fatherland.
O God, You have given me more than my due;
It lies beyond my means to pay my debts to You.
But I see no point in declaring bankruptcy,
Since Christ has settled the accounts for me.

(2)

Why, then, should my Birthday song wail like a
    dirge?
Why such waves of agony within my bosom surge?
But when the whole world is stinking with blood of
    man,
Smile, if you can!
I know very well that life is but a play,
But a tragedy is a tragedy, whatever you may say!
When you see the massacres of women and chil-
    dren, there is no way
Of keeping your hair from turning grey.
Who says that life is a dream?
A nightmare, it would seem!
No joy in my smiles, no tears in my weeping,
I feel like one whose soul is no longer in his keeping.
Can it be that God should treat His creature like a
    clod?
Can it be that my heart is kinder than the Heart of
    God?
No, I only hate the rapacity of our enemies,
And regret the waywardness of the Democracies.
Ah for an International Fire Brigade!
Else the whole world will soon be on fire, I am
    afraid.

(3)

My eyes have already visualized the day
When heaven and earth shall have passed away;
But my poor little heart lingers still
Over the ant-hill!
For a man is no more than an ant,
Even if he had the mind of a Kant.
A few glimpses into the splendid Whole
Do not lift you from your wretched hole.
Look! How the ants fight in their struggle for exis-
    tence!
By and by I too shall have to put up a tough re-
    sistance!
Looking around me I yearn for chloroform,
My heart is like the wick of a burnt-out candle,—
    still a little too warm!
The miseries of men I can no longer endure:
When, O when will the rich cease to suck the poor?
Listen to the Voice of St. John, the son of Thunder,
Pouring his vials of wrath on man's chief blunder!
So long as a single person dies of starvation,
To store up superfluous food entails eternal damna-
    tion.
So long as a single person in cold shivers,
To store up superfluous clothes causes heats of
    fevers.
Don't say that Spirit can dispense with Matter,
Seeing that the Universe itself is made of the latter.
Do you think that the Creator is not so spiritual as
    you?
You are playing to the gallery of the Devil if you do.
To use Matter wisely is to be spiritual;
To talk about Spirituality is a empty ritual!
By feeding yourself, you only satisfy your hunger
    temporarily;
By feeding others, you satisfy your hunger eternally.
By arranging Matter harmoniously, you produce
    Beauty:

Where ugliness appears, the artist surely has not
   done his duty!

(4)

Don't you see the eighteen Lohans gone hopelessly
   wrong?
They fasted and tortured themselves lifelong.
As though any narrow path were a road to salvation!
As though humanity would be fed by our own
   starvation!
As though the miseries of men could be cured by
   insensibility!
As though by burying our heads in the sand we
   could evade Reality!
I on my part would rather be a sinner than a Lohan.
A Lohan is a monster, while a sinner is a man!
If there were no God, then let us eat and drink and
   avoid sorrow,
For all of us shall be dead tomorrow;
Then it would be the best plan
To follow the ways of man;
Then let all ethics go hang,
Let us form a pleasure gang:
With a pretty girl on each hand,
Let us feel grand;
In politics, a Machiavellian;
In other things, a practical Epicurean!
When we live, let us enjoy the best we can;
When we die, everybody will say, "He was a de-
   lightful gentleman";
But neither of the two would I follow:
The Lohan is wrong, the gentleman is hollow!
To do the will of Christ is my only joy;
I will be a humble laborer in His employ;
To prepare the way for His second coming
By hook or by crook, by drumming or by humming!

But it was not until October 18, 1939, that I received

Confirmation, that is, almost two years after my Baptism. Being a new Catholic whose faith was not deeply rooted in his mind, I did not realize the importance of Confirmation. I dilly-dallied about it. I did not even present the introductory letter which Father Germain had written to Bishop Valtorta. I enjoyed going to Mass and receiving Holy Communion without being known of men, whether priests or laymen. Was I not an exile in Hongkong? The War might come to an end any day, and we would be returning to Shanghai, where there would be ample opportunity for me to be confirmed. *In my procrastination, St. Thérèse again intervened!*

On October 15, 1939, which was a Saturday, I went to the Church of St. Thérèse of the Child Jesus to hear the Mass. At the Comunion I knelt before the rail along with many others. It happened that there was no server; so the Communion plate was being passed from one communicant to another. But I was so absorbed in the thought of Jesus coming under my roof that I forgot to take the plate from the one on my right. The priest waited and waited, and I looked and looked at the Host. Finally, he said, "Have you ever received Holy Communion?"

"Yes," I answered, "many times."

"Take the plate and hold it in your hands," he said. I did, and received the Communion. Then the priest said, "Please come to see me after the Mass."

I went to see the priest. That was Father Granelli, who afterwards became one of my best friends. But at that time he thought that I had acted like a fool. I had to tell him when I was baptized, and that I had a letter of introduction to the Bishop. He phoned the Bishop to tell him that I wanted to see him. The Bishop, who had heard about me, appointed the next day for my interview with him. On the

16th I went to the Cathedral for the first time to see him, and, presenting the letter of Father Germain, I expressed my desire to receive Confirmation in the due course of time. To my great surprise, he said, "Day after tomorrow at the St. Teresa Church!" Being confirmed on St. Luke's Feast, I was given the name of "Lucas."

As I think of it now, if that little episode of absent-mindedness before the Communion rail had not happened—*and such a thing had never happened to me before*—for all that I know I might still remain unconfirmed even now! St. Thérèse never does anything in half-measures. Having converted me, she went ahead to hasten my Confirmation. What a blessing it is for a wayward man like myself to possess a resolute patron like the Little Flower of Jesus! By this time, I have given her a blank check.

It was only after my Confirmation that I began to live a full Catholic life. Since then my faith has not flagged for a single day. I came to realize that each Sacrament of the Church is a channel of special graces, and that Confirmation has a special relation with the receiving of the Holy Spirit, increasing the zeal and fortitude of a Christian. I have felt a certain warmth and unction in my spirit which I had not felt before Confirmation. After Baptism one feels the beginning of a new spring, but there are still some chill days and the weather is none too constant, alternating as it were between fitful sunshine and fitful showers. After Confirmation one feels as in early summer, when the trees become luxuriant and flourishing, when, in the words of Tu Fu:

> A gentle breeze is blowing, butterflies are frolicking.
> Flowers are blazing, honey bees are buzzing.

A most providential thing happened in those days. As I

came out from my first visit to the Bishop, my eyes were
attracted by the books exhibited in some glass cases. Just
as I was looking a young priest came out from his office and
asked me, "Are you Dr. Wu?" "Yes," I said, "But how do
you know me, Father?" He told me that he had received
some letters from the Jesuits in Shanghai inquiring about
me. The priest was so gentle and friendly that I liked him
from the beginning. His moustache contributed no small
part to his charm. It was Fr. Nicholas Maestrini, one of the
holiest priests I have ever known. He became my spiritual
director, and recommended for my reading one book after
another, such as St. Francis of Sales' *Introduction to the
Devout Life*, his *Treatise on the Love of God*, Tanquerey's
Spiritual Life, Scupoli's *The Spiritual Combat*, Marmion's
Christ: the Life of the Soul, Petitot's *St. Thérèse of Lisieux*,
and many other books and pamphlets. He initiated me into
the beauties of the Daily Missal. He expounded the philosophy of Holy Mass as the ladder of perfection. But it was
not so much his knowledge as his charity that impressed
me. I have seen more learned priests, but I have not met a
more charitable priest. He was on fire with the love of God,
and his enthusiasm for the glory of God was infectious. It
was also through him that I came to know the Carmelites;
and we did no apostolic work without first enlisting the support of their prayers. Practically all the rudiments of my
spiritual life were formed in those days, and Father Maestrini
was the principal instrument that God employed to enlighten
me on the fundamentals of the Catholic faith and spiritual
life. Another wonderful priest whom I saw pretty often was
Father Don Hessler. He had recently been ordained, and his
first convert was a Jewish gentleman, Dr. Allen Spitzer, who
became my godson. For a wild olive to be the godfather of a
natural olive! How proud I am of Allen and his wife, who

are model Catholics. Jesus knows that I love the Jews more than my own countrymen, for they are His countrymen.

No sooner had I received Confirmation and become a soldier of Christ than the Holy Spirit worked on my expansive nature and turned me into an apostle. Recently I have come across in the writings of one of my dearest godchildren, Dr. Paul K. T. Sih, a passage in which he has presented with as much love as understanding my humble philosophy of apostolate. "In him," he writes, "a personal knowledge of Christ is not a thing to be folded away and secretly treasured; it is to be put to work for others. . . . In his own words, 'The best way to keep an experience of Christ is to pass it on.' " I do not remember when I said this, but whoever said it, it is nothing but the truth. Anyway, I became a fisher of men, and of women too, shortly after my Confirmation. The first fish that God drove into my net was Francis Chiu-yuan Yeh, who was then my colleague in the T'ien Hsia office. He was one of the most stubborn men that I have ever met. I worked on him for full two years before he was caught. He himself wrote an account of his spiritual Odyssey in the name of a third person. Let me quote a paragraph which reveals what a stubborn soul he was:

Early in 1938, Francis found himself in Hongkong. There he met Dr. John C. H. Wu . . . who had already become a Catholic. John had been a Methodist, and his embracing the Catholic faith interested Francis. They use to walk together and John would invariably drop into the wayside church to pray. Francis would always wait for him outside the church. He thought as he had not become a Catholic, he had better not go in. But as Francis was deeply interested in Catholicism, they had lengthy discussions on religion and life.

This reminds me of what happened in the winter of 1939. One day, as we were taking a promenade together in Kowloon, we passed by the Rosary Church on Chatham Road. I said to Francis, "Let's go in for a few minutes." "No." he said, "you go in, but I will wait here." I went in, and threw myself upon my knees right before the altar. I said to Our Lady, "Look here, Mother! I have led a beautiful soul to the threshold of your Church. I have done my best. You will have to do the rest. How can you fail me, Mother! After all, Mother, this is not my own business. Every one of us who loves Christ should cooperate!" Hearing my own voice which sounded like that of a man in a desperate mood, I cried like a baby before our Blessed Mother. In fact, I am again crying as I am thinking of it now. I am crying now because I am grateful to her for having answered my prayer so quickly. When I had wiped my tears with my handkerchief, I went out to join Francis who was still tarrying at the door. Of course, I did not tell him what had happened when I was in the Church, trying to appear as jolly as possible. We parted, each going to his house. I refrained from calling on Francis for three days. The fourth day, he came to see me and told me, "John, I don't know why, for it is the first time that I have had such an experience in my life. I feel *a driving force* within me; I want to be baptized as soon as possible. I will write a letter to Father Maestrini announcing my decision." Even then I did not reveal my secret; but I wept again, this time for joy and for wonder. Francis was baptized on February 2, 1940, the Feast of the Purification of Our Lady. After a few years of full Catholic life, he passed away on March 1, 1948. He worked for the Church up to the very day of his death!

Another beautiful soul that the Lord threw into my way was Alice Chow, who was also working in the *T'ien Hsia* Office. One evening we were invited to a dancing party. It was a big party. As I knew Alice I danced with her. During the dance Alice wanted me to recommend some spiritual books for her to read. I whispered into her ears, "I am reading a new translation of Thomas à Kempis's *The Imitation of Christ*. I shall present you with a copy of it tomorrow." I wonder how many times the name of Thomas à Kempis has ever been mentioned during a dance!

When the party was over, Alice said to me, "John, will you take me home? I have something to tell you." I called a taxicab, and gave her a lift. In the cab, Alice told me that for some reasons she had stayed away from the Communion rail for a period of fourteen years, although she was an old Catholic. She had a good cry in the car. I suppose that the cabman must have thought that we were making love. In a way we were, only making love with Christ. I told her, "You miss Him; He misses you even more. He has been waiting for you all these years. Nothing is so sweet as a reunion with an old friend. All that is necessary is to make a confession. I will introduce you to a wonderful priest called Father Maestrini."

"Can he be as holy as Father Jacquinot in Shanghai?" she asked.

"Well, you will see," I responded.

In a few days, we went together to Father Maestrini, and Alice was reunited with Christ. Ever since then she has been one of the most devout Catholics I have known.

While I was doing apostolic work among my friends, my own family had not yet come into the fold. Faith is such a personal matter that I never wanted to impose my own religion upon my wife and children. I did try to sound her out several times, but each time I was repulsed. She said, "You may change again, this may be just another temporary infatuation." On another occasion she said, "What is God

but one's own conscience? So long as one does not do anything against one's conscience, I do not see the need of a
religion." Well, what can you do with such a lady? So far
as I knew, and so far as I could judge subjectively, she was
more sinned against than sinning. I could not remember a
single instance in which she had committed anything approx-
imating a mortal sin or even a deliberate venial sin. Further,
as she could not read at all, even the best spiritual books
would not do in her case.

As I was at my wits' end, St. Thérèse again intervened!
Francis Yeh had announced his decision to be a Catholic
to Father Maestrini on January 17, 1940. On January 18,
something happened to our little girl Lan Hsien, who was a
year and three months old. In order to give an accurate
acount of the whole thing, I will let my diary of those few
days to speak for itself:

Thursday, January 18, 1940

This morning Lan Hsien suddenly became very sick! 103.5°
is her temperature. O God, I cry for Thy help! O little
Mother Thérèse, help me and my wife! O most merciful
Holy Mother, save us from the complete wreck! O Jesus, I
am not yet strong enough, I am a baby, I know Thou wilt
not send anything more than Thy little one can bear.

My wife would not hear of calling for a priest. That would
kill her. We have called for a doctor.

Forgive my sins and wash them clean!

The Devil is tormenting me.

If anything should happen so unexpectedly, where shall
I be?

Let me die for her!

To call a priest would frighten my wife out of her wits,
and she is pregnant now and could not bear it. O all-merciful
Father, I simply can't imagine that such a thing could happen

in Thy universe. To let the child go without Baptism could easily kill me. To have her baptized now would kill my wife. Let *me* be killed. But Father, I am still a weak child—it takes time for me to grow in Faith.

O thou of little faith, it would not happen!

Whenever God has accomplished something through me, Satan becomes envious of me, and I suffer at his hands. After the confession of Alice, my wife and youngest son Chi-wen were ill, and I was ill too. After the conversion of Francis, my most beloved Lan Hsien is sick. Well, even Christ has to suffer at the hands of the Satan. But God is almighty! All that I *need* is a complete abandon in His hands.

God would not strike a frail reed like myself as though I were an oak.

He permits such trials, because He wants to make me more and more humble. But have pity on my wife, who is going to deliver another child next month!

God has opened my eyes to one fundamental truth: *Nothing really good can be accomplished without genuine suffering.* The higher the achievement, the higher the price. There is no greater thing than sanctity, and therefore one must be ready to pay the highest price. Even the Son of God had to pay the supreme price for His Christhood, had to swallow the bitter cup, had to be the Man of Sorrow before He could redeem mankind from its sins. If one wants to follow Christ but at the same time shrinks from pain, it is like crying for the moon.

My wife prayed to St. Thérèse with Lan Hsien in her arms. She knelt although big with child. Lan Hsien's temperature has fallen to 102!

My wife said that all this is meant for the punishment of our sins, aware or unaware.

Father Maestrini came to call in the afternoon! In the morning I had intended to phone him, but hesitated. There was naturally a wish that he would call of his own accord. O God, Thou art spoiling me. Every whim of Thy little one is gratified. The Father told me the formula of Baptism. He also told me that he had received a letter from Francis, announcing his decision of Baptism! I thank Thee, God!

Friday, January 19, 1940

I baptized Lan Hsien this morning between eight and nine in the morning, for her temperature rose again to 103.5°. I had just come from Holy Communion, and I told my wife that baptizing her would cure her without a doctor. After the Baptism I went to sleep and upon my waking Lan Hsien walked in with her mother, bringing to me the evening paper!

Saturday (No diary)

Sunday, January 21, 1940

Early this morning Lan Hsien's temperature rose to 104! My wife prayed to St. Thérèse: "Lan Hsien is too hard to rear up, *I resign from my motherhood. Be you a mother to her!*" This sentiment is so sincere and so fundamentally Catholic that the sweet Saint listened. In the afternoon, while still having a temperature of 100 something, Lan Hsien walked and knelt before the bust of St. Thérèse, which Father Maestrini had given us,—smiling and prattling and making impressionistic crosses. My wife marvelled.

At the Mass, I prayed for Lan Hsien: "If Thou preserve her, I should be all the more willing to bear all the little crosses that Thou hast sent me during the last few days. But if it be Thy will to call her back to Thee, Thy will be done, not mine. All that I ask for in that case would be that Thou endow me with a gift of fortitude and peace."

Upon my coming back I found she was sitting up and smiling, although her temperature was still 104. My wife had a strong suspicion that it is a similar case with that of our deceased boy Hsiu Sze. But in the afternoon the temperature subsided, and she was to all appearances well. She has been sick for a week, and I do hope that St. Thérèse has compassion on my wife, who is virtually a saint.

Monday, January 22, 1940

Doctor Pao has come, and discovered that Lan Hsien has developed pneumonia.

O my heavenly Father, no sacrifice is too great to make to Thee. What are we but grass? Grass that today grows and tomorrow withers. But our souls are immortal. If Lan Hsien is wanted to go to Thee now, I shall join her in the time appointed for me long ago. The day, be it near or far, will come anyway. I hold the rest of my life in trust for Thee. I abandon myself completely in Thy hands.

If Lan Hsien recovers, Thy will be done. If she dies, Thy will be done.

I have spoken to my wife about a formal Baptism by Father Maestrini. God has moved her to consent to my suggestion willingly and soberly. I told her that if Lan Hsien dies, we shall meet her some time later. Life is a brief dream anyway. In the twenty-first century, all will be gone. My wife understood my words. *It is not for us ephemera of a day to judge the plans of the Lord of Eternity.* Rash judgment against men is bad enough; rash judgment against God is a sin against the Holy Spirit.

O merciful Father, who am I to compete with Thee for the custody and care of the child? In Thy hands she will be a little saint. In my hands, she may turn out to be not as good as I might expect. I rather envy her. But O Father, Thou rememberest that we are flesh, and that I am not entirely detached from human affections. I trust, O Loving Father, Thou wilt satisfy this childish wish of mine.

I prayed to Christ for a long time, ending by: "I leave everything to Thy hands."

My wife wept; because I said to Lan Hsien some words too touching to be recorded even here.

Father Maestrini came at about 3 p. m. He baptized her, christening her "Teresa." During the Baptism, I was praying to the Little Flower. *The peace of Christ filled my soul.*

Father Maestrini said, "When you and I go to Heaven and find ourselves face-to-face with God, we shall feel grateful for this day!" I was so touched by these words that I suddenly wept.

Francis came. He said, *"God has never failed you, and will never fail you!"* I wept.

Went to the Rosary Church to pray for Lan Hsien's recovery. God will do a miracle!

O God, whether my dearest child goes to Thee or remains with me, she is *Thine!* Hereafter, let me seriously and earnestly start for the goal of sanctity.

Have pity on my wife.

Tuesday, January 23, 1940

To all appearances Lan Hsien is much better than yesterday! I am more grateful than I can express in words. *My wife is completely confirmed in faith. She said there was a marked improvement after the Baptism at four yesterday.* Glory be to the Father and to the Son and to the Holy Ghost! Amen.

My wife said that at six o'clock in the morning she smelt an intense gush of frankincense,—the first time she ever did in her life. I said it was the Little Flower, giving an assurance of Lan Hsien's recovery.

If all these miracles should fail to convince anyone of the Truth of Christianity, then he would not believe even if dead men should arise.

On my part I vow solemnly to God a saintly life: but as all sanctity comes from the grace of God, I must pray for this highest of blessings.

When the Doctor came at ten o'clock in the morning, he examined Lan Hsien, and found she had recovered completely. The pneumonia was gone! He had said yesterday, that it would take at least one week or nine days. *My wife said, "It must be the work of Our Heavenly Father."*

This morning T. K. Chuan phoned to say that he had found a doctor especially good for pneumonia. I answered, "No, thanks, it's no longer needed." "What!" the good man exclaimed, apparently frightened.

It was this experience that converted my wife and all the members of our family. Within half a year, thanks to the zeal of Father Maestrini and the catechist Miss Ellen Chow, all of them were baptized, one batch after another. Their baptismal names are as follows:

>My wife—Mary Teresa (October 19, 1899)
>Our children—Thomas (November 25, 1918)
>Edward (May 3, 1920)
>Theodore (April 4, 1925)
>Agnes (April 21, 1926)
>Margaret (April 11, 1928)
>Nicholas Bosco (February 3, 1930)
>Francis (April 30, 1931)
>Peter (July 6, 1932)
>Vincent (December 25, 1933)
>Stephen (May 6, 1935)
>Therese (September 19, 1938)
>Lucy (February 19, 1940)

God has given us twelve children and Christ led them to His fold; may the Holy Ghost sanctify them all! As to the birth of our thirteenth and last child John Jude, it will be treated in another chapter. Frankly speaking, I do not deserve such a good wife and such filial children; but Christ deserves even better disciples.

One other conversion round this time gave me great joy. During the War of Resistance against Japan, my sister's husband was in free China with me, and he joined the Church. He became a member of the staff of a certain bank in Kuei-yang. My daughter Margaret once visited him and witnessed an interesting scene, proving that he acted like a perfect Catholic. A hot-tempered youth was quarrelling with my brother-in-law; he went to the extent of spanking him on the face several times. After each spank, my brother-in-law said, "We Catholics don't return blow for blow." The whole scene became so comical that even long afterwards when Margaret related the story to me she could not help giggling.

Before I conclude this chapter, I must mention the invaluable friendship that God gave me in those days with the Carmelites of Stanley, especially with the saintly Prioress, Mother Thérèse of the Child Jesus. The Carmel was a powerhouse of prayer for all my apostolic work. While living in the world, I carry the interior Carmel within me. I have reaped in the world what the holy Sisters have sown in their cloisters. No Catholic works alone. He may appear to be lonely, but he is in company.

The good Mother Thérèse went to her reward in September 1948. I want to reproduce a touching letter which Bishop Henry Valtorta wrote to me about her joyous death:

Hongkong, 8 September 1948

Dear Dr. Wu,

I regret I have bad news. Rev. Mother Thérèse, a former Prioress of the Carmelite Convent, is dying. She had two big operations at Queen Mary's Hospital for cancer trouble: too late. I saw her today in her cell in the Carmel at Stanley. *She asked me to write to you and tell you that she prays for you and will always pray for you in Heaven. She is so happy and enjoys such great peace!* Her agony is very edifying: a Saint is dying. She hoped to go on this beautiful Feast of the Birthday of our Heavenly Mother, but—although she remarked that the day was not over yet—she may linger for a few days more. The Sisters are all very sad, yet they feel greatly consoled at the sight of her. She has arranged everything, even giving encouragement to the Sisters to ask her what is to be done for the funeral according to Carmelite traditions (as she is the first to go and nobody knows from experience what course to follow in such cases). She will be buried in a special Carmelite Cemetery in the garden of the carmel. Going to Heaven! *You cannot imagine how happy she looks!* Well, I am sad, but for us who remain behind, and surely not for her. She has finished well her task of starting Chinese Missionary Carmels and now she goes for the crown. I envy her. . . . . . .

Best regards to you and blessings!

+ Henry Valtorta

There are literally no bounds to the generosity of some of the missionary Sisters. Mother Thérèse was a Belgian. I will tell the story of another Belgian Carmelite, Sister Susanna, now Prioress of the Carmel at Macao. Some time in 1941, Father Maestrini with his usual spirit of charity and sincerity, told me, "John, a Sister is gravely ill in the hospital. She was so generous as to offer her life to our Lord for the conversion of Mrs. Averil Tang. Averil has been converted; and the Lord seems to have taken the Sister's offer seriously. To all appearances she is going to die!"

"Well, what can I do?" I said.

The good priest said, "Anyway, let us visit her in the hospital."

At that time, Father Charles Meeus happened to be in Hongkong. After praying together, the three of us went to the hospital. On seeing her in the sick bed, the two priests looked at each other like fools, and did not open their mouths at all. I had to break the ice. I said, "Sister Susanna, we have come to make a request of you."

"Say it, Doctor," she replied.

"Sister," I resumed, "you were so generous as to offer up your life for winning the soul of Averil. Now, the Lord wants you *to offer up your death* for our apostolic work in the world. Are you willing to live and spend your life in praying for us and millions of other souls?" I felt sure that the Holy Spirit was speaking through me.

The Sister answered, "Yes, Doctor, I am willing to live

and offer all my sufferings and prayers for your work of apostolate."

She recovered gradually and was transferred to the Carmel of Macao, where she was later elected Prioress. In September 1946, hearing of my appointment as Minister to the Holy See, she wrote me a long, edifying letter which I treasure very much; but I will only reproduce a short passage:

As for myself, I confess humbly I could not restrain a smile when I heard of the Lord's choice of you. I felt deeply moved and very happy, because during the War, often when I prayed, I wondered, thinking of our conversation and of the offering you made for me; very often I told Our Beloved Lord and Savior that really I was not worth all this, and that really it was not fair at all, begging Him to sanctify you and to make of you an ardent apostle. How could we ever reach His generosity, or love Him as we are loved by Him, unless by surrendering ourselves completely, entirely to Him? Dear Doctor Wu, I shall never forget you, nor what I owe to your generosity . . . but please beg our Beloved Lord to give me the grace of living my missionary life as the Little Flower would have done it. I think I may say that you have a "certain obligation" to help me,—is it not so? Excuse my simplicity in writing to you, but I feel you understand my intention in so doing.

But why do I reveal all these secrets? In fact, these are only a fraction of the countless ineffable consolations I have received from the hands of Christ and the Blessed Virgin. Not all the pages of one's life will ever be read on earth. All that I want to testify here is that a Catholic is never alone in the world; he never suffers or enjoys alone, although he may be living in a desert; he has numberless relatives in Heaven and on earth, many of whom he does not even know; he is an integral member of the Mystical Body of Christ, and his family is but a corporate member of a great family. In this light, one can fully realize the truth of Paul's words: "In all things we suffer tribulation, but we are not distressed; we are sore pressed, but we are not destitute; we endure persecution, but we are not forsaken; we are cast down, but we do not perish; always bearing about in our body the dying of Jesus, so that the life also of Jesus may be made manifest in our bodily frame"(2 Cor. 4.8–10). Nobody has written better of the communion of joys and sorrows among Christians than the Apostle himself, who said, "For whether we are afflicted, it is for your instruction and salvation; or whether we are comforted, it is for your comfort; which shows its efficacy in the endurance of the self-same suffering, that as you are partakers of the sufferings, so will you be also of the comfort" (2 Cor. 1.6–7). So closely knit is the Mystical Body of Christ that "if one member suffers anything, all the members suffer with it, or if one member glories, all the members rejoice with it."

To sum up my life in Hongkong, I would say those days were the kindergarten of my Catholicism. May God grant that I ever remain a little child and never outgrow the spirit of the kindergarten!

Is my Catholic life "a temporary infatuation," to use the former words of my wife? In a way, it is! For our life is temporary, and one lifetime is not sufficient for the full development of such a passion. My good friend Father John Monsterleet has written kindly of me: "In the degree that he was restless in his search for pleasures before abjuration, in that degree has he been stable in his faith and his fidelity after his conversion." On the whole, he has said the truth, although I wish I had been more faithful and docile to my Beloved. By nature I am an extremely changeable man, but

I don't rely only on my nature, but on *His grace*. His grace has changed my natural changeableness into a feeling tentacle for discovering every day new beauties of Christ and of His Church, thus ministering unto my constancy. Has St. Paul not said, "For when I am weak, then I am strong"? Shall I not say, "When I am changeable, then I am constant"? The Lord has transmuted my natural fickleness into supernatural fidelity! When Christ asked the Twelve, "Do you also wish to go away?" the Prince of Apostles answered, "Lord, to whom shall we go? Thou hast the words of everlasting life, and we have come to believe and to know that Thou are the Christ, the Son of God" (John 6.68–70).

Before concluding this chapter, let me give a brief account of how I came to write "The Science of Love."

Sometime in March of 1940, my *T'ien Hsia* colleague Chuan Tseng-ku told me that the April number of our Monthly stood desperately in need of an article, and that he expected me to write something to fill up the pages. I said to him, "It is a short notice, but if you leave me free to choose the subject, I will try to meet your deadline."

"Anything you like," he said.

Now at that time I was completely enamored of the spiritual doctrine of St. Theresa, and I proceeded to write about it after I had prayed to the Blessed Virgin: "Mother, help me to paint a portrait of your beloved child Thérèse, my beloved spiritual sister." In ten days or so, the article was ready, and I christened it "The Science of Love." After its publication, Father Maestrini approached me for printing it as a pamphlet under the auspices of the Catholic Truth Society of Hongkong. Since then it has been translated into German, Dutch, Italian, Spanish, Czechoslovakian, Indian, twice into French and twice into Chinese. I do not know of any instance of a soul being led by it to Christ, but I know of innumerable cases where it has been instrumental in bringing consolation to priests and Sisters, and in strengthening the faith and rekindling the love in the hearts of laymen. It has also won me many friends in all parts of the world. I want to mention two great Indian Catholics whom I hold especially dear. One is J. P. de Fonseka, who wrote a most delightful review of the Indian edition of my booklet. "With her science of love she fits in anywhere. There would be the same need of this Teresian love in Chungking as there is even in our corner of concentrated hucksterdam which goes by the name of the Pettah." Then he said it would be good news for the Saint of Lisieux to hear "that she has taken a flying leap over the Great Wall of China and found response in the heart of one of the noblest sons of ancient Tartary. Let her report to the Mother Superior of the Carmel of Lisieux that she has caught a Tartar! The angels of heaven would smile so angelically at the old joke." In fact, everything that De Fonseka wrote could easily make the angels laugh. But the climax is not yet. Here is a passage that made even me laugh:

In urging the comparative ease of the Little Way of the Little Flower as against the more exacting way of the great saints, the Chinese client of Lisieux falls back on a delightful specimen of ancient Chinese wisdom surpassing that of the Wallet of Kai Lung which says: "If you fail in painting a tiger the result is liable to turn out a dog. Whereas if you fail in carving a swan, the result may at least resemble a duck."

So the Wu family preferred to be ducks in the event of failing to turn out swans. (Tiger, tiger, burning bright in the forests of the night, what mortal hand or eye dare frame thy fearful symmetry—of a dog?)

It is indeed a pity that De Fonseka should have gone to Heaven so soon! The other Indian friend whom I treasure is Joseph Thaliath, retired Chief Justice of Trivandrum, who has sent me a booklet in his own language containing an article on the Little Flower's influence on me. Although I cannot make head or tail of it, I know that he has written it in the Teresian spirit of love. What thrills me is that my "Science of Love" has been received in the home of Buddha to whom I owe so much. I met Joseph's son, Father Jonas, in Rome, and felt as elated as if one of my own sons had become a priest. Oh, the fun of being a Catholic!

17. ESCAPE FROM A LION'S DEN

On December 8, 1941, early in the morning, I went to Mass in the Rosary Church in Kowloon. After the Mass was over, my friend Alice Chow and myself prayed together before the statue of the Sacred Heart for a hundred and one things, including the peace of the world. No sooner had we stepped out of the Church than we heard the bursting of bombs; and when we lifted up our heads we saw a couple of aeroplanes dropping bombs at a place about one mile away from us. What was all that about? Could it be war? Were we not celebrating the Feast of the Immaculate Conception of the Blessed Virgin, who is Our Lady of Peace? The fact is we did not know that the Pearl Harbor affair had taken place on the Vigil of the Feast and that the war had already started.

As we came near our houses in the Terrace of the Fairy of the Moon, we heard a voice from the veranda of one of the flats, calling out to us, "Hey! the War has entered our door! Ha, ha!" That was Francis Yeh, who never announced any news, good or bad, without ending it with "Ha, ha!" or "Hi, hi!" May God bless his memory! He was one of the sweetest souls I have known, and I doubt not that he is *hi-hi-ha-ha*-ing in Heaven before our all-merciful Father.

So, war had actually come. Yet I did not feel my heart beat any faster, partly due to my low blood-pressure, but mostly due to my sheer trust in the wisdom and power of Our Lady. It was impossible that anything which had started on her Feast should result in any harm to those who trusted in her motherly care. Moreover, had St. Paul not said that "everything helps to secure the good of those who love God"? (Rom. 8.28). Did I love God? Certainly I did, although I wished to have loved Him more. What then was there to worry about? Anyway, "to live is Christ and to die is gain." These were some of the thoughts welling in my mind.

But war came nearer and nearer. In five days the soldiers had broken into Kowloon. My eldest son Thomas pressed me to ford over to Hongkong, while he offered to remain with the family in Kowloon. In that parting I tasted something of death. To leave the whole family in a territory already fallen to the enemy, and to go all alone to Hongkong, which would be the next to fall! The chances of our reunion were meagre indeed. Add to this the fact that my wife was expecting a baby the next month, and you can imagine what a pathetic situation it was for all of us. I would not leave my family; I said, "Let us live and die together." But Thomas reasoned differently. He said, "Daddy, you simply cannot afford to fall into the hands of the Japanese. In going to Hongkong you still have a chance to escape. I shall take care of the family, which would be safer without your presence. Go in peace and trust everything to God."

I still shillied and shallied, but the rattle of the machine guns came nearer and nearer. So Thomas caught me by the arms and dragged me to the ferry just like a policeman dragging along a criminal. I caught the last boat.

I went to the *T'ien Hsia* office and found all our friends there. Some of them wanted to go back to Kowloon to see their families, but the communications were already cut. All of us were mad with grief. I remained grimly silent like a convict waiting for the execution. The most pathetic scene was when the philosopher Chuan Tseng-ku suddenly burst into a fit of wailing on thinking of his Annamese cat. He said, through his sobs, "Who is going to feed my cat?" At the eventide, each of us went to seek for his own refuge. Francis and I went to the Cathedral, and we remained there many days among thousands of refugees.

In the meantime, the war was following upon our heels. Cannon balls came incessantly from Kowloon, and bombs were raining from the skies. One day, a little before Christmas, the fire was concentrated on our sector. Our building shook violently, so much so that a priest stood up and announced to all the refugees, "Let us get together and prepare ourselves for death. The Lord is calling us back today, and the Bishop has kindly given to all of you a general absolution. Let us sing the Psalms appropriate to the occasion." He led, and we followed. Strangely enough, I sang very loud and did not feel panicky at all. I only thought that if I was to die, my soul would fly over to visit my family. I also prayed that if the building fell it should crush me so thoroughly and so quickly that I might die before I had time to feel pain.

But the fire subsided gradually, and we survived! All of us looked at one another with amazed faces. Francis Yeh came up to me and whispered in my ears, "Hi hi! John, do you know what happened? You see my sleeves are all wet. The old lady who sat on the floor next to me was so frightened that she urinated!"

As soon as the fire had entirely died down, my dear friend Averil Tang, who was living not far away and who had seen the concentrated fire and heard that our buildings were demolished and all the refugees killed, came in the hope of finding my corpse so that she could bury it. Upon seeing me, she embraced me and wailed over my shoulder, saying, "Oh, John, I thought you were dead!" I said, "Averil, don't wail any more; I am still alive!" Really it was most touching to hear the wailing of your friends over your death while you were still alive! It is a luxury that one enjoys in war-time.

Afterwards we learned that the reason for the ceasing of the fire was that the British had hoisted the white flag. It was wise of them to do it, because to continue to resist at such odds would only entail unnecessary loss of lives without any chance of warding off the invaders. A surrender was declared on Christmas, and the Japanese soldiers came to take over Hongkong. As the ferry system was not restored, we had no way of going back to Kowloon. So we stayed on as refugees in the Cathedral. On January 7, 1942, I received a notice from the Japanese military authorities, who had their headquarters in the Hongkong Hotel, "inviting" me to go there to have a talk. So my whereabouts had been known by them! As I could not possibly escape, I decided to go to see them. Francis Yeh said, "Be bold, John, I will go with you."

On January 8 I asked Father Maestrini to offer a Mass before the altar of St. Joseph, and to beg the great Saint to guide us in our dealings with the Japanese. Francis and I received Holy Communion and prayed ardently for protection and guidance. At ten o'clock we went to the Hongkong Hotel. A Japanese officer came to talk to us. He spoke Chinese fluently. I asked him what he wanted to see me for. He said in a roundabout way how desirable it would be for

China and Japan to make peace. I said, "I certainly love peace more than you do. It is most easy for Japan to make peace with China." He pricked up his ears and asked, "How?"

"Oh, it is very simple," I replied. "Withdraw all your troops from China, and there will be peace." He said, "But we cannot withdraw our troops. If we do, your troops will follow us to Japan." I answered, "As to that, I can guarantee. China has never wanted war. It was your honorable country that started it, we have always been on the defensive. If you withdraw your troops, I cannot imagine that our troops will ever invade Tokyo."

I was as polite as I could be, but evidently he did not like my logic. After a few moments of ominous silence, he said, "You will stay here!" Addressing himself to Francis, he said, "You too!"

Poor Francis! This time he did not say "Ha, ha!" With me there is a very peculiar quality. In the midst of the worst circumstances, I have often been surprised to find myself in a humorous mood. I said, "General, you are too polite with us. We dare not be your guests. We have our homes in Kowloon. We should be very grateful already if you could let us go home. As to staying here, I am afraid that it will cause you too much trouble." He smiled, apparently tickled by my naiveté, but said resolutely, "You had better stay here."

Francis and I were shown the room we were to live in, and were told not to come out of the door. When we were left alone, Francis looking all misery, whispered to me, "John, we are imprisoned!"

"Don't I know it?" I said, "But take it easy, everything will turn out all right." When I said this, I really did not see any human way out, but I put my whole confidence in the intercessory power of St. Joseph. I felt deep within me a wonderful peace, such peace as only Christ could give.

In the first few days, we were served with sumptuous meals, including *poulet garçon*, fish and even turkey. They were evidently the left-overs in the refrigerator of the Hotel. But gradually we got worse and worse food, so bad that Francis was afraid that at this rate we might be executed pretty soon!

In the meantime Father Maestrini, knowing that we were imprisoned, managed to send us some spiritual books to read, among which were Karl Adam's *Christ Our Brother* and a Chinese prayer book. In that enforced retreat, we prayed and recited the Rosary together day and night. I read the prayer book from cover to cover, underlining almost every line. When one is in distress, prayer becomes such a real thing. On January 16 I discovered in the book a prayer to St. Jude, "the Patron of hopeless cases." I said to Francis, "Read this prayer. It seems as though it were specially written for us!" He said, "Let us then start a novena in honor of St. Jude." We turned the wardrobe into a kind of altar, and every day we recited the prayer together with the Rosary. Sometimes I would imitate the celebration of Holy Mass, with Francis as the server. We succeeded in memorizing many prayers and ejaculations.

One day I was praying alone to St. Jude. A thought came to my mind: my wife was going to give birth to another boy, and I was going to name him after St. Jude. Somehow I was sure it was going to be a boy.

Francis expected some great news to happen on the 29th, the feast of his Patron, St. Francis de Sales. We would be released on that day. But nothing happened. Francis was most restless on that day, pacing up and down in the room, and going to toilet every five minutes. I was as quiet as ever, enjoying *Christ Our Brother*. Francis looked at me and said, "John, how can you be so serene in such a hopeless situation?"

I replied, "Well, Francis, the more hopeless we are, the more hopeful!"

"Ha, ha!" he said. That was the first time he had laughed since the imprisonment.

On the morning of the 30th, we heard a loud knock on the door, louder than any we had heard. I was really frightened this time. I thought that was the end of us. On opening the door, we saw a Japanese officer solemnly announcing to us the coming of the Bishop. The Bishop? Did he come to administer Extreme Unction to us? But the Bishop was smiling, he told us that Sir Robert Kotewall had kindly undertaken to bail us out, and that we could return home this morning! That was heavenly!

Sir Robert is one of my dearest friends. He is not only a statesman, but also a poet. He used to contribute his translations of Chinese poems to T'ien Hsia. He was so good as to render one or two of my poems into English. To make a long story short, Sir Robert and I had taken to each other and I saw him quite often before the War. This time he was out hobnobbing with the Japanese *in order to protect his friends.* In fact, he told this to me confidentially in so many words.

Well, Francis and I ferried over to Kowloon and made a beeline for the Terrace of the Fairy of the Moon, where our home was. We found all of our folks alive! I felt as though I were really in Fairyland. It was too good to be true; yet it was true all the same!

My wife said, "I knew you would come back today!"

I said, "How could it be?"

"I had a dream last night," she resumed, "I saw you coming into my room with a walking stick, calling out, 'Second Sister!' This is the most vivid dream I have ever had in my life. I was just telling our old maid about it."

This remains one of the mysteries I have not been able to

solve. Was it merely psychological? How was it then that she did not have such a dream any other night? Or was it a prevision? How was it then that I did not have a walking stick when I came? Or was it meant just as a consolation to my wife? I think this is more likely.

My wife is so matter-of-fact and honest a woman that it is impossible not to believe in her words. Therefore, I will tell a remarkable vision she had seen about a week before the Battle of Hongkong. One night I was out playing bridge at T. K. Chuan's house. I returned home a little after midnight. She had gone to bed, and at about midnight she woke up, and saw Our Lady standing on the left side of her bed. Our Lady was dressed in blue, with a red hood extending from her right shoulder to the waist on her left, holding the Infant Jesus on her left arm. Our Lady was wreathed in smiles. The Infant Jesus held in his hands a rosary and was moving His arms. I will let my wife continue the story in her own words: "At first I thought that it must be a dream or an illusion, for it is impossible that an ignorant and unworthy woman like myself should have seen Our Lord and Our Lady. So I rubbed my eyes and closed them for a few seconds. But when I opened my eyes again, they were still there! I shut my eyes once more, and upon my reopening them, they had gone."

I am perfectly convinced that it was a genuine vision. I myself have never seen any vision in my life. Even for my wife, it was also the only vision she has ever seen. Such visions are granted only to the humble of heart and for a very special purpose. On that particular occasion, it evidently was vouchsafed to my wife, as our dear friend Sarah Wong afterwards told me, "in order to fortify her against the forthcoming calamity, especially as she was expecting a baby."

After this long digression, let me resume the thread of narration. It was on the 30th of January, the Feast of St.

Martina, that I found myself reunited with my family. I went to Mass next morning to offer my thanksgiving to God and to satisfy my thirst for Holy Communion. After my return home, Father Maestrini called on me, and we had a most joyful time together. It was not so much a conversation as a duet of praises of the wonders of God and His Providence. As we were still talking, we heard the cries of the newborn baby in the next room! It was a boy. In half an hour, the doctor gave orders that we could come in. I asked the Father to baptize the baby right away. This he did. As it was the feast of St. John Bosco, he suggested christening him John. I explained to him about my commitments to St. Jude. The good Father said, "Then why not call him John Jude?" I agreed.

Although I was bailed out from the Hongkong Hotel, I was really not quite free. I was supposed to be interned at home. But I said to the Japanese officer that it was a spiritual necessity for me to go to church every day. He asked, "How far is it from your home to the nearest church?" I said, "It is about five minutes' walk from my house." Then he drew a narrow zone as the scope of my freedom of locomotion. Well, I thought, so long as I can go to the church, that is all the freedom that I want.

In the spring something happened which really vexed me. The Japanese municipality was organizing a "representative council," composed of the "leaders" in all walks of life, such as banking, law, medicine, journalism, culture and education. An officer approached me and showed the list of the names. My name headed the list as representing "culture"! Well, I thought, this is a greater calamity than the war itself! I said to the officer, "I appreciate the Mayor's good intentions. Please convey my thanks to him. But as to being a member of the representative council, I think you know as well as I do that I am an officer of the Chinese Government. After all, China and Japan belong to the same civilization, and the foundation of that civilization is *loyalty*. Without loyalty there can be no talk of culture and education. Please ask the Mayor to cancel my name!" I expected some spanks, but the officer seemed to be impressed by my logic. In my life, I have found that logic and reason go a long way in dealing with people, whoever they may be. The result in that particular case was that my name was cancelled, and the Japanese respected me all the more!

But it was a very uncomfortable predicament for me to be in. Meanwhile the municipality issued an order that all laborers from Shanghai and other parts of Japanese-occupied territory should go back to their native places by travelling on land, because there were not sufficient boats. That furnished a golden opportunity for us to escape. Francis Yeh and I registered ourselves and all the members of our families as laborers under assumed names such as "King Ah-pao," "Wang Ah-mao," "Chang Hsiao-ti," "Li Mei-mei," and so forth. We dressed ourselves in the most shabby clothes you can imagine. I shaved off my beard, which I had grown during my imprisonment. But Thomas was scared while we were still planning our exodus. He said, "Daddy, do you realize what you are doing? Can we seriously hope to break the net of secret intelligence for which the Japanese are so famous? You are running into death! If you are prepared to die, we are willing to die with you. If you are not, don't try."

"I am!" was my answer. As I look back upon those days, I still tremble. But I did not feel any danger then!

Before I took the step I had duly considered how my escape would affect Sir Robert Kotewall. All my friends said that it would not affect him seriously, because the Japanese had too much respect for him to do him any harm. Another

consideration was even more serious. Was I telling a lie when
I said that I was going to Shanghai? I was sorely afraid that
anything that was founded upon a lie would not be blessed
by God. It was a terrible thought. So I went to confession
to a Chinese priest. I exposed to him the whole situation,
and asked his advice: "Father, whatever you will say, I will
obey."

"Go ahead!" he said. "It would glorify Christ and His
Church by showing to the world how patriotic a Catholic
can be!"

I pricked up my ears at those words and said, "Is this
Christ talking?"

"Yes," the voice came from within the confessional, "it is
Christ talking!"

"Then, Father, will you follow me with your prayers?"

"Certainly. Our Lady will never forsake you!"

"But Father, is it a lie to say that I am going to Shanghai?"

"Well, you are going to Shanghai by way of Chungking!"

That settled the matter for me. Running into death or
running into life, I had Christ to back me up.

On the evening of our planned escape, I stayed up late,
writing a letter to the Japanese officer who was in charge of
our case. I enclosed a poem to him, of which I can only
remember two lines:

> Excuse me for going away without saying Goodbye!
> Loyalty requires the skipping of minor courtesies.

I wrote that just in case we should be caught. I thought it
might serve as an extenuating circumstance. So I left it on
the desk.

On the day of our departure (May 2) we borrowed a truck.
Before we started I went to St. Teresa Church and prayed to

Our Lady of Fatima. We were about twenty, all dressed up like the poorest of laborers. We drove westward to Sa Tou Ku. On the way, four Japanese gendarmes mounted onto our truck. Now, I thought, has come the end! But I treated them very courteously. I offered the one of them who sat next to me a cigarette. "Arigato!" he said. That means "Thank you!" I lighted the cigarette for him; and again "Arigato!" I took out my rosary and said it quietly. Apparently he was impressed by my piety, because Japanese are a religious people. But all the time I was wondering when the gendarmes would go, and for what purpose they had come to our truck. After about ten miles of riding, they made a sudden signal to the driver to stop. Every one of us looked pale with fright. But they went away, saying "Arigato!" All of us responded, "Arigato!" All that they wanted was a free ride!

We continued our journey; but when we reached Sa Tou Ku, it was already eventide. We waded over to the boat, but the boatmen said we could not start for the other shore, because the Japanese would machine gun any vessel sailing in the dark. So we had to spend a night in the boat, and we had a good showerbath, as it was raining. As soon as dawn came, we sailed toward Ch'i Ch'ung. From Ch'i Ch'ung we walked to Ping Shan. When we reached Ping Shan, it was late in the afternoon. I kissed the ground with tears of joy, because that was the beginning of Free China.

We travelled through Hong Tse, Tam Shui, and many other villages until we arrived at Wei Yang. We stayed there for a few days. I went to the church, and met Father Ma Chun-hsien. I went to confession to him, but he said, "You have done well, and you are welcome to Free China! For your penance say three 'Glory's.'"

From Wei Yang we took boat and sailed along the Tung

Kiang (East River). It took us fifteen days to reach Lao Lung. We visited every church we could find along the River. One has to travel far and wide in the world to realize how universal the Catholic Church is. We were told afterwards that bandits flourished in the regions we had passed through. But we being so awfully poor, the bandits evidently were frightened away, lest we should borrow money from them. As a matter of fact, every home where we stayed overnight was very cordial to us. I remember we had a grand banquet in one of the houses.

From Lao Lung we took a truck and travelled through Chung Hsing, Shao Kuan, Hung Yang. Whenever possible, we started each day's journey with Holy Mass and Holy Communion. We met many good priests. Finally, we arrived at Kueilin, in the evening of June 12. We heard that on that day there had been a big air battle in which six of the enemy planes were shot down by the American fliers.

We put up in a hotel quite near to the Catholic Mission. We went to see Monsignor Romaniello, whom I had met years ago in Hongkong. He wrote me a poem called "Touchdown," which I treasure very much:

> Doctor Wu, you are so true,
> To the spirit of fighting men.
> Whiskers long: from a lion's den,
> Hidden with Mary's mantle of blue,
> You led your brood of five and ten,
> Over water, road and fen,
> Into the land of free men.
> That is why I rejoice with you.

How narrow the escape was in reality can be gathered from some of the facts we came to know only afterwards. On

May 3, the day after our escape, a couple of Japanese officers came to our house and knocked at the door. Receiving no answer, they broke in. They immediately sent out telegrams to Macao and Kuang Chow Wan to have us arrested. But they could not imagine that we had taken the land route. Then they approached Sir Robert Kotewall. Sir Robert said, "I only guaranteed that they are good men. I did not say that they would not escape. Furthermore, I am in Hongkong, and they are in Kowloon. How was I to know that they were running away? If there is any negligence, it is on the part of the military authorities in Kowloon." These words were reported to me in Kueilin by a mutual friend of Sir Robert and myself who had come out from Hongkong. She further told me, "Sir Robert asked me to tell you that he was delighted with your escape." So generous he is!

The more I think of that experience, the more I marvel at the goodness of God. All our children, except John Jude who was only three months old, keep vivid memories of the exodus, and whenever we talk about it at our family Rosary, our talk becomes a chorus of praises to our all-merciful Father and to the Blessed Virgin, the Mother of good counsel. I can find no better words to describe our feelings than verse four of the Psalm of the Good Shepherd:

> Though I should walk in a dark valley,
> I will fear no evils, because Thou art with me.
> Thy rod and Thy staff: these comfort me.

A very dear friend of mine, Father Maur Fang, who was then the chief editor of the Catholic daily, *Yih Shih Pao*, published, when he heard of our wonderful escape, my earlier translation of Psalm 123 to mark the happy occasion. The

psalm fits our case so well that I want to quote at least the
two concluding verses:

> Our soul was freed as a bird from the snare of the
>   trappers:
> The snare was broken, and we were delivered.
> Our help is in the name of the Lord,
> Who made heaven and earth.

18. THE POETRY OF LIFE

So at last we were in Kueilin. I loved Kueilin at first sight. The streets were clean, the mountain air refreshing. Some of the hills are formed in such a way as to resemble the old-fashioned pen-stands of China. I thought, "What a natural setting for poetry!"

There was a personal reason why I took to Kueilin. The word literally means "Cassia Forest," thus reminding me of the name of my little mother! I felt as though I were in the womb of my mother again. I wished to settle down for some time at least, but I had only about a thousand dollars in my pocket—that is, about forty dollars in United States currency. Just as I was thinking of such things, a friend, Li Tung-ch'un, called at the hotel. He was the General Manager of the Ta Yeh Trading Corporation. I had seen him only once when in Hongkong, but we took to each other. Seeing me in such a miserable condition, he said, "Teh-son, we are like brothers, and recently it happens that I have made lots of money. As

285

you know, the fortunes of a businessman are like a see-saw or the ebb and flow of the tides. You must beat the iron while it is hot. I am quite hot now. Don't miss the chance of calling upon my help, while my pocket is full. Just say a word, and the money will be yours!" Well, well, I thought, it must be the landscape of Kueilin that had made him so poetic! I said, "Tung-ch'un, I need ten thousand dollars."

"What!" he exclaimed, amazed at my modesty, "Say another word! What about fifty thousand?"

"No," I said, "I will not accept a single dollar more than ten thousand. This is all that I need at present."

We were arguing back and forth for half an hour! We had apparently reached a stalemate, when another friend, Chen Kung-chieh, who had been listening to our interesting controversy with a great deal of amusement, intervened without our invitation. "Let me suggest a compromise," he said, "Mr. Li will not offer less than fifty thousand, and you will not accept more than ten thousand. Each party should yield somewhat. How about making it twenty thousand?" Both of us responded, "Okay!"

That interesting episode happened on the very day of our arrival at Kueilin, June 12, 1942.

Early the next morning, the air-alarm sounded. We started at once for the Seven-Star Cave, which is the greatest natural cave in the world. Near the cave was a tea house, and we sat down for some tea while waiting for the second whistle. We recited together a whole chaplet of the Rosary, prayed to Mary to help us find a house in the neighborhood of the cave, so that we would not have to run such a long way at every alarm. As it happened, the enemy planes did not come that morning, so it was soon "All clear." We rose and walked in a leisurely manner, knocking at almost every house and asking if there were rooms to rent. One lady told us that there was a house behind the hospital, but that it was for sale. We went there all the same. It was a shabby hut built of thin boards against the foot of the mountain. A fruit tree grew slantwise from the hall, stretching a part of its trunk outside the hut through a hole above the windows. The tree was there long before the hut was built, and the present owner, instead of cutting it off, had accommodated the house to the tree. At the back of the hut was a small grotto, used as the kitchen. At the front was a cassia tree. On the left side was a huge stone stairway of about a hundred steps leading to a cave called "The Cave of Morning Cloud." *Cassia* and *Cloud!* Was not my little mother's name "Cassia-Cloud"? This was the house destined for me! I asked the owner how much he wanted for the house, and he wanted twelve thousand dollars. I agreed immediately, and the contract was made. My wife wanted to bargain him down, but I stopped her, saying, "I will tell you the reason later." I felt as though I had got a precious pearl, and no price was too high for it. I had always been searching for a mother, and I found her in the person of the Blessed Virgin. Having found the Blessed Virgin, I found also my little mother! Right then, I had a glimpse into the marvellous ways of God. Moreover, had I not received twenty thousand from Tung-ch'un last night? Even objectively speaking, the price was quite fair.

A few days later, we moved into the house. It was the first time I felt myself in the bosom of nature, which I had missed so much in Shanghai. About fifty steps from our door was the mortuary of the hospital. Coming in and going out, we had to pass the mortuary. Every time I saw a new corpse lying there, I recited a "Hail Mary" for him. All of us were so accustomed to it that the border between life and death seemed to thin down to something like transparency. That was certainly one of the happiest periods of my life.

As I wanted to enjoy life a little after such a strenuous journey I did not go up to Chungking till September 1. At that time, my good friend Foo Ping-sheung was the Political Vice-Minister of the Foreign Ministry. He lived in the Hostel of the Ministry, and was so kind as to invite me to live with him there as his guest. I spent two months with him. The longer I stayed, the more welcome I received from him. Such is the constancy of his friendship.

As I was in economic stress, and as no official salary was enough to support my exceptionally big family, I had to look for something to do. I was even thinking of returning to the practice of law. Meanwhile I had an offer from the American Embassy to serve as a regular legal adviser at a handsome salary. Just as I was considering the matter, Madame H. H. Kung phoned me to tell me that her sister Madame Chiang wanted to have a talk with me. I went, and there was a nice quarrel between the First Lady and myself. She was opposed to my practising law. I said, "Look here, we must be reasonable. I have a big family, and I have to work to support them. Law being my profession, I don't see anything wrong in practising one's profession. Either ask the Generalissimo to send me to America, where I may do some useful service for our country, or else I have to practise law."

Madame Chiang looked at me with sharp eyes, "Have you forgotten about the translation of the Bible? The Generalissimo would be glad to support your family."

That enraged me. "I live *by* the Bible," I said proudly, "but I do not live *upon* the Bible. The translation of the Bible is not my profession, but my avocation. . . ."

I thought that ought to settle the matter once and for all. But the First Lady asked me tauntingly, "Dr. Wu, have you ever read the Bible?"

"Of course, I have!" I replied, without even looking at her face.

"Then," she said, "do you remember what St. Paul said: A *laborer is worthy of his hire*"?

Her ready wit and intimate knowledge of the Bible impressed me so much that my anger subsided. I remained silent, wondering why St. Paul should have said such a thing. Did he foresee that nineteen centuries later those casual words of his would shut up the mouth of a John Wu? The First Lady, observing that I was in a talking mood, asked, "What do you think will be enough to support your family?"

After thinking for a moment, I concluded that the only way of getting out of this predicament was to raise my demands so high that the Generalissimo would drop the matter automatically. So I said, "No less than six thousand dollars a month!"

That was about two hundred dollars in United States currency, but it sounded extremely high in my own ears. What was my surprise, then, when Madame Kung, who had silently listened to our stormy conversation, spoke up, "Oh no, Dr. Wu, that's hardly sufficient for such a big family. You must remember you will have to buy stationery, and you will have to invite some priests to dine with you once in a while for discussing doubtful points. Nowadays a single additional dish costs hundreds of dollars."

The following day, I received a note from the Generalissimo to the effect that I was to receive ten thousand dollars a month for the period of one year, in which I was to translate the Psalms and the New Testament. I was jubilant, and told all my friends about my good fortune. A former student of mine, who was quite high in the government, remarked, his mouth watering, "Dr. Wu, you are indeed 'an uncrowned king!'" Now this was the title that Chinese scholars had given to Confucius. But I wondered if Confucius had ever been so happy as I was at that time. If you can imagine that you were to be paid for riding your hobby horse for a year or so, you will know something of the happiness I felt then.

Nothing could have been farther from my mind than to translate the Bible or any parts of it with a view to publishing it as an authorized version. I had rendered some of the Psalms into Chinese verse, but that was done as a part of my private devotion and as a literary hobby. When I was in Hongkong in 1938, I had come to know Madame H. H. Kung, and as she was deeply interested in the Bible, I gave her about a dozen pieces of my amateurish work just for her own enjoyment. What was my surprise when, the next time I saw her, she told me, "My sister has written to say that the Generalissimo likes your translation of the Psalms very much, especially the first, the fifteenth, and the twenty-third, the Psalm of the Good Shepherd!"

"Oh," I said, "you have sent them to Chungking? I did not know that." But as no harm was done, I dropped the topic and talked about other things.

In the Autumn of 1940, when I was in Chungking, the Generalissimo invited me several times to lunch with him, and expressed his appreciation of the few pieces that he had read. So I sent him some more. A few days later I received a letter from Madame Chiang, dated September 21, 1940, in which she said that they both liked my translation of the few Psalms I had sent them. "For many years," she wrote, "the Generalissimo has been wanting to have a really ade-quate and readable Wen-li (literary) translation of the Bible. He has never been able to find anyone who could undertake the matter. By many leading Christians to whom he has spoken of this matter, the answer was given him that the word of God is so wonderful that the truth shines through even the bad rendition in Chinese. But we feel that this is dodging the question, for if, in spite of the bad text, some have found comfort and understanding, how much more powerful the Bible could be, as an agent to enlighten men's hearts and minds, if a really clear and readable translation could be had!" The letter ends up by saying that I should take up the job and that "the Generalissimo would gladly finance the undertaking of this work."

I did not take this suggestion seriously. China was in the heat of war, and I had other duties to attend to in the Legislative Yuan. So the matter had been dropped at that. But this time I was caught.

Taking my first month's subsidy with me, I took a plane back to Kueilin in November. As soon as I arrived home, I danced on the mud floor to the great amusement of my wife and all our children. I presented a thousand dollars to the old maidservant who had been with us for almost twenty years, saying, "Accept it as a gift on my birthday."

"So you have changed your birthday?" she said.

"Take it," I replied, "for every day is my birthday!"

After some preliminary study of the commentaries, I started my work with the Psalms on January 6, 1943, the Feast of the Epiphany. I followed no definite order at all. I just picked up whatever Psalm suited the mood of the day. I promised myself that I would translate one piece each day, no matter how long or how short it happened to be. The first piece I did was Psalm 35. I don't remember why I picked that up first, but I do remember how wonderful I felt when I sang out aloud the following verses:

O Lord, thy mercy reaches the heavens,
Thy faithfulness unto the clouds.
Thy justice is as the mountain of God,
Thy judgments as the deep sea.
Thou preservest men and beasts, O Lord.
How precious is thy grace, O God:
The children of men flee for safety under the
    shadow of thy wings,
They are filled with the treasure of thy house,
And thou makest them to drink of the torrents of
    thy delights.
For with thee is the fountain of life,
And in thy light we see light.[1]

When I had rendered them into Chinese verse, they sounded very Chinese indeed! For Chinese poetry is most at home in the use of parallelisms; and when they are put in rhyme they sound better than in French or English versions. It was promising! But something happened that I can never forget. Just as I had written down with my brush the Chinese equivalent of "the torrents of thy delights," I overturned by accident a cup of clean water, and my whole drafting-book was soaked. I called to my wife, "Look, look, the torrents of delight!" We dried it together, and everything proceeded smoothly. Practically all the good things of my life have begun with some unpleasant accident.

On June 29 I found myself translating Psalm 83, which was the last one to be taken up by me. That is a piece least susceptible of versification, because it is full of proper nouns. But I muddled through all right.

That half year was for me a continuous feast of singing days. Although the hut we were living in was extremely shabby, so shabby that my dear friend Lin Yutang, who

[1] Unless otherwise noted, this psalm and those which follow in this chapter are quoted from *The Psalms: A Prayer Book*, published by Benziger Bros., Inc.; reprinted with the permission of the publishers.

visited us when he was in Kueilin, said that it was more like a pigsty than a house; yet some of my happiest days were spent there, and I cannot look back on those days without a wistful yearning.

There were only two drawbacks about that hut. One was the tree. As the hole above the windows was just large enough to allow it to stretch out, whenever the tree was shaken by a storm, the whole hut shook with it. Once the situation was so bad that I held a crucifix in my hand and stood in the middle of the hall and howled at the wind: "In the name of Christ, I forbid you, O wind, to rage a minute longer! Don't you know that I am translating the Bible?" It was only after ten minutes that it subsided. So stubborn was the wind!

The other drawback was that it was leaky. One midnight, it was raining more heavily than usual; my wife and I were wakened by an unwelcome showerbath. So we got up and moved the bed to a dry corner. No sooner had we got into the bed than that place leaked again. If I remember correctly, we had to move four times before we finally settled in a truly dry spot. But both my wife and I derived a great deal of fun from it. We giggled until our sides almost burst. My wife was very much impressed by the fact that the manuscripts of my translation were not wetted at all.

O the fun of being miserable, of being miserable to a point, at any rate! And when a man and his wife can bear it for the love of God and for the love of each other, it is heavenly! Where there is love, even a "pigsty" is a paradise: where there is no love, a palace is no better than hell.

The goodness of the Maryknollers in Kueilin contributed not a little toward our happiness in those days. It was Father Edwin J. McCabe who taught three of my boys, Bosco, Francis and Peter, the art of serving Mass. He transliterated the Latin words syllable by syllable into Chinese monosyllabic sounds, and had the boys memorize them. When they recited them quickly, it sounded exactly as though they were speaking in Latin. So ingenious are the missionaries!

Monsignor John Romaniello, the Apostolic Prefect of the Kueilin Mission, is one of the most popular priests in China. He is not only holy but humorous. He told me that his patron saint was Chesterton, and as I, too, am extremely fond of G. K., we became great friends, admiring each other's taste. There were, however, some subtle shades of difference between his sense of humor and mine. His humor took the form of telling interesting stories, while mine took the turn of playing practical jokes. On one rainy day we invited him to lunch with us. It happened that it was leaking at the middle of the hall. About every minute there was a big drop of water. I hit upon the idea of placing the Monsignor at the head of the table, and arranging it in such a way as to ensure that the water should drop right on the crown of his bald head. When the lunch was ready, everybody took his seat. Just as I was serving the wine, I heard a voice coming from the head of the table, "Ugh, ugh, what is this?" I pretended to be entirely innocent and offered to change places with him. No, he would not, because it was "nice and cool." Everybody was edified by his sweetness; and thus a practical joke was turned into a living sermon.

It must not be imagined that I was practising such jokes all the time. Nor was Monsignor Romaniello always reading the detective stories of Chesterton. In fact, he furnished me with many useful reference books for the work of translation, among which were Callan and McHugh, *The Psalms Explained*, and Callan's commentaries on the New Testament.

Father Francis Daubert gave me Spencer's version of the Testament; and Father Anthony Paulhus gave me James

M'Swiney, *Translation of the Psalms and Canticles with Commentary*. Both these works I found extremely useful. Of course, I consulted some Protestant versions too. It was war-time, and one had to be contented with whatever one could lay one's hands on. Like Our Lord Himself, my version of the Psalms and the New Testament saw the light in humble surroundings. The Maryknollers were able midwives. By the way, in those days, I chose Father Thomas O'Melio for my confessor, because he was the mildest of all. In fact, one easily forgets sinning when one is singing the love of God. In those days, the Maryknoll House was a guest-house for priests of all Orders. Father Thomas Ryan, S. J., was there, and also Father B. G. Schneider, O. P. I admired both of them.

Whenever Father Charles Meeus came to Kueilin, he visited me every day and we had a jolly time together. He knew Chinese well, and he sang many of the Psalms in my new version. He did it so well that even my wife was convinced that I could write poetry. He is one of those priests who radiate the joy of Christ wherever they go. Being a naturalized Chinese, he did a great deal for China by way of publicity in his trips to America during those years of war. Knowing my poverty, he once brought fifty yards of Indian serge over the Himalayas in the hope it would fetch a good price. Now, he thought, poor John is going to get a fortune. But when the stuff was unrolled, it was found to be all moth-eaten! The result was that he could only get fifty dollars for it, and gave the money to us apologetically. O the charity and humility of that priest! It was not a fortune that I wanted, it was his love, and with that we were rich enough.

Once I was so cruel as to say to the good Father, "Look here, you come every day, and my translation is interrupted. I love you, Father, but I love Christ more. Let us offer a mortification for the success of the translation. From now on, suppose you come every other day."

"But I am going away to the States day after tomorrow," he said.

"Good," I said, "then don't come tomorrow. Let us offer this sacrifice to God to His greater glory. Goodbye, Father, and God be with you!" And we kissed each other.

The following day, just as I was cudgeling my brains over some fitting phrase, the good Father appeared at the door again. I gave him a white eye. But he said, "John, I tell you a secret. I have a weak heart. In the past I have fainted twice while walking on the road. I don't know whether we shall meet again. So don't be angry with me for coming to see you once more."

"Oh, Father," I said, "I didn't know that. But be sure that a man of such a good heart will live long. God love you!" So we enjoyed another holiday together. Nothing is so sweet and edifying as the friendship of a holy priest. We have seen each other many times since then. But now he is in Shanghai, and no one but God knows when I shall see him again.

It would take a whole volume to tell how much I enjoyed the Psalms and the translating of them into Chinese verse. Even from a purely literary point of view, the Psalms are a supreme work of art. Now, as Laurence Binyon has so well put it in *The Spirit of Man in Asian Art*, "It is the miracle of art that what is in a man's mind, not only his conscious aim but the imponderable stirrings and promptings that colour his conception of life, passes into what he makes." In the case of the Psalms, the difficult thing is not to render them literally, but to catch at least some of the imponderable stirrings and promptings of the mind of the Psalmist, and to transmit them to the mind of the reader. In order to do it successfully, the translator must have experienced the same kind of events and feelings as those of the authors themselves. For this task, God had prepared me not only by my interest in poetry and my love for the Psalms, but also by giving me an experimental knowledge of the workings of His grace, by subjecting me to various heart-rending trials, by infusing into me a sincere contrition for my sins, a taste of His sweetness, an unquestioning trust in His Providence, a love for Nature, which is His handiwork, and a delight in His Law. He had also given me the heart of a child with an ever-fresh sense of wonder. In short, He had prepared me to enjoy immensely the Psalms and to produce such a paraphrase of them as to give a similar joy to Chinese readers. As I once wrote to Father John Monsterleet, "I am not a poet, but God has made a poem of my life, a poem full of sorrows and joys."

The authors of the Psalms were passionate people. They were good lovers and good haters. When they were joyful, the whole universe seemed to ring with laughter. They would write:

> Let the heavens be glad,
> And let the earth rejoice;
> Let the sea roar and the fulness thereof;
> Let the field exult and all that is therein.

> Then all the trees of the forest shall be joyful
>   before the Lord,
> For he comes, for he comes to rule the earth.

> Shout joyfully to the Lord, all ye lands,
> Be glad and rejoice and make melody.
> Make melody to the Lord with the harp,
> With the harp and the sound of the psaltery,
> With trumpets and the sound of the horn:
> Shout joyfully before the Lord the King.

When they were sad, the whole universe seemed to
mope with them:

> I am like a pelican of the wilderness,
> I am become like an owl in the ruins,
> I am sleepless and I lament,
> Like a bird all alone on the housetop.

> For I eat ashes like bread,
> And I mingle my drink with weeping,
> By reason of thine indignation and thy wrath,
> For thou hast lifted me up and cast me down.

> I am wearied with my groaning,
> Every night I wash my couch with my weeping,
> I bedew my bed with my tears.

> My tears have become my bread day and night,
> Whilst they say to me daily: "Where is thy God?"

They loved the Lord and His Law with their whole heart:

> Thy laws become my songs in the place of my pil-
> grimage.

> Thy precepts are my heritage forever,
> For they are the joy of my heart.

> I hate half-hearted men, and I love thy law.[2]

> I love thy commandments more than good and fine
> gold.

> I rejoice at thy words, as one who finds rich spoils.

> My soul waits expectantly for the Lord,

    [2] The following verses and those quoted on pages 299–303, also the
second excerpt on page 305, are from *The Holy Bible*, Catholic Book
Publishing Company (1949).

More than night watchmen for the coming of the
    dawn.

I would rather stand upon the threshold of my God
Than dwell in the tents of sinners.

Because they loved God so passionately, they hated the
enemies of God with an equal intensity:

Do I not hate, O Lord, them that have hated thee?
Am I not weary of them that assail thee?
I hate them with a perfect hatred;
They are become enemies to me.

My zeal consumed me,
Because my enemies forget thy works.

I thoroughly enjoyed the translating of the imprecatory
Psalms, which were addressed to people who had made themselves enemies of God. I liked some of the striking images
therein:

May they pass like the snail that melts away,
Like the aborted foetus of a woman which sees not
    the sun.

Some of the Psalms in praise of creation are exquisite
nature poems, which appealed to me as very Chinese:

Thou commandest the springs to flow into the rivers
Which run among the hills,
They give drink to every beast of the field:
The wild asses quench their thirst;
The birds of the air dwell near them,
They sing among the branches.

Thou waterest the hills from thy chambers,
The earth is filled with the fruit of thy works.
Thou bringest forth grain for cattle
And herb for the service of man,
That he may bring forth bread out of the earth,
And wine to cheer the heart of man;
And he may make his face cheerful with oil,
And that bread may strengthen the heart of man.

The trees of the Lord have their fill,
The cedars which he has planted.
There the birds make their nests;
As for the stork, the firs are her home.
The high hills are a refuge for wild goats,
The rocks, for rabbits.

Thou hast made the moon to mark the seasons:
The sun has known its setting.
When thou makest darkness, and night falls,
All the beasts of the forest rove in it.
The young lions roar after their prey,
And seek their food from God.
When the sun rises, they disappear, and lie down in
    their dens;
Man goes forth to his work and to his labor until
    the evening.

And what a wonderful rural piece this:

Thou hast visited the earth and hast watered it,
Greatly hast thou enriched it.
The river of God abounds with water,
Thou hast prepared the grain for them;
For thus hast thou prepared it:
Its furrows thou hast watered,
Its clods thou hast made smooth,
With showers thou hast softened it,
Thou hast blessed its sprouting seed.

Thou hast crowned the year with thy kindness,
And thy paths drip with fatness.
The pasture lands of the desert drip,
And the hills gird themselves with great joy.
The fields are clothed with flocks,
And the valleys are covered with grain:
They cry aloud and sing.

In translating all such pieces, I had three thousand years of Chinese literature to draw upon. The Chinese vocabulary for describing the beauties of nature is so rich that I seldom failed to find a word, a phrase, and sometimes even a whole line to fit the scene. But what makes such Psalms so unique is that they bring an intimate knowledge of the Creator to bear upon a loving observation of things of nature. I think one of the reasons why my translation is so well received by the Chinese scholars is that I have made the Psalms read like native poems written by a Chinese, who happens to be a Christian. Thus to my countrymen they are at once familiar and new—not so familiar as to be *jejune*, and not so new as to be bizarre.

Perhaps the most oriental trait of the Psalms is the pervading philosophy of retributive justice. If the fear and love of the Lord form the warp of the Psalms, the idea of spiritual causality forms the woof. Let a few illustrations suffice:

He dug a trench and hollowed it out,
But he fell into the pit which he had made.
His wickedness will revert upon his own head,
And his violence will return upon his crown.

The nations have fallen into the pit which they
    have dug,
Their foot has been caught in the snare which they
    hid.

> Many are the afflictions of the just man;
> But the Lord delivers him from all of them.

The beauties of the Psalms are innumerable. Who can ever forget such striking images and touching sentiments as the following:

> And I say: O if I had wings like a dove,
> I would fly away and be at rest.

> Thou hast noted the ways of my exile;
> My tears are stored in thy water-bag:
> Are they not recorded in thy book?

> I have seen a wicked man in his pride
> And spreading himself out like a cedar.
> And I passed by, and lo, he was not;
> I sought him and he was not found.

> For his anger endures for a moment,
> But his kindness for a lifetime.
> In the evening weeping comes,
> But gladness in the morning.

> If my father and my mother should abandon me,
> Yet the Lord will uphold me.

> He who planted the ear,
> Shall he not hear?
> He who formed the eye,
> Shall he not see?

> Man's days are like grass;
> Like the flower of the field, so he flourishes.
> The wind has scarcely passed over him,
> And he is no more;
> Nor does his place know him any longer.

They who sow in tears,
Shall reap in joy.
Going they go and weep,
Carrying the seed to be sown:
Returning they shall return with exultation,
Carrying their sheaves.

Your wife, as a fruitful vine within your house,
Your children as olive-shoots round about your table.

Awake, O my soul;
Awaken, psaltery and harp!
I will awaken the dawn.

Before I was afflicted, I erred,
But now I keep thy word.

It is good for me that I have been afflicted,
That I may learn thy laws.

When anxieties are multiplied in my heart,
Thy consolations delight my soul.

Let the rivers clap their hands,
Let the mountains exult together before the Lord.

The mountains skipped like rams,
And the hills like lambs.

Personally, for special reasons, I liked two of the Psalms
best. One is the Psalm of the Good Shepherd, which has
revealed to me the three stages of interior life. My whole
course on Christian Mysticism, which I have been giving in
the School of Religion of the University of Hawaii, is based
upon this one Psalm. The first stage, which the spiritual
writers usually call the purgative way or the age of the
beginners, is symbolized by the following verses:

> The Lord is my shepherd: I shall want for nothing.
> He makes me lie down in green pastures.
> He leads me to waters where I may rest.
> He gives refreshment to my soul.

The second stage, which is usually called the illuminative way or the age of the proficients, is symbolized by:

> He guides me along right paths for his name's sake.
> Although I walk in a darksome valley,
> I shall fear no evil, for thou art with me.
> Thy rod and thy staff: they comfort me.

The third stage, which is the unitive stage or the age of the perfect, is symbolized by:

> Thou preparest a table for me before the eyes of my
>   foes;
> Thou anointest my head with oil;
> My cup brims over.

> Goodness and kindness will follow me all the days
>   of my life,
> And I shall dwell in the house of the Lord days with-
>   out end.

I expounded these stages to President Chiang Kai-shek, who was deeply impressed by this Psalm.

The other Psalm which I have liked in a special way is Psalm 107, which seems to sum up the whole course of my life, both interior and exterior. The Psalm begins like this:

> Give Praise to the Lord, for he is good,
> For his mercy endures forever.
> Thus let those speak who have been redeemed by
>   the Lord,

Whom he redeemed from the hand of the enemy,
And whom he gathered out from the lands,
From the east and the west, from the north and the
    south.

Then it continues to enumerate four classes of men whom
the Lord has saved from their respective dangers and distresses. The first class is composed of wanderers in the desert:

They wandered in the desert, in the wilderness,
They found not the way to a habitable city.
They were hungry and thirsty,
Their life was growing faint within them.

And they cried to the Lord in their anguish;
He delivered them out of their distresses.
And he led them by the right way,
That they might come to a habitable city.

Did I not cry:

O God, if You are there,
I wish to know Your secret will.

Was I not a traveller, a lonely wanderer in a desolate world?
Did I not write:

Travelling has its advantages, the chief among which is
that it drives home to you that you are but a *traveller on
earth*. Your wife, your children, your friends are really no
more than your chance acquaintances. Your own body or
even your personality is something you have casually acquired. *You are a guest in a world without a host*, for all the
people you meet are as much guests as you are.

Has God not led me to a home, to a habitable city, to
the Vatican and to the interior castle of my soul?

The second class consists of captives:

> They sat in darkness and gloom, in bonds of misery
>   and iron.
> For they had rebelled against the words of God,
> And they have despised the counsel of the Most
>   High.
> And he humbled their heart with labors,
> They staggered and there was none to help.
> And they cried to the Lord in their distress.
> He delivered them from their troubles,
> And he brought them out of darkness and gloom,
> And broke their bonds asunder.

Has God not delivered me from the triple bondage to the
world, to the Devil, and to myself? Even physically, did He
not break gates of brass and burst iron bars for me?
    The third class consists of the sick:

> They were sick because of their wickedness,
> And were afflicted because of their offences.
> Their soul abhorred all food,
> And they drew near to the gates of death.
> And they cried to the Lord in their distress;
> He delivered them from their troubles.
> He sent his word to heal them
> And to rescue them from death.

Was I not a sick soul, whom the Divine Word has healed
and the motherly hand of the Blessed Virgin has nursed to
a new vigor of life?
    The last class consists of the shipwrecked:

> They that had gone down to the sea in ships,
> To ply their trade on the high seas,
> These have seen the works of the Lord,

And his wonders in the deep.
He spoke, and called forth a stormy wind,
Which lifted the waves on high.
They mounted up to the heavens, they went down
    to the depths;
Their soul was wasting away amid evils.
They staggered and reeled like drunken men;
And all their skill was swallowed up.
And they cried to the Lord in their distress,
And he brought them out of their troubles.
He soothed the storm into a gentle breeze,
And the waves of the sea grew quiet.
And they rejoiced because they were still,
And he brought them to the haven where they
    longed to be.

This was exactly how I felt in the world of politics in those stormy days. Didn't I stagger and reel like a drunken man? In my interior life, too, I felt I was sailing in a stormy sea. Holmes once said to me, "My inference was that you alternated violently between exaltation and discouragement," and I think he was right. I myself wrote, "The older I grow, the less I know about the meaning of life. All currents of thought, all winds of doctrine, have crossed in my mind; I stand baffled and bewildered like Alice in Wonderland." Christ alone has given me His peace.

With Christ, there is peace even in war. Without Christ, there is war even in peace. With Christ, the poor are rich. Without Christ, the rich are poor. With Christ, adversity is sweet. Without Christ, prosperity is bitter. With Christ, the ignorant are wise. Without Christ, the wise are fools. With Christ, life is a prelude to Heaven. Without Christ, life is a prelude to Hell.

19. A CHINESE TUNIC FOR CHRIST

I do not think that I am a hard-boiled man. But I am no sentimentalist either. The reason why I remember so well all the occasions on which I have wept, particularly since my embracement of the Catholic Faith, is because I have so seldom shed tears that they are precious for their scarcity. In the nursery days of my Catholic life in Hongkong, it is true, I did weep quite a few times. I don't know why, but whenever I read a particular passage in the last chapter of the Gospel according to St. John, I could not refrain from weeping. It seemed as though there were tear gas in it. The passage is as follows:

There were together Simon Peter and Thomas, called the Twin, and Nathaniel, from Cana in Galilee, and the sons of Zebedee, and two others of his disciples. Simon Peter said to them, I am going fishing. They said to him, We also are going with thee. And they went out and got into the boat. And that night they caught nothing. But when day was breaking, Jesus stood on the beach; yet the disciples did not know that it was Jesus. Then Jesus said to them, Young men, have you any fish? They answered to him, No. He said to them, Cast the net to the right of the boat and you will find them. They cast therefore, and now they were unable to draw it up for the great number of fishes. The disciple whom Jesus loved said therefore to Peter, It is the Lord. Simon Peter therefore, hearing that it was the Lord, girt his tunic about him, for he was stripped, and threw himself into the sea.

Every time Simon Peter threw himself into the sea, there arose in John Wu an ocean of tears. You cannot analyse tears any more than you can analyse laughter and love. I love Peter more than any other Apostle or saint, because he was the most *childlike* of all. I suspect that it was the principal reason why Christ made him the rock upon which He has built His Church. The naive simplicity of Peter, I venture to think, was what endeared him to the heart of Our Lord. Do you remember the scene of Jesus washing the feet of His disciples, and the impulsive words successively uttered by Peter on that occasion? "Lord, dost Thou wash my feet? . . . Thou shalt never wash my feet! . . . Lord, not my feet only, but also my hands and my head!" He was simply like a drunken man in that if you help him on the right side he falls on the left, and if you help him on the left side he falls on the right. He was the weakest, simplest, but at the same time the sincerest of the children of man. This is the kind of quality that Our Lord likes best, because it gives the amplest room for His grace to work.

I used to flatter myself in thinking that I was by nature akin to Peter, because I too am endowed by God with a high degree of impulsiveness and impetuosity. My students used to call me "Doctor of Jurisimprudence," and even my children have often been tickled by my impetuous actions. I

once asked my confessor Father Maestrini, "Father, I think
I am akin in nature to Peter. Shall I take him for my model?"

"Frankly," he said, "you are more akin to St. John than
St. Peter. Your impulsiveness takes the form of quickness of
perception rather than promptness of action."

I have thought over this matter many times, and finally I
have come to the conclusion that my confessor was right. But
how is it then that I love Peter more than John? For the
simple reason that John himself had a secret admiration for
the pristine simplicity and utter sincerity of Peter. I am
really not as naive as I thought myself to be or as some of
my naive friends still think me. My naiveté is post-sophistica-
tion, whereas Peter's was primordial. I have *become* simple
in the same way as Mary Magdalen *became* a virgin by her
contact with Christ; whereas Peter's simplicity was on a par
with the Virginity of Our Lady.

But where am I? I am again digressing. It is a sign of sen-
ility to digress this way. I was starting with the tearful topic
of weeping, and now I am making comparisons between St.
Peter and myself! Let us return to weeping.

During the two years (from November 1, 1942 to October
31, 1944) when I was engaged in the translation of the
Psalms and the New Testament I wept over the Bible only
once. One night, as I was translating Chapter 19 of St. John's
Gospel, I came across this: *Now the tunic was without seam,
woven in one piece from the top. They therefore said to one
another, Let us not tear it, but let us cast lots for it, to see
whose it shall be.* Suddenly I burst out weeping. The whole
scene flashed upon my mind like a sudden illumination.
This seamless tunic had been woven by the motherly hands
of the Blessed Virgin, and had been worn by her grateful Son
Who was now hanging on the Cross! And now the soldiers
were making merry over such a precious tunic, turning it into

an object of lottery, in the very presence of Our Lady! But what made me weep was the lightning-like flash of intuition that whatever Our Lady had woven could not be divided, being without seam from the top! Wherever Our Lady is, there is seamless unity. I thought that it was just a childish fancy on my part. But when I was in San Francisco in 1945 as an adviser to the Chinese Delegation to the United Nations Conference, Father Reilly, who was serving as the secretary of Monsignor Yupin, lent to me a copy of Lagrange's *The Gospel of Jesus Christ*, in which I was pleasantly surprised to find a confirmation of my mental vision:

A seamless robe was of some value; the high priest wore one like it. The one worn by Jesus had most probably been woven by the hands of some woman who believed in Jesus, perhaps one of the wealthy Galilaean women who had followed Him; or it may have been made for Him by His Mother. Ever since the time of St. Cyprian it has been regarded by the faithful as the symbol of the Church, which must remain undivided. Woe to those who stir up schism and rend her apart![1]

When I was translating the New Testament, I often prayed to the Blessed Virgin to the following effect: "Holy Mother, Spouse of the Holy Ghost, help me to weave the Chinese tunic for your Son, the Divine Word. Make it a seamless robe, beautiful and wearable. Give it an oriental touch; perfume it with frankincense, preserve it with musk, line it with gold, but at the same time make it as light and as comfortable for Him to wear as possible! Share with me some of those gifts which you received from the Magi, plus the blessing. In one word, Mother, do it for me, for no one knows your Son's measure and taste better than you; I will cooperate with you as an apprentice tailor."

[1] Marie-Joseph Lagrange; Benziger (New York, 1939).

In the spring of 1944, I completed my first rough draft of
my versions. I went to Chungking for a short visit. Meanwhile the Japanese soldiers launched a great offensive westward into the provinces of Hunan and Kwangsi. The troops
were nearing Kueilin. I tried desperately to return to Kueilin
to bring out my family. I booked the plane twice, but I was
prevented from boarding the plane each time *by the most
unaccountable causes*. I will not enter upon the details of
the wondrous Providence of God. Suffice it to say that had I
not been prevented from returning, I could never have
escaped from Kueilin. God has truly treated us like the apple
of His eye, because we have cast all our cares upon Him.

Being unable to go back to Kueilin, I sent a telegram to my
family to move immediately to Kueiyang. In the meantime,
I took a long-distance bus from Chungking to Kueiyang. In
a few days, my family, under the leadership of Thomas,
escaped from Kueilin under the most terrifying conditions.
When we were reunited in Kueiyang, my wife told me that
if I had come back then, it would have been practically impossible for the whole family to escape in time. The train was
so congested that they were literally thrown into it by Thomas
through the windows! And it was the last train to leave
Kueilin!

Although most other things had been lost or thrown away,
I was happy that my family had brought my manuscripts
with them. At first we stayed at a hotel; but whenever we
were in distress God always sent somebody to help us, and
this time it was Professor Chang Yung-li, a native of Kueiyang
and a zealous Catholic, who invited us to live in his country
house. I did not know him. He must have heard of our arrival
from some of the good French priests in the Diocese. We
moved in, and I resumed the work of translation by revising
and copying out the manuscripts. Meanwhile, the Seminary

at the Loh Chung Kuan ("Pass of the Fullness of Joy") on the mountain invited me to do my work up there. I often lived there two or three weeks at a stretch, while my family lived at the foot of the mountain. Both the French missionaries and the native priests were extremely hospitable to me.

The Holy Spirit timed everything well. When I was in Kueilin translating the Psalms I enjoyed the blessings of the Old Testament. We could live very comfortably with the monthly allowance of ten thousand dollars, National Currency. When I was translating the New Testament in Kueiyang, the national currency had depreciated beyond recognition; but I did not ask for an increase of the allowance. One day, as I was riding in a rickshaw, I entered into a conversation with the rickshaw man. I asked him. "How much do you earn every month?" He replied, "Very little, just barely enough to support my family. I earn about a thousand dollars a day. That makes only thirty thousand dollars a month!"

As I was earning only a third of his income, you can imagine what a hard time we went through the second year of my translation work. One morning we found ourselves literally penniless. We had some leftovers in the kitchen, so far as the food was concerned; but my stock of cigarettes was exhausted. I actually did not smoke for a whole day. If necessity is the mother of invention, it is also the father of renunciation! I wish the money had not come in the afternoon of that very day! Otherwise I could easily have cut off the habit of smoking. "Sweet are the *uses* of adversity," says Shakespeare. Judging from my own experience, the *uses* of adversity are sweet, but its taste is not so sweet. Two years before, I had been an "uncrowned king"; but now I was actually "a king of patches and shreds." Still a king! For, as Our Lord says, "Blessed are ye poor, for yours is the kingdom of God."

I finished the revision and copying of the manuscripts on
October 31, 1944. Fathers Chung and Chen had helped me
in the copying. I still treasure their copies. But the most
strange thing was this. As I have mentioned, my work started
from November 1, 1942. Originally the time set was one year;
but it proved impossible to complete both the Psalms and
the New Testament in one year. So I approached the private
secretary of the President, Mr. Chen Pu-lei, for an extension
of a half a year. Mr. Chen said, "Make it a year." That meant
that I had to hand in the translation of the New Testament
on or before the end of October. As it happened, it was the
lunar birthday of the President. It was a remarkable coincidence. I explained to the President that God wanted to show
His deep pleasure at his interest and co-operation in the
translation of His word.

In the winter of 1944, my family moved to Chungking.
Dr. Sun Fo housed us in the Sun Yat-sen Institute for the
advancement of Culture and Education at Peipei.

From time to time the President wanted to see me and
I got to know him very well. I was deeply impressed by his
personality and spirituality. Although he liked my version
of the Psalms better than that of the New Testament, yet I
could see that he was absorbing more and more the spirit of
Christianity. He marked my manuscripts with red and blue
pencil, and made quite a few thoughtful corrections in the
wording. Among his special markings, I found to my greatest
satisfaction the passage in the Gospel of St. Mark, where
Christ laid down the principles which have been the very
foundation of Democracy in the West: "You know that
those who are regarded as rulers among the Gentiles lord it
over them, and their great men exercise authority over them.
But it is not so among you. On the contrary, whoever wishes
to become great shall be your servant; and whoever wishes

to be first among you shall be the slave of all; for the Son of Man also has not come to be served but to serve, and to give his life as a ransom for many" (10. 42–45).

In the spring of 1945 I went to San Francisco to attend the United Nations Conference. I spent three months there, and by the end of July I returned to Chungking. The President and myself continued to work on the New Testament.

On August 15 I reported before the Legislative Yuan meeting on the U.N. Charter. Just as I finished my report, we heard a tremendous sound of fire-crackers outside the Hall. "What is it?" I asked. "We are celebrating the Victory!" was the reply. And it was the Feast of the Assumption of Our Lady! I thought that from thenceforth there would be peace for China and for the world.

On December 9, as I was taking breakfast with Dr. Sun Fo in his house at the Lonely Stone Bridge, where the Legislative Yuan was situated, he told me, "The President expressed the desire that you should go to the Vatican." I said, "When did he tell you?" He replied, "The day before yesterday, when I was taking supper with him, he said that to me." I smiled, although Dr. Sun himself was not pleased with the suggestion, because he always wanted to see me appointed Minister of Justice. I smiled, because it was on the Vigil of the Feast of the Immaculate Conception of Our Lady that the Head of the State had expressed this desire.

For me, whatever our Blessed Mother Mary had decided was not to be gainsaid. For my political friends who were not Catholics, it seemed ridiculous to appoint me as a Minister to the Vatican, which was only as big as Peipei. I was the Chairman of the Foreign Affairs Committee in the Legislature for quite a few years. Some of my members had been sent as Ambassadors to bigger States. Was I not under-selling myself? I told them that I would never accept a ministership to any other State; as to the Vatican, I would even go as a secretary or attaché of the Legation. On the other hand, some people who were not my friends opposed my appointment, on the ground that I was a Catholic. I told them that the first duty of a Catholic in public service is to be faithful to the duties of his state and to be loyal to his country. The opposition was rather formidable, but in the heart of my heart I never doubted for a moment that what the Blessed Mother had planned she would push through.

My appointment was not decided officially till September 8, 1946, the Birthday of Our Lady!

In the spring of the same year I participated in the Political Consultation Conference where all parties, including the Communists, took part. I was in great hopes that all the problems between the Parties could be ironed out and our poor people spared the ravages of Civil War after they had suffered so much already during the eight years of the War of Resistance against Japan. But somehow or other the Conference came to no results.

In early summer, my family and I returned to Shanghai. I thought of the words I had heard in Hongkong four years before: "You are returning to Shanghai by way of Chungking." One day I went to visit the chapel in which I had been baptized nine years before. As soon as I knelt down before the statue of Our Lady, I wept like a baby in thinking of all the motherly care she had taken of me and of my family, during all those stormy years. But although the years were stormy, my interior peace had not been disturbed for a single day. Even during the air-raids, when I found myself in a dugout, I often, though not always, recited the Rosary and felt as though I were in a grotto of Our Lady. When I happened to meet an interesting friend there, we would discuss philosophy, literature and religion and forget about the raid. I remember one day in Chungking, I had the good fortune of meeting for the first time Professor Paul M. A. Linebarger in a dugout, and I was especially drawn to him as being the son of my old teacher in International Law. We discussed so many interesting questions together that we did not even notice the passing of time. Afterwards, in one of his books on China, I have found an account of me, which, to be sure, is overgenerous, but which I deeply appreciate because generosity is a quality that runs in his blood, knowing as I do the kindness of his father. I hesitate to quote it, but then, as an ancient Chinese poet has put it:

> Man's life is like the sojourning of a traveller,
> A little friendship is no little matter.

Therefore let me quote his kind words, which have kept me, as the Chinese would say, warm for three winters:

Dr. Wu is one of the most extraordinary personages of the modern world; he has taken all knowledge—East Asiatic and Western—for his province. He writes a spirited, graceful English and is capable of discussing anything from modern politics or abstruse points of Anglo-American law to ancient Chinese hedonism or the philosophical implications of the *Autobiography* of St. Thérèse of Lisieux. Dr. Wu, in a bomb-shelter, possesses much of the moral poise and profound personal assurance for which Westerners like T. S. Eliot seek in vain.

By nature I am a coward, but by grace I have felt in times of danger like a baby in the arms of its mother. And since Mary is my Mother, how could I help feeling grateful for her ever-watchful care of me, in season and out of season?

That half year in Shanghai, from the summer of 1946 to our going to Rome, was a season of harvest for me. For one thing, my version of the Psalms was published, dedicated to Mary, Mother of China. To my greatest surprise, it sold like hot dogs. The manager of the Commercial Press, Mr. Wong Yuen-wu, told me that it was the best seller for many years. I suspect Our Lord has a special predilection for things of humble origins. The version was born in a pigsty.

The popularity of that work was beyond my fondest dreams. Numberless papers and periodicals, irrespective of religion, published reviews too good to be true. I was very much tickled when I saw the opening verse of the first Psalm used as a headline on the front page of one of the non-religious dailies. They arranged the ten words in such a way as to surround my picture like a crown on the head. Thus was "the uncrowned king" crowned! The words, if rendered back into English, would read as follows:

Happy only is the gentleman who does good,
God will shower on him infinite blessings!

From this you will see how little accurate my version is. But I did not publish it as a literal translation, but only *as a paraphrase.* My chief object was to interest the Chinese public in the Holy Scriptures.

I will tell you how I discovered the write-up in that particular daily. I was taking breakfast with Father Joe Sweeney, commonly known in China as "the Father of Lepers." A couple of my little boys came in and told us that they had seen my picture on one of the papers pasted on a wall. "Don't tear it down!" I said, "It is not lawful to do so."

Father Joe, being a most practical theologian, remarked, "It depends upon whether it is today's paper or yesterday's. If it happens to be yesterday's paper, I don't see anything wrong in tearing it off and bringing it home."

Off went the boys, and in a few minutes they came back with the paper. It was yesterday's. When I saw it, I was very glad that the Psalms had gone into the secular papers; but I was extremely tickled that they had given me out as "the gentleman who does good"!

"This is Shanghai, the scene of my wild days," I said to Father Joe. "What would the sing-song girls think if they should see the picture?" The good Father said, "I guess they must be pretty old by now. Don't worry about your past, Doctor. God is capable of curing even the lepers!"

Father Joe is a typically Yankee "saint." He does much, but speaks little. Whenever he was praised, he would say, "Oh skip it! Let's have a drink."

Now to return to the Psalms. Not only Catholics but other Christians took to my version very much. In an excellent book-review, two Protestant missionaries of *The Bible Treasury*, signing themselves as Taddao and Anli, were good enough to make such comments as the following:

This issue of the Psalms in Wenli is a piece of art unexcelled in Chinese Christian literature.

Considering the narrow confines Mr. Wu has set himself by conforming to the rules of Chinese poetry, whereby he had to divide his lines into 3, 4, 5, and 7 characters in each line, and at the same time see to it that the last characters of each first, second and fourth line in each verse of four lines rhymed properly, he has produced a work of literary art beyond all praise. That his language is, in spite of its poetic artificiality, lucid, and in general a fair rendering of the Hebrew original is a feat of which he may well be proud.

While defending the current vernacular version of the Psalms, they did me justice by saying that "Rhymes in Chinese are probably more important than in other languages," and that therefore my version was "a great help to many readers in popularizing the Psalms." That was exactly my principal objective.

How can I thank God enough for having deigned to make use of such a humble instrument as my paraphrase of the Psalms to lead souls to the light and comfort them! From time to time I have received letters to that effect. I have also seen public accounts of its salutary influence on people unknown to me. Here is a story written by Dom Thaddeus Yang about the conversion of an old General in Changtu:.

"I have read the Four Gospels several times and Dr. John C. H. Wu's translation of the Psalms twice, and I feel that nothing in our Confucian Classics is comparable to the religious and moral doctrines contained therein." This conviction had led seventy-five-year-old Mr. Yang Tsin to the threshold of the Catholic Church. Before a congregation of more than five hundred people, he was baptized recently by the Rev. John Yang, pastor of the Cathedral, with Msgr. A. Poisson, Vicar General, serving as godfather . . .

But the most touching story is one told by Thomas Cardinal Tien in one of his published papers. As it was written in Chinese, I have to do it into English:

Mr. Wu's version can be chanted like songs. It is so fascinating that once you have begun to read it, you are no longer able to let it go out of your hand. I have heard of a certain Catholic who could not cease humming over it in his sick bed until he died with the version on his breast!

Another consolation to me is that my version is read and appreciated even by non-Christians. Yu Yu-Jen, perhaps the greatest living calligrapher of China, has often picked up verses from the Psalms in writing for others.

Aside from the publication of the Psalms, God made my

wife and myself into instruments of many conversions, especially among our relatives. My elder brother Joseph and his family (about fifteen in all, including the grandchildren), my sister Gertrude and her family, my wife's younger sister and her family, my wife's nephews and nieces, and quite a few friends and their families came into the Church, one batch after another. One day, when some new converts were being baptized in the Church of St. Thérèse, the late Bishop of Shanghai, Msgr. Haouisée, made a casual remark to me: "By the time you go to the Vatican, you will have made a whole rosary of converts!" When I was on board the S.S. *Joffre* I counted the fish in my net; they were fifty-one, but then one had already gone to Heaven! That particular one was my beloved sister Gertrude.

When, at the end of the war, I returned with my family to Shanghai (in May 1946), I found my sister sick in bed. Her philosophy of life had entirely changed—you may remember how she had felt about the question of bribery, when I was a judge. Nothing is purifying like suffering. She was willing to embrace the Catholic faith, and was instructed. My good friend Father John Monsterleet, S. J., baptized her in June, giving her the name of Gertrude. Then she was confirmed, had Confession, Holy Communion, and finally Extreme Unction. Five Sacraments in a little over a month! The Extreme Unction she received at the hands of Father Mark Tennien on the midnight of August 3; and she passed away in the small hours of August 5, Feast of Our Lady of the Snows. As Father Tennien has written something about the last rites, I will let him speak:

Late one post-war night, when Shanghai's wandering bootblack had curled up on the sidewalks to sleep until daybreak, I was keeping vigil with an interesting book. The telephone bell suddenly startled me. Who could be calling at such an hour?

A soft, deep voice moved rapidly in worried urgency: "Father, my sister is very close to the end. I know you stay up late, so I called you. Would you be so kind as to come and give her the last rites?"

"Certainly, I'll be glad to come."

"Then I'll be right over to get you in my car."

I slipped on my cassock and went to the chapel for the holy oils and the Communion pyx. A little man in long Chinese gown and cloth shoes quietly slipped through the door and knelt in prayer. This Chinese gentleman, who fingered his beads as the car sped through the narrow streets, was John C. H. Wu, China's Minister to the Holy See. We sped to the bedside of his dying sister, who had been converted by Wu a month previously, and I administered the last rites to the sick woman.

Six weeks later, the deceased sister's other relatives, fourteen in all, became Catholics. "They were so impressed with the last rites and the funeral," Wu explained, "that they asked for instruction."

However, the Father has omitted some interesting conversation which he had with my sister and which I interpreted for them. "Tell your sister," said the good priest, "that when she goes to Heaven, she must remember to pray for me." I interpreted accordingly, adding, *"Sister, don't forget that the name of the priest is Tennien!"*

"Yes, I'll remember him," was her answer. Then I said to her, "Sister, you are going to Heaven to see God. Don't fail to visit us. Help your family from Heaven. Soon I expect to go to Rome to see the Holy Father. Pray that we may be reunited in Heaven." She nodded and appeared very happy. So wonderful is the grace of God!

Afterwards, I heard that Father Tennien was making thousands of converts in South China. I should be surprised if my sister's prayers had nothing to do with that remarkable fruitfulness of his apostolate.

On September 8, my appointment was formally announced. I sailed on December 17 with my whole family (except Thomas, who was married) on the *S.S. Joffre*, bringing the manuscripts of the New Testament with me. I had just completed the ninth year of my Catholic life.

In Rome I continued to revise the manuscripts with the help of Monsignor Lokuang; we also went to consult on special points such authorities on the Holy Scriptures as the late Father Vosté, Msgr. Ricciotti, and Father Dyson. In 1948, my version got the *Nihil Obstat* from Dom Lou, the *Imprimatur* from Archbishop Yupin, the Approbation from the Congregation de Propaganda Fide, and a Letter-Preface from the living Vicar of Christ himself! In 1949, it was printed in Hongkong. It was dedicated to Our Lady of the Rosary. After all, it was she who helped me in weaving a seamless Chinese tunic for Christ. Dom Lou wrote to Msgr. Lokuang: "I don't see any reason why this translation should not become the authorized version. His use of the classical phrases and idioms furnishes the key to a living synthesis of the East and the West, a synthesis like a seamless cloth, like the pieces of coal melted into one fire in the furnace of Divine Love. Could all this have been attained without the inspiration of the Holy Ghost?"

Why have I quoted this? Is it because I wanted to show how clever I am? Well, one does not become a saint and go to Heaven by cleverness, while sanctification is my sole ambition now, and the Beatific Vision my sole objective. No, it is not for vanity that I have quoted these words, it is to show that the Blessed Virgin has not failed me any more than she has failed anyone else who has appealed sincerely to her for help. If you compare the above words of Dom Lou, who did not know at all in what words I had prayed to our Holy Mother, with the words of prayer recorded in the preceding pages, you will find that every word of my prayer has been answered in letter and in spirit! As for myself, I have not forgotten for a moment what St. Paul so candidly said: "*For God Who commanded light to shine out of darkness, has shone in our hearts, to give enlightenment concerning the knowledge of the glory of God, shining on the face of Christ Jesus. But we carry this treasure in vessels of clay, to show that the abundance of the power is God's and not ours.*" I should be a liar if I denied that I am a vessel of clay; but I should equally be a liar if I said that the light of God has not shone in my heart, or that the Blessed Virgin has not helped in my work. For where there is the Mother, there is the Holy Spirit.

20. *THE DIPLOMACY OF LOVE*

It was the 16th of February, 1947—Quinquagesima Sunday. The weather was fine; the skies were smiling; my heart was singing for joy. I was to present my credentials to the Holy Father, Pius XII. It was the first time in the diplomatic history of the Holy See that a Catholic ever represented a non-Catholic nation.

After presenting my letters of credit, I made a speech before His Holiness in conformity to diplomatic usage. I spoke in English, and His Holiness responded in English. My speech was as follows:

Holy Father:

It is a great honor for me to come to this "mountain of myrrh and hill of frankincense" to present to Your Holiness the credential letter, wherewith I am charged by His Excellency, the President of the Republic of China, to represent the Chinese Government at the Holy See. I am keenly aware of the importance of my mission, and of my own unworthiness of it; for my mission is nothing less than to confirm and increase the intimate relation between the greatest spiritual power of human society and a people of the oldest oriental culture. The wedding between the two will be such a momentous event in the history of this, God's world, that the marriage of Cana would be viewed in the light of eternity as its prefiguration.

With States as with individuals, true friendship is built upon mutual understanding and sympathy. Let me assure Your Holiness that no nation appreciates more than China Your Holiness's message that Peace, whether it takes the form of interior peace of the individual soul, or of peace in the family, or of peace in a State, or of peace in the world, can only be achieved through love. No nation sympathizes more deeply with Your Holiness's most candid query: "What age has been, for all its technical and purely civic progress, more tormented than ours by spiritual emptiness, and deep-felt interior poverty?" (*Summi Pontificatus*). For China, as a nation, has lived long enough to learn by experience that in the long run it is Spirit, not Matter, that triumphs; Right, not Might, that prevails. This historical insight has taught China in many a national crisis to hope against hope; it is the secret spring that keeps China perennially young in outlook and spirit in spite of her age. And it is thanks to this same historical insight that her last victory has not inflated her with pride and self-complacency, but has, on the contrary, made her more conscious than ever of her dependence upon the Providence of God, and more eager than ever to rebuild her war-torn house upon the rock of love and justice. The President of the Republic of China, who is a sincere believer in Christ and a great lover of the Holy Scriptures, has taken to heart these inspired lines of the Psalms:

> Unless the Lord build the house,
> They labor in vain that build it.
> Unless the Lord keeps the city,
> The guard keeps watch in vain.

Your Holiness has repeatedly stressed the importance of the

law of universal charity—"of that charity which alone can consolidate peace by extinguishing hatred and softening envies and dissensions" (*Summi Pontificatus*). This again finds an echo in the heart of China. For the traditional Chinese philosophy of life teaches that "all men are brothers." Thus, the water is there in the old water-pots, waiting with eager patience to be turned into wine. May our Blessed Mother hasten once more the coming of the hour of Jesus! I will not enlarge upon this vision, for fear that my fervor transport me beyond the duties of my state. For in imitation of St. Paul, I would say: When I am beside myself, it is to God; when I am sober, it is as an official representative of my country.

Before I come to a conclusion, I cannot help adding a few words on behalf of my country in appreciation of what the Holy Catholic Church has done for our people. His Excellency President Chiang, in his book on *The Destiny of China*, has referred to the great contribution that Father Matteo Ricci, Ven. Paul Hsu, and their contemporaries made to the scientific education of China. The missionaries, during all these centuries, have been like zephyrs carrying with them the perfumes from the garden of Christ. The merits of those loyal soldiers of Christ can be told only in Heaven. Of recent years, the people of China have learned to admire more and more the unflinching moral courage with which the Holy See has stood for justice and worked for peace. The establishment of the diplomatic relation between China and the Holy See is but a tangible sign of this admiration. And this admiration was changed into sincere gratitude when Your Holiness with a special kindness created the first Chinese Cardinal, the Catholic Hierarchy and the Apostolic Internuntiature in China, and, on the top of it all, beatified the Chinese Martyrs. This gratitude has been reinforced when the Chinese people remember what great services the native Catholics and the Missionaries rendered to the nation during the war. We are convinced that during the period of our national reconstruction, the Catholics will continue to give their best contributions, for, as Your Holiness has on some occasion observed, a good Catholic must be a good citizen. It is my

sincere hope that there will soon be a great spiritual renaissance in our country, and the Church in China will be a
flourishing garden "full of pleasant fruits, new and old." For
I am confident that, with the wise guidance and constant
encouragement from Your Holiness, the Church in China
will produce many "a scribe steeped in the Kingdom of
Heaven" who will "bring forth out of his treasure new things
and old," and transmute them in the crucible of white-hot
Love into that Beauty which is yesterday, today, and ever
the same.

With that admiration, gratitude and hope, I am going to
begin my mission. I will do my best, with the grace of God,
to strengthen the good relation between the Holy See and
my country, and I am confident that the benevolence of
Your Holiness will certainly alleviate and sweeten my grave
burden.

In the atmosphere of warmest cordiality, I present to Your
Holiness the best wishes of His Excellency, the President of
the Republic of China, for a long and prosperous reign.

The Holy Father responded as follows:

Mr. Minister,

In the determination of His Excellency the President of
the Chinese Republic to entrust you with the high office of
Envoy Extraordinary and Minister Plenipotentiary to the
Holy See, We discern a gesture whose deep significance can
escape no one.

It is a gesture of particular consideration which will not
only be appreciated in all its importance by the entire
Catholic world, but above all, will it be greeted by the
Catholics of China with profound satisfaction and lively
gratitude.

Hence, We heartily welcome Your Excellency as a son and
representative of a people of more than 400 millions, whose
country was the cradle of Asia's oriental civilization. After
thousands of years and despite all sorts of trials and misfor-
tunes they have kept their vigor and their youth—for which
not a few other nations could envy them; and aware of their

reserves of material and spiritual energy, they look to the future with that calmness and security, which is characteristic only of the strong and the brave.

At the same time We greet Your Excellency as a loyal son of the Church, whose journey to the Catholic faith was illuminated by Dante's *Divine Comedy* and whose thought and actions unite in an exemplary way the love of God and the devotion to your native land.

The noble words you have just pronounced in the presentation of your credential letters reveal, together with your religious and patriotic sentiments, a thorough and sincere acknowledgment of the serious duties that are common to mankind.

There is no place where such an acknowledgment could find a truer echo than in the House of the Father of Christianity, Who cherishes an equal benevolence for all peoples regardless of any limitations of time and space, of origin and language, of race and culture.

But in every country the more noble, farseeing and mature minds have learned in the school of suffering in the recent past that despite all their differences they have a common element so essential that no one can tamper with it without imperiling the very foundations and the prosperity of his own people.

For this reason We regard the exalted sentiments of Your Excellency as the reflection of the mind of a people that after sombre experiences in the past, rises to a wider and truer knowledge of reciprocal functions and duties, determined to adapt its thought, its will and its action in the international field, to the moral concept that each member of the great family of nations be assured of what belongs to it—*suum cuique tribuere.*

As an outstanding jurist and an active member of Legislative Commissions and International Conferences, Your Excellency is in a better position than many others to judge how far the present results obtained by the rulers of the nations concerning the fundamentals of a secure and lasting peace have satisfied or deluded the legitimate expectations of humanity. It is because We observe that Your Excellency, an authority in post-war international questions, affirms principles of brotherhood and love among nations as indispensable factors of international justice, that Our hope increases that such sentiments be realized and that they may overcome the opposing forces that aim at preventing or delaying the advent of a true peace.

The fact that, in the presence of representatives of the whole world, and for the first time in the history of the Church, We chose to elect a son of China to be a member of the Sacred College; the establishment there of the episcopal Hierarchy; the privilege that was Ours in raising to the honors of the altar a glorious band of Chinese Martyrs; Our sending to your beloved country an Internuncio Apostolic, and now the entrusting of Your Excellency as the first Catholic Minister Plenipotentiary with such an important mission in the center of Christendom: all these show the progress and the happy development in the relations between the Holy See and China. We have no doubt that the value of this for the welfare of the entire nation will be recognized even by those who do not belong the Catholic Church.

The mission of Your Excellency now consists in promoting and extending what has been so successfully attained. To your task you bring rich gifts of mind and heart united with an experience that has been acquired and perfected through many years of tireless labor. You are beginning with such lofty sentiments that We feel particular pleasure in assuring you that in the exercise of your high office you will ever find in Us the most ready and benevolent support.

While We reciprocate with equal cordiality the kindly good wishes you brought Us from His Excellency the President of the Chinese Republic, Our thoughts go out with paternal affection to Our Beloved Sons and Daughters of China, to all of whom We lovingly impart Our Apostolic Benediction.

And as the Colonnade of the Vatican Basilica opens its large arms towards the East, so We now lift Our Hands towards the Orient and invoke the protection of the Almighty over the rugged and arduous journey of the Chinese

people from twilight to dawn, which We hope will soon
shine forth in a secure internal and external peace.[1]

After the exchange of speeches, the Holy Father led me into
his private study, and we had a tête-à-tête for twenty minutes.
My very first impression of him was so profound that I almost
could not speak. He appealed to me as father and mother at
the same time. He was not only dignified, but humble, tender
and most democratic. The first question he asked me was,
"Do you find anything objectionable in my speech?" I was
taken aback by his extraordinary humility. I never had expected that question. So I at once lowered my eyes and
mused for some moments before I could make any answer.
At last I lifted up my eyes towards him and said, "I think
the speech is perfect. The only thing is that Your Holiness
has spoken too well of me." The Holy Father smiled most
sweetly, and we talked about other things more strictly
diplomatic.

My speech on that occasion was well received by the public.
My good friend Dr. Frank Buchman, who happened to be in
Rome at that time, told me that some of his friends in the
Vatican circles were remarking that they had not heard such
a diplomatic speech in twenty-five years! That was perhaps
because I was such an amateur in diplomacy. Mine was the
diplomacy of love.

A few weeks later, Monsignor Montini, the Acting Secretary of State, appointed a day for me to present my whole
family to the Holy Father. He said that a photograph would
be taken of the Holy Father together with my family. I
asked if this was customary. He said that it was not. Then
I said, "Don't you think it would be better to skip photo-

[1] L'Osservatore Romano, February 17, 18, 1947.

graphing? The Holy Father is busy enough; and if every diplomat wants to have his family photographed with His Holiness, it would add another unnecessary burden upon him." What was my surprise when the Monsignor replied, "Don't worry about that. A diplomat must have at least thirteen children before he can cite the present case as a precedent!"

When the day came, I presented my wife and twelve of our children together with a daughter-in-law and a godson to the Holy Father. We were accompanied by my Ecclesiastical Counsellor, Monsignor Stanislaus Lokuang. That was a most informal audience. The Holy Father was in his most natural mood. On seeing such a big family, he was extremely delighted, and complimented me in the warmest of terms. I said, "Holy Father, it is all the merit of my wife." But the Holy Father, with his finger pointing directly at me, replied, "But you, too!"

When the time came for photographing, the Holy Father stood together with us. But I felt that this was not quite right. So I moved a chair to him and insisted that he should sit down like a father. In doing so, I was solely motivated by my Chinese sense of filial respect. But as it turned out, it became one of the factors that made the picture unique. I was told that it was the first time that a Pope was ever pictured sitting with a private family! Poor Holy Father, he was caught in the meshes of Chinese courtesy!

The Holy Father's affection for me and for my family has been growing with time, and, I trust, will grow to eternity. Only recently I have received a most touching letter that Monsignor Montini has written me in the name of his Holiness. I take the liberty of quoting a paragraph:

His Holiness was deeply touched by the warmth of filial

affection and regard to which your letter gave expression. The Supreme Pontiff was likewise much consoled to know that you and your beloved family make a daily remembrance of him and of his special Holy Year intentions in your prayer. As an earnest of his heartfelt gratitude and paternal benevolence the Holy Father cordially imparts to you and Mrs. Wu and to the members of your scattered family his special Apostolic Blessing.

On the purely natural plane, as I have said, a big family can be a source of deep pathos. As the proverb goes, "No feast in this world can last forever." The members of my family are now scattered all over the world, from China to Ecuador. But the Mystical Body of Christ binds all of us together. No matter where we are, the love of the living Vicar of Christ broods over us all.

21. MY LAST TRIP TO CHINA

On February 19, 1949, I received a telegram from Dr. Sun Fo, who was then the Prime Minister of China, calling me back for urgent consultation. He asked me to be in Canton before the end of the month. At that time, the country was already in the worst of conditions, as the Reds were nearing Nanking. It was dangerous to return to China then, and furthermore to leave the family in a foreign land under such circumstances was certainly agonizing. However I did not want to play the coward by refusing this challenge. Even though it was not likely that I could render any valuable help, I wanted to see the actual situation with my own eyes. So I made arrangements to fly on the 21st. On the 20th, I wrote a letter to the Holy Father, asking him:

O Holy Father, pray for me that in whatever I may do, in whatever I may say, in the world of politics, I may be guided by the Holy Spirit; that I may face my tasks fear-

334

lessly in the interests of love and justice and for the glory of Christ and His Church. By nature, I am a weak child, afraid of danger and sacrifice. Only the grace of God can make me strong and ready to make sacrifices whenever they are called for.

I started at midnight on the 21st. It was a dark and gloomy night, symbolic of the night of my soul. My family and many friends saw me off. Monsignor Lokuang wrote a poem of farewell to me, which read like a funeral dirge more than anything else.

> The steel wings reflect the chill lamplights.
> He waves his hat in front of the departing plane.
> Leaving his family in a foreign country,
> He returns alone to the homeland.

> No moon peeps from the clouds, the night is at its
>   darkest.
> He starts for the homeland by way of the air.
> Fog fills the sky; sorrow fills his heart.
> Relying upon the Providence of God, his soul rests
>   in peace.

I was booked for Hongkong, but on the day my plane arrived there it was so foggy that the plane could not land, so the pilot decided to fly northward to Shanghai. We arrived at Shanghai in the evening, and I took a taxi directly to my home in the Jessfield Road, where my eldest son, Thomas, was living with his family. They were so surprised to see me back that there was more astonishment than welcome. I found that Thomas' wife had given birth a few days ago to another male child. I went upstairs to look at him. As I looked at him, he burst into a fit of crying. A few days later, Thomas told me, "Daddy, will you please come up to baptize the baby?

I am afraid he is dying." I baptized him, and gave him the name of Bernard. Next day he died.

As my arrival was reported in the papers, three of my best friends came to visit me the following morning. They were lawyers, my former colleagues at the Comparative Law School of China. The first thing they said was, "Do you know why you are called back?"

"No," I replied.

"But we know," they said. "You will be asked to join the Cabinet as Minister of Justice. We have come to beg you *not* to accept it."

"Why?" I asked.

"The Cabinet has reached the height of unpopularity and is bound to fall," they said. "Why should you plunge yourself blindly into it, thus inviting calamity and disgrace on yourself?"

I replied, "Don't you know I am a Christian, and don't mind any calamity or disgrace so long as I am doing the right thing? If everybody stays off when the Government is collapsing, it will only hasten its fall."

They were angry at my stubbornness and said, "Do what you like, Dr. Wu. But if you accept, please don't expect us to join you. Your knowledge of the situation is not up to date."

In the meantime, Dr. Sun Fo was disappointed by my landing at the wrong place. In a few days, however, he came to Nanking, and we met there. He said to me, "I am so glad that you have come. You see, I have been Prime Minister for two months, but my Cabinet is still half empty. I intended to include you at the very beginning, but I thought I had better spare you because you have such a big family. But now people are criticizing the Cabinet for its emptiness. That was why I wanted you to come back to help me. I am not pressing it upon you, but if you are willing to make the sacrifice, please choose between Education and Justice."

"Don't talk of sacrifice to me," I said. "I am a Christian, and sacrifice is my vocation. I will choose the Ministry of Justice. But listen, I have some conditions to submit."

"Say it!" he said.

"I have three conditions," I began. "The first condition is absolute non-interference on the part of any of my superiors. Neither you nor the Generalissimo nor the Acting President will be allowed to interfere with judicial independence. I have no concrete evidences of such interferences, but what I want to do is make judicial independence a sacred principle, so that a really solid foundation of government by the rule of law may be laid down, and a living tradition may grow out of it."

Upon hearing this, Dr. Sun clapped his hands like a little child, and exclaimed, "Good! Good!"

"In social dealings," I continued, "you know I have always been courteous and yielding, but when I ride on the horse of Justice, you may be surprised to find a steeliness in me. You did not know me as a judge; at that time I had absolutely no respect of persons."

"Understood!" he said. "Now what is your second condition?"

"My second condition is with regard to the salary of the judges. As you know, judges have little social life. They are almost like cloistered monks. Their livelihood must be amply provided for. Other officers have more friends, and in times of need they can borrow money. In the case of a judge, he cannot go out to borrow money without losing his dignity. He must guard his integrity with the utmost jealousy. That is why in some Western countries the judges are treated as a class apart."

Dr. Sun did not clap his hands this time, but became rather pensive. After reflecting for a few moments, he said, "I think this can be done. Just now the Ministry of Finance is trying to issue silver coins, and you may be sure that the judicial officers will be given the first consideration."

"My third condition," I went on, "is with reference to the education of the prisoners. As you know, I am a Christian, and all men are my brothers and all women my sisters, and all the criminals are my fellow-sinners. When they are sent into the prison it is the Law that does it, not I or any man. The Law does not forbid me to turn all the prisons into training schools of character and trade. For this I do not require a single cent from the Budget. I will call upon the cooperation of the missionaries and priests of all religions and of all sects to help in educating the prisoners. I think they will only be too glad to render this service."

Upon hearing this, Dr. Sun was so happy that he almost danced from his sofa to his desk, and said, "John, in a few days your name will be announced as the Minister of Justice!"

Then I thought of those friends who had advised me so strongly against accepting it. I said to Dr. Sun, "Wait a minute! I cannot do the work all alone. I must get my Vice-Ministers and other helpers. Let me return to Shanghai for a few days so that I can secure the services of my friends."

He agreed, but suggested that before I went to Shanghai I should as a matter of courtesy pay a call on the Acting President Mr. Li Chung-zen. I phoned my old friend Kan Chiai-hou, who was a personal secretary or adviser to Mr. Li, and asked him to arrange for an interview. The following day I went to see the Acting President. It was the first time we had met. But I went directly into the subject, and told him what I had said to the Prime Minister, repeating all my conditions to him. His response was very warm and spontaneous. When he heard my first condition, he said, "Tsai Hou Mu Yu!" which means, "Nothing can be better!" "Just the other day," he said, "I announced to a group of my friends exactly the same principle. I told them that there is no Emperor in a Republic, and that Law is the only Emperor." The other conditions were also acceptable to him, and he pledged his wholehearted support of my program. He went to the door with me and watched me disappear into a jeep.

I went immediately to Shanghai and invited the friends who had advised me against accepting the post to come to have a talk. When I told them that I had accepted it, they looked aghast without saying a word. They did not say it, but judging from the expression on their faces I was pretty sure they were thinking in their hearts, "What a hopeless man!" However, I continued to report to them all the conversations I had with Dr. Sun and the Acting President. To my great surprise their faces began to beam, and after I had concluded my narration they exclaimed, "If you go into it with this spirit, the spirit of a martyr, let it be known to you that we are no cowards either! We will all help you." So it was all settled.

I stayed in Shanghai for a week and had happy reunions with my friends and relatives. The priests and sisters were especially happy to see me back. Those days were one of the happiest periods of my life; and although I had left my wife and children in Rome, I was not the least homesick. I realized that to be a Catholic is to be a member of a big family, a family co-terminous with the whole universe.

After a few days, the Cabinet fell, before Dr. Sun had time to put up my name. I was neither happy nor sorrowful at the news. With the grace of God I had secured a moral victory, and that was all that mattered. I told my friends, "You see it pays to be generous!" They all laughed.

In the meantime, the political situation was becoming worse every day. Friends advised me to go back to Rome immediately. But how could I leave China without saying goodbye to my dear elder brother Joseph in Ningpo and to my good friend President Chiang Kai-shek, who was living a retired life in his home town near Ningpo? So I took a boat to Ningpo, accompanied by a group of young folks, including my son Thomas, my nephew Joseph Cheng and my godson Paul Chu. We had a wonderful trip. We visited all the places that were dear to me, such as the schools I had attended, the old house I was born in, the old relatives I had not seen for years, the city temple where my father was allegedly deified, and finally the Catholic churches of Ningpo, which I had never entered before, although they had been there even at the time of my birth. I was saying Goodbye to my home town; for it might well be my last visit to it. During that visit I saw much of my brother. He is still in Ningpo with his family. After the summer of that year, we did not hear from each other for a whole year, due to the difficulties in postal communications. Then I got a message to him. I have had a reply from him, in which he said, "As soon as I got your letter, I wept for joy and went to the church bringing the letter with me and thanking the Blessed Virgin for everything." He also tells me that the spiritual life of his whole family is still growing, but the most devout of all is his son Chu K'ang, who is dumb and deaf. He often goes to the church, praying silently. He works hard to support his parents. This dumb boy is truly a filial child of God.

When the President heard of my arrival in Ningpo, he was so kind as to send his car to fetch me to Feng Hua, about thirty miles from the city. I presented to him a manuscript copy of the version of the New Testament which he had helped to translate. I said to him, "I am just fifty now, and at fifty a man should know the will of God with regard to his own life-mission. I think I shall devote the rest of my years to education and the spiritual life. I shall no longer waste my time in politics." To which he answered, "Oh, that is wonderful!"

At the suggestion of his secretary, I had a picture taken with the President. Two chairs were placed in the courtyard; but he sat down first, taking the chair on the right. Now, according to Chinese etiquette, the left side is higher than the right. I refused to sit down in the other chair; I begged him to move. No, he would not, but just said, "Please sit down." I had to sit down. To obey the order of the host is better than to stand on ceremony, as a Chinese proverb has it. He was wonderfully calm and affable, in spite of all the adversities and trials he was going through. He is truly a man of deep spiritual culture.

I spent about a week in Ningpo, then returned to Shanghai. From Shanghai, I flew to Hongkong. There I met again my dear friend and confessor Father Nicholas Maestrini. I handed over to him all the manuscripts of the translation of the New Testament to be published in the name of the Catholic Truth Society of Hongkong. I flew to Canton, where Dr. Sun Fo had returned with his whole family. After a few days, I flew back to Hongkong; and from Hongkong I flew back to Rome, arriving there on the 20th of April, just two months from the day of my departure. The next morning I attended the wedding Mass of my second daughter, Margaret, and Stanley Ho.

As I have already said somewhere, practically all the important events of my life came in a most casual way. My coming to Hawaii is no exception to the rule. Sometime in the summer of 1948, Dr. Gregg M. Sinclair and Mrs. Sinclair, who were making their world-tour, came to Rome. One day, I received a telephone call from Dr. Sinclair, saying, "Hello, Doctor, this is Sinclair of the University of Hawaii. Do you remember me?" Yes, I had seen him several years ago in China. He then expressed the wish to come to see me. I invited the couple to a tea party. During the party our conversation turned to the interesting people we had known. Then he asked me who were some of the new friends I had made in Rome. I mentioned among others Jacques Maritain whom I had seen a great deal, saying, however, that I missed him because he had resigned his diplomatic post to take up a professorship at Princeton. Incidentally I remarked that in a way I was glad that he had taken that step, because really the life of a teacher was much more interesting than the life of a diplomat. Then Dr. Sinclair asked, "Would you take the same step? We would be glad to invite you to be our Visiting Professor of Chinese Philosophy. Or would you think it a demotion for you?"

"What? A demotion?" I replied, "I should say it would be a promotion!" Two days later we invited the Sinclairs to a dinner, and they showed us some movies of Hawaii. Both my wife and my children were greatly impressed, and I got more and more interested in coming to Honolulu. I accepted the invitation right then. It was agreed that I was to come for the year 1949–50.

At that time, the political situation of China was still quite normal. The reason why I was willing to quit diplomatic life was that there were too many parties and other functions to leave any time for private study, and study, after all, has been the dominant interest of my life.

In the Spring of 1949, the University of Hawaii sent me

a formal invitation, and we made preparations to come over. In early July, about two weeks before our boat was to sail, Archbishop John Mitty of San Francisco and Bishop J. J. Sweeney of Hawaii came to Rome in order to make their five-yearly reports to the Holy See. At that time, Archbishop Paul Yupin was also in Rome, staying with us in the Legation. He told me that he knew the Archbishop of San Francisco and Bishop Sweeney, and he desired to introduce me to them. Now it happened that I had just been appointed by the Holy Father to be a Papal Chamberlain of the Cape and Sword. So Archbishop Yupin thought it was a proper occasion for a celebration, to which Archbishop Mitty and Bishop Sweeney should be invited. But I said, "Look here, I have no spare money to spend on the vestments of a Papal Chamberlain, and a function like that would cost hundreds of dollars. Better skip it." But the Archbishop was so kind as to undertake to make a present of the vestments to me, and Monsignor Lokuang undertook to pay for the expenses of the party. As it did not cost me anything, I allowed them to do it, with my heart full of gratitude. On the day of celebration, Archbishop Mitty put the cape on me, Bishop Sweeney placed the cap on my head, and Archbishop Yupin gave me the sword. Suddenly an idea dawned upon my mind: I was predestined to go to Honolulu. The presence of Bishop Sweeney was a sure sign from God that He was pleased with my decision. Lit up by this light, the whole function acquired a new significance.

My stay in Honolulu has been most fruitful in intellectual and spiritual life and in friendships. In many ways, it is the beginning of a new chapter of my life. I am yet too near to it to write about it. Life goes on, and can never be brought up to date. All that I say now is that my experiences here have deepened my knowledge of the providential ways of God and confirmed my trust in Him.

Epilogue

"GOD HAS BEEN GRACIOUS"

An English Carmelite Sister, herself a convert, once wrote me that although a convert I had never really been a "pagan"! The whole passage from her letter (dated August 24, 1948) is worth quoting: "Intuition tells me we have never been really 'pagans' or 'heretics.' The very inmost—the most precious—of our souls has always, consciously or unconsciously, asleep or awake, sought the Face of Jesus, seeking *truly* the Truth and catching glimpses of it in all values. Sometimes perhaps captious as wilful 'children' but always in love with our God,—because in His Infinite Mercy He loved us first."

Yes, as I look back upon these fifty-odd years of my life, it appears all of one piece, the keynote being Love. My whole life has been surrounded by God's Love. All the scattered leaves of my life have been gathered together by His loving hand and bound into an harmonious volume. Indeed, the

Spirit of Love has arranged all things sweetly. Even in human relations I have received more love than I have given. But if I am a debtor to men, how much more am I a debtor to God! This is why I have always had a feeling of being a bankrupt. It is not a comfortable feeling, but I know too that this feeling itself comes from above, the very salt that the loving Father infuses into me in order to preserve all the other flavors. Speaking of certain souls, St. Teresa of Avila wrote, "Sometimes the many favors they receive leave them overwhelmed, and afraid lest they be like an overladen ship sinking to the bottom of the sea." This is how I feel. Yes, sometimes I feel so utterly helpless in requiting the love of God that my very helplessness makes me turn to Christ. I say to Him, "Beloved Lord, pay all my debts!" And He has done it once for all and every day anew!

I think it is not too much to say that in the Chinese soul one quality stands out above others, and that is the sense of gratitude. The very institution of "ancestor-worship" (this is a misnomer, for in reality it is nothing more than the *remembrance* of one's ancestors) is based upon the sentiment of gratitude towards the origin of one's physical being. This feeling of gratitude can easily be transferred to its proper place, that is, in our relations with God, the Father of all mankind, the Living Source of all things physical and spiritual. When a Chinese is converted, it is but natural that gratitude should constitute the dominant note of his spirituality. I think it is true in my own case.

My gratitude towards God has something of a wholeness about it, which does not admit of analysis. Furthermore it is a growing process; for the more I know of the ways of His loving Providence, the more I adore Him, and the more grateful I feel. Even in the days of greatest trials I have had an implicit confidence in His infinite Love and Wisdom. I may not know His purpose in sending the crosses; but He knows what He is doing, and that is enough for me. I have often been disturbed but never mystified. I am too mystical to be mystified. I have taken to heart the words of St. Paul: "Now we know that for those who love God all things work together unto good" (Rom. 8.28). My only worry is that I do not love God enough. As for all other things, such as prosperity and adversity, honor and disgrace, life and death, whatever may happen, Christ seems to be constantly whispering to my interior ear, "Fear not. It is I." The Chinese trust in Heaven is bred in the bones and runs in the blood. There is a saying on the lips of every Chinese: "Men have a thousand plans, but Heaven has only one plan." Here is another: "Heaven does not drive any man to the wall." You simply cannot trust Heaven too much. It is true that many Chinese tend towards fatalism. But the trouble with the fatalists is not that they have too much trust, but that they put their trust at a wrong place, and this is due to the fact that their conception of Heaven is none too clear. If they had conceived Heaven as the Loving Father of all creation, a Father who is too considerate towards His children to deprive them of their free will in order to compel them to obedience, they would have arrived at the necessity of our cooperation with His will. At least, this was how Confucius conceived of Heaven; and I think that most Chinese think the way he did. The Chinese are too practical and industrious a race to be purely fatalistic and quietist. The proverb which is most frequently quoted is: "The making of plans depends upon man; but their success depends upon Heaven." I submit that this comes very near to Christianity. St. Ignatius would have approved of the saying wholeheartedly. In fact, I have heard a good friend of mine, Father Martin J. Burke, who was a former missionary in South China, quote the very proverb to me in the Cantonese dialect, in illustration of the Christian doctrine of free will and predestination.

However, there is no denying that without the light of Revelation a Chinese is in danger of becoming a fatalist, just as an Occidental who has forgotten his Christianity is in danger of becoming an activist. As Monsignor Fulton Sheen has so keenly observed, "It is apt to be an error of the Eastern World to think that God does everything and man does nothing; it is apt to be the error of the Western World to believe that man does everything and God does nothing. The Oriental thus ends in Fatalism, and the Occidental in Pride. Fatalism can stand catastrophe better than Pride, for Fatalism can take a disaster in its stride, but to the proud Humanist, disaster is the negation and overthrow of his whole philosophy of life."[1] To my mind, the one is just as bad as the other. But in view of the fact that the Western influence has practically permeated all corners of Asia, there is no question that the virtue of trust in Providence has a higher market-price than the doctrine of strenuous action. (You see how I talk like the son of a banker.) In his *Christian Perfection and Contemplation*, Father R. Garrigou-Lagrange lays the greatest emphasis on the spirit of recollection as against what is called the "strenuous life." "As a matter of fact," he says, "it is not life, but a fever, a deadly illness; it is materialism in action. After turning away from God and from the true life of the soul, it seeks its equivalent in multiplied and increasingly intense activity, which is often a complete loss; for the finite can never equal or become the Infinite. To a true contemplative, people who are devoted to an exaggerated intensity of life must seem like walking corpses; dead men running, as an old ballad says."[2]

[1] *Philosophy of Religion*, Appleton (New York, 1948), p. 253.
[2] Herder (1937), pp. 391-2.

When I first came into contact with the Western world in Shanghai, my head swam on seeing the ceaseless motions of the motor-cars and the streetcars, the bicycles and rickshaws. I felt as though I were in the midst of a gigantic circus. Did happiness depend upon so much hurried movement? Was I not happy in Ningpo, angling on the bank of a river, flying kites in a wide field, playing shuttlecocks in the courtyard, or cutting capers in front of my mother? But now I had to watch my every step in order to keep from being run down. It was all like a much-ado-about-nothing, and it was more a tragedy than a comedy! Perhaps my feeling was mostly due to my lack of adaptation to the "modern" environment. My own children have adapted themselves perfectly to it. Practically all of them are mechanically minded. They take to driving as naturally as I took to rowing a boat. As to bicycling, which I have never mastered except in my dreams, they can do it almost as easily as I walk. It is therefore quite natural that their valuation of the Western civilization differs from mine. I am open-minded enough to admit that my judgment is biased in favor of a quiet life in the country. But one thing that I can never subscribe to is the crazy idea that our happiness depends upon an abundance of external possessions and exterior activities. I once wrote: "To a happy soul, pleasures are no longer necessary; to a pleasure-seeking soul, happiness is not yet possible." With all the marvellous progress that natural sciences have made, humanity has not yet found happiness, and that is why it is seeking pleasures so desperately and trying to forget itself in deadening activities. O Humanity, Humanity, you are running fast, but you are running in the wrong direction!

The other night I was out in a party, and a professor of chemistry asked me, "What do you think is the best definition of happiness?" I answered, "Peace of mind." He was impressed by the answer, but I did not have a chance to expound it. In my view, peace of mind is the result of complete self-realization, and no one can realize himself fully unless he is first awakened to his own insufficiency. As it is, Humanity is seeking to realize itself apart from God. As Jeremias put it, "Be astonished, O ye heavens, and ye gates thereof, be very desolate, saith the Lord. For my people have two evils. They have forsaken me, the fountain of living water, and have digged to themselves cisterns, broken cisterns, that can hold no water" (2.12). These words seem to have more point now than when Jeremias announced them. No one has offered a better diagnosis of unhappiness and frustration than Frank Sheed. "Unhappiness," he said, "is always unused or ill-used spiritual energy; and man has within himself so many energies made for God, that, lacking God, these energies cannot be satisfied, and can only turn in upon man and rend him." [3] He further said, "For fullness of being, man must have a knowledge of and a co-operation with that which maintains him in existence, that which is the very condition of his be-ing at all . . . There is an abyss of nothingness at the very heart of our being, and we had better counter it by the fullest possible use of our kinship with the Infinite, who is also at the very heart of our being." [4] Our pilgrimage is therefore neither eastwards nor westwards, but inwards; and this is what I call moving beyond East and West.

It is not fair to Christianity to call it "Western." Christianity is universal. In fact, the West has something to learn from the East, for, on the whole, the East has gone farther in its *natural* contemplation than the West has in its *supernatural* contemplation. To take just one instance, the average Buddhist in China knows something about the three stages

[3] *Theology and Sanity*, Sheed & Ward (New York), p. 337.
[4] *Ibid.*, p. 330.

of Abstention, Concentration and Wisdom; while the average
Christian has no idea of the three ways, the purgative, the
illuminative and the unitive. The spiritual education of the
Christian is sadly neglected. As I told a group of Carmelite
Fathers in Rome, the East has entered upon the contemplative stage before its time, while the West has lagged in the
stage of discursive reasoning too long. The East is a thief,
while the West is a son who does not resemble the Father.
The son will have a great deal to learn from the thief. My talk
delighted the Carmelites so much that Father Gabriel took
notes of it and made an article out of it. I entirely agree with
Frank Sheed that "the real job of the moment is to re-Chris-
tianize the world—beginning with ourselves, of course, but
not postponing the rest of the world till our own Christianiza-
tion is completed." And the great paradox is that unless the
West recognizes humbly its own need of re-Christianization,
the East will not be Christianized so easily. It is most gratify-
ing to see that the importance of the mystical element in
religion is being more and more recognized in the West. It
is to be hoped that the mysticism of the saints will gradually
leaven the whole lump of Christendom.

It was Count Hermann Keyserling who said, "The Chinese
are men of long, and we of short, breath; for us mobility, for
them quiescence, is the normal condition." [5] There is a great
deal of truth in these words. But it is not exactly "quiescence," but rather a slow tempo of life that a Chinese likes.
Any hurried movement is disconcerting to him. In this, again,
I am a Chinese of the Chinese. For instance, I have always
taken delight in serving the Mass, whenever there is no altar-
boy. But I feel more at home in serving a priest who says the
Mass slowly. I know slowness or quickness has nothing to do
with the sanctity of the priest. I hear that St. Francis Xavier

[5] *The Travel Diary of a Philosopher*, II, p. 107.

said a pretty quick Mass. But there is no denying that I prefer
to serve a priest who says every word distinctly and slowly,
and waits patiently for your *"Deo gratias."* The first time
that I ever was able to give all the responses was when I
served a Mass said by Father Donald Hessler, who is a man
of long breath.

But whether long breath or short breath, Love is all. In
dealing with the Orientals, one cannot too much emphasize
that God is more motherly than a mother. The Chinese
respect the father, but love the mother. One of the things
that attracted me so strongly to St. Thérèse of Lisieux is
that she knew well the maternal quality of God's love. As
she said, "I had long felt that Our Lord is more tender than
a mother, and I have sounded the depths of more than one
mother's heart . . . Fear makes me shrink, whereas under
love's sweet rule I not only advance—I fly." When I read it,
I said to myself, "How Chinese she is!" There is in the bosom
of every Chinese a secret pride, which can only be melted
by the fire of love, but cannot be uprooted by a surgical
operation. You may rough-handle him, you may beat him to
his knees; but you can never win his heart by such means.
On the contrary, his knees may kneel, his heart will ever rebel.
But if you treat him nicely, he is too sensible to take advantage of your kindness and generosity. We must remember
that he belongs to an old nation rich in experience and
worldly wisdom. You can only make him humble by making
him generous, and you can only make him generous by being
generous yourself.

One of the reasons why I feel so much at home in the
Catholic Church is that most of the priests and sisters I have
met have been so motherly to me. I have gone to confession
to priests of many nationalities and orders. Whether they
are Chinese, American, French, English, Italian, German,

Swiss, Indian or Belgian, I have only heard one voice, the voice of a mother. Whether they are Jesuits, Dominicans, Maryknollers, Lazarists, Scheuts, Benedictines, Sulpicians, Carmelites, Passionists or secular priests, I have only experienced one wisdom, the wisdom of a mother. There is unity without uniformity, there is diversity without division. In the confessional, the Father is there, the Son is there, the Holy Spirit is there. The forgiveness is there, and so is the medicinal grace. I have heard some superficial critics of the Sacrament of Penance saying, "You Catholics go to Confession in order to sin more." Nothing of the sort! I will relate one experience. When I was in Chungking, I fell into a certain sin, and I went to confession to an old benign French priest. The very next day, the same temptation came and I fell again. I felt some hesitation in going to confession again. But I steeled my will and acted as my own policeman; I put my hand on my own shoulder and dragged myself along to the same divine tribunal. I thought the Father must be awfully upset and would give me up for hopeless. But he was very mild and counselled me to rely on the grace of God and be patient with myself. A wonderful thing! The same temptation has never come back again in all these years. To say that one goes to confession in order to sin is just as absurd as to say that one goes to the hospital in order to get sick.

One of the greatest charms of the Catholic Church for the Chinese soul is its monastic tradition. The Chinese people are on the whole attached to the world; but they have a secret admiration for those who have heroically sacrificed all their worldly pleasures and relations in order to devote themselves to a life of union with God. At the bottom of their heart, the Chinese realize that all honors and riches will soon pass without leaving a trace; and therefore they admire those who abandon what is temporary in singlehearted pursuit of what is eternal. This is why, although living in the world, my heart is with those who are living in cloisters. I often told the holy monks and nuns to pray for me that I might live in the interior cloister of my soul, wherever I might find myself and whatever I might be doing. To my mind, the cloisters are the hothouses for raising and cultivating the flowers of spirituality. But the hothouse exists for the garden, not the garden for the hothouse. Those flowers of spirituality must, therefore, be made to spread into all parts of the world, until the whole world becomes one big cloister. Every one of us carries a cloister within himself, in which he can have a perpetual rendezvous with his Beloved. When the love of God reigns supreme in a family, the family itself becomes a cloister and the duties of state constitute a cell for each member of the family. If one performs one's domestic, professional, and social duties for the love of God, one is a monk or a nun in spirit.

Another thing about the Catholic Church that makes me feel at home is the Liturgical Year. As I have said somewhere in this book, I was born under the Lunar Calendar, which was studded all over with seasonal feasts; and when the Lunar Calendar was abolished, the year appeared to me like a bare tree without leaves and flowers. Since my embracement of the true Faith, the year has become a living presence again. Nay, the Liturgical Year is so wonderful that the Lunar Calendar with all its festivities was but a faint foreshadowing of it. It often reminds me of "the tree of life" in the Apocalypse of St. John, bearing twelve fruits, yielding its fruit according to each month, and the leaves for the healing of the nations" (22.2).

The Chinese people are syncretically minded. Men of different religions or denominations have no prejudices against one another at all. In fact, if a Catholic tries to live up to his professions, all people will respect him. President Chiang Kai-shek, a Methodist, co-operated wholeheartedly with me on the translation of the Psalms and the New Testament. In the history of China, many beautiful friendships have existed between men of avowedly different faiths.

Perhaps, the most characteristic quality of the Chinese soul is a certain playfulness flowing spontaneously from an interior harmony. At his best, a Chinese is in tune with the Universe. The rhythms of his life are in perfect accord with the cosmic rhythms; or, rather, the two blend into one. Whether he is a Confucianist, a Buddhist or a Taoist, the feeling of oneness with the Universe forms, as it were, the inarticulate substratum of his soul. This feeling is a direct aesthetical intuition beyond words and images. Of course, words and images have to be used, but they serve only to point to it, just as the finger serves to point to the moon but is not itself the moon. All language, according to Buddha, is "like a man calling the attention of another to the moon by pointing his finger toward it. The other man ought to look at the moon. If instead of looking at the moon, he looks at the finger, he would not only miss the moon, but also the finger."

To illustrate the sense of oneness with Nature, let me quote a poem by a Taoist scholar, Lu Yun:

> Beyond the dusty world,
> I enjoy solitude and peace.
> I shut my door,
> I close my window.
> Harmony is my Spring,
> Purity my Autumn.
> Thus I embody the rhythms of life,
> And my cottage becomes a Universe.

Thus, a Chinese can live in isolation without being an isolationist, because his spirit is in tune with the Macrocosm. The same spirit dictated the famous words of the great Confucianist Mencius: "All things are present within me." It is because the typical Chinese regards himself as a microcosm that he feels at home in the bosom of the Macrocosm. Here is a poem by another great Confucianist, Chen Hao:

> When leisure comes, I take everything easy.
> I sleep until my east window is radiant with the sun.
> Quietly I contemplate all creatures enjoying themselves.
> Heartily I join my fellow men in seasonal festivities.
> My insight penetrates beyond the visible cosmos,
> While my thoughts enter into the changes of wind and cloud.
> To keep pure in prosperity and happy in poverty,—
> This is the way of true manhood.

If one feels at home in the Universe, one naturally acquires a serenity and a playfulness like a baby at the breast of its mother. All the interesting personalities in the history of China are just big babies. Confucius, for instance, played music and sang when he was surrounded by his enemies and his life was in jeopardy. The great scholar-general Chu-ko Liang, so the popular legend has it, once saved himself by a wonderful ruse. He had no soldiers at hand, and he was literally driven to the wall by his enemies. He mounted the city wall, and sat in a conspicuous place playing music in the most leisurely manner imaginable. He beckoned with his hands to the enemies, saying, "Please come in!" The enemies were frightened, suspecting that the city was full of soldiers in ambush, and took to their heels immediately. This is one of the most popular plays on the Chinese stage.

It is in the light of this spontaneous playfulness that we

can understand the queer actions of the Zen masters and the Taoists. Let one anecdote suffice. Wang Hui-chih, the son of Wang Hsi-chih, who is regarded as the greatest calligrapher of China, was travelling by boat. He saw Huan Yi, a famous flute-player, travelling by land along the bank of the river; and he sent a messenger to request him to play the flute. Huan Yi, who had heard of Hui-chih and had an admiration for him, descended from his chariot, sat on a chair, and played the flute three times. When the music was finished, he immediately ascended his chariot and went away. The two men did not exchange a single word.

This is a beautiful event, an event without reason but not without rhyme. The silence of these two artists has evoked a continual echo in the soul of every Chinese intellectual. This kind of romance is typically Chinese; and yet it is not entirely alien to the spirit of Catholicism. In fact, a true Catholic enjoys the peace and happiness of the Pantheist at their very Source. Recently, running through Maisie Ward's *The Splendor of the Rosary*, I was thrilled to find a similar meeting between St. Louis, King of France, and Brother Giles, disciple of St. Francis. The saintly King of France was making a pilgrimage to the sanctuaries of Europe. Hearing of the great fame for holiness of Brother Giles, he went to see him in Perugia. The holy Brother knew by inspiration that it was the King of France, although he was travelling *incognito*. With great fervor he left his cell and ran to the gate to meet him. Without speaking a word the two men knelt down together with the greatest devotion, embraced and kissed each other with as much familiarity as if they had been friends for a long time. After a great while, they parted from each other, St. Louis going on his way and Brother Giles returning to his cell, without breaking their silence for a single moment. Later, the other Brothers, upon learning that it was the King of France, murmured at Brother Giles for his queer action, saying, "Oh, Brother Giles, wherefore hadst thou so country manners that to so holy a King, who had come from France to see thee and hear from thee some good word, thou hast spoken nothing?" Brother Giles answered, "Dearest brothers, wonder not ye at this that neither I to him, nor he to me, could speak a word; for so soon as we had embraced, the light of the divine wisdom revealed and manifested, to me, his heart, and to him, mine; and so by divine operation we looked each in the other's heart on what we would have said to one another, and know it far better than if we had spoken with the mouth, and with more consolation, because of the defect of the human tongue, which cannot clearly express the secrets of God and would have been for discomfort rather than comfort. And know, therefore, that the King parted marvellously content and comforted in his mind."

Clearly Brother Giles was Chinese, whereas the other brothers were Europeans. I submit that he was as good a Catholic as they.

Finally, the Catholic devotion to the Blessed Virgin has been prefigured in all the religions of the East. The Oriental love for the Mother—whatever form she may take—is apt to be a lifelong passion. This passionate affection for the Mother runs through all the religions of the East like a common strain. There is a touching story about the great disciple of Confucius, Tseng Tzu. His family was poor, and he had to support his mother by collecting fagots on the hills. One day, during his absence, some of his friends called on him, and his mother did not know what to do. In her embarrassment she gnawed her fingers. At that very moment Tseng Tzu felt a sudden spasm of pain in his heart; and, taking up his bundle of fagots, he returned. When mother

and son loved each other as they did, it is not incredible that
they should have some mysterious physical communication.

Lao Tzu, literally the "Old Boy," was not noted for his
filial piety toward his mother; however, he loved the Tao as
his mother. In one of the chapters of the *Tao Teh Ching*,
after describing how stupid and helpless he appeared compared with the brilliant and clever men of the world, he
concluded with an apparent sense of complacency:

> However, in one thing I differ most from others:
> I prize only the sustenance that comes from the
>   Mother's breast.

One of the reasons why Buddhism has been so popular in
China is the cult of the feminine deity, Kuan Yin. Whether
at sea or on land, the Chinese people appeal to her help in
times of danger and distress. It is significant that originally
Kuan Yin, the Chinese for Avalokita, was a man-god; it was
only later that he was metamorphosed in popular imagination
into a goddess of mercy. She has served in China as the tender
mother of the poor and hapless.

This predilection for the Mother is found also in India.
The great Hindu, Sri Ramakrishna, drew his inspiration from
his devotion to Kali "the Divine Mother." It is most touching
to read that on his last day, August 15, 1886, he cried in ringing tones three times the name of Kali, his Divine Mother,
before he entered into his final ecstasy.

To whatever religion he may belong, an Oriental will hardly
feel at home where there is no mother. This is one of the
reasons why, although I was a Methodist for nineteen years,
my spirit found no rest; I somehow missed the Mother. Was
God not enough? Of course He is; nay, more than enough.
But it is precisely His will that we should adopt the Mother
of Christ to be our Mother. So long as this will of His is not

complied with, our filial piety toward Him is not complete. The Mother of His Son is good enough to be the Mother of His adopted children.

Have I lost anything by being a Catholic? Absolutely nothing. On the contrary, I have gained Christ, and in gaining Christ I have gained all. It is true that I have had crosses, but the crosses are the greatest treasures to me. Like medicine, they may taste bitter, sometimes so bitter that I could not help knitting my brows; but they are salutary to my spiritual health. The Truth has made me free, and grace has helped me to enjoy the new-won freedom. Oh, what joy I feel in my heart! The Second Spring has dawned in my soul, carrying with it the song of Love:

may this be true of me today 22-7-19

For winter is now past, the rain is over and gone.
The flowers have appeared in our land,
The time of pruning is come.
The voice of the turtle is heard in our land.
The fig tree has put forth the green figs.
The vines in flower yield their sweet smell.

The sorrows are there together with the joy; but they only serve to sweeten the joy. For the sorrows are the sorrows of the ages; but the joy is the Joy of Eternity!

EXPLANATIONS AND ACKNOWLEDGMENTS

To write an autobiography or a book of confessions when one is still a baby—for, after all, life begins at fifty—is, to say the least, a hazardous undertaking. I should never have started this book were it not for the persistent pressure of my friends, especially my dear confessor, Father Nicholas Maestrini, who has been praying for it more than ten years. Other priests, including Father Pasquale d'Elie and Father F. Legrand, have also pressed me to do it. Their reason is, perhaps, that the capturing and taming of one dragon might lead to the capturing and taming of all the other dragons. Of course, they know as well as I do that everything depends upon the grace of God, but they think that the story of my conversion may throw some light on the spiritual physiognomy of my countrymen and give the missioners some hints on the ways of approaching them. Moreover, as I was the worst of the prodigal sons, my return sets the mercies of the Almighty Father in the clearest relief.

As early as 1941, Father Maestrini offered a votive Mass to the Holy Spirit for the book which he wanted me to write. I began to write some paragraphs, but I stopped for lack of sustaining interest. There are many ways of glorifying God, I thought, and of helping other souls to see the Light, and the writing of a book of confessions is the least desirable of all. To my mind, one Hail Mary said devoutly would lead more souls to Christ than a dozen autobiographies. In the meantime, I addressed myself to the translation of the Sunday Missal, the Psalms and the New Testament. I told Father Maestrini that his votive Mass to the Holy Spirit was not in vain, because his prayers had been answered in a far better way than we had dreamed of.

In 1948 I was in Rome. It happened that Father Maestrini

had his sabbatical year just then. He returned from Hong-kong to Italy to visit his parents and relatives in Perugia. When he was in Rome, he visited me in my Legation. One of the first questions he asked me was, "Have you forgotten about the book?"

"Which book?" I said.

"Your Life, of course!" he said.

"So you want my life!" I rejoined. "Frankly, I cannot do it. When one is in love, one is too much absorbed in one's beloved to think of oneself. I am just preparing a book on the spiritual life, based on the Beatitudes, and I have no time to deal with my own life."

"But your life is not your own, it belongs to God. To write about your life is to give an account of the graces that you have received from God, and the wonderful ways of His Providence."

"Yes, Father, but one's Life should be the last book, not the first book. Take St. Augustine, for instance. He must have written *The City of God* before he produced his *Confessions*. If you can show me that the *Confessions* came before his other works, I should be willing to reconsider my decision."

Somehow I was quite sure that at last I had shut the mouth of Father Maestrini. But he would not yield so easily. He immediately took down from my shelves Cayré's *Patrologie et histoire de la théologie*, and, after some feverish searching, said to me, "John, you are wrong. The *Confessions* was written long before *The City of God!*" I felt like a man who had fallen into his own trap. The joke was on me. However, I did not start to write. The duties of my state were my excuse.

In the early days of June 1949, I had an unexpected visit from Frank Sheed and Maisie Ward and their son Wilfrid, accompanied by the Passionist Father Alfred Wilson. Although it was the first time I had the pleasure of meeting the famous couple, I had known them through their books. Only recently my good friend Monsignor Charles Duchemin, the Rector of the Collegio Beda, had recommended for my reading Sheed's *Theology and Sanity*, which he himself had been using as a book for meditations. As to Maisie Ward, I had also been enjoying her *Young Mr. Newman*. I thought it was a God-sent opportunity to submit the project of my book on *The Way of Love*, which has to do with the three ages of the spiritual life. If Mr. Sheed should approve of that project, that would be something to tell Father Maestrini. What was my surprise when Mr. Sheed said that, while he was delighted with the project, he would like to have me do a spiritual autobiography first! Was he in conspiracy with Father Maestrini? But that could not be, for the two did not know each other.

It happened that my dear friend Alice Chow was also in Rome. She too pressed me to do the autobiography. I requested her to pray to the Holy Ghost; but the only immediate result was the Prologue, after which I laid the manuscript aside.

In the spring of 1950, the University of Hawaii, at the suggestion of Bishop James J. Sweeney and Dr. Harley Zeigler, asked me to offer a course on Christian Mysticism at its affiliated School of Religion. The classroom was full, and my lectures were so well received as to surprise myself. At the end of the semester, Mrs. Jean Charlot, who had been attending the class, mailed a set of my lectures to Mr. Sheed without knowing my former relations with him. Sheed wrote me that he was delighted with the lectures, but ended his letter by asking, "What about the autobiography?" This was only a polite way of saying that he would not publish the lectures unless I should write that book first! So there was no running away from it. Happily, I was in a position to do it, because I was free in the summer recess.

In the writing of this book, I have received many helps from priests, Brothers, Sisters, and other friends, by way of prayers, advice and encouragement. It is impossible to mention them all. I imagine that their names are written in Heaven anyway. In short, my sojourn in Honolulu is so fruitful in friendships and rich in consolations that, were I to render an account of them, it would constitute a new chapter of my life.

John C. H. Wu

Honolulu
February 11, 1951
Feast of Our Lady of Lourdes

European Reminiscences

(an appendix to *Beyond East and West*)

My stay in Rome and my occasional excursions to other parts of
Italy and Europe were so full of interesting experiences that were I
to write them down they would make a goodly sized guide-book
for pilgrims. Here I can only set down in a rather disconnected
manner some episodes having a direct bearing on my interior life.
They may look like loose leaves of a book, but they are bound together by God's love.

1. A DILAPIDATED CHURCH

On January 20, 1947, early in the morning, I started with my family
by a special train from Marseilles. In the afternoon we reached the
Italian frontier, Ventimiglia. We went down for an outing. We went
into a church near the railway station. It was a dilapidated church,
having been bombed during the War. Wrecked as it was, yet I felt
no sense of desolation; a warm homely spirit seemed still to swell
in it. I saw the statues, more or less disfigured, of St. Joseph and St.
Thérèse. Another statue of a beautiful lady, with a crown of thorns

This chapter was written in 1950. It was originally intended to be a part of
this book, but was left out for reasons of space—Author.

on her head, I saw for the first time. They told me that it was the famous Santa Rita, to whom the Italians have a particular devotion. There was a notice that the church was being repaired, and that all contributions would be welcome. So I thrust into the contribution box all the *lire* I had in my pocket, my only regret being that I did not have more of them with me.

One and a half years later, as I went to France by motoring, I passed by Ventimiglia again, and went to visit the old church. I found it all repaired, and marveled at the zeal and industry of the Italians. This quickness of recovery betokens to my mind the perennial virility of the Church.

2. STANISLAUS

On the morning of January 21, while I was reading on the train a French book of prayers, I chanced upon a prayer to St. Stanislaus Kostka, which had a special bearing on the spiritual well-being of the youth. So I taught my children to remember the name "Stanislaus." It sounded very interesting as they pronounced it, so we had a jolly time over it, until the train resounded with "Stanislaus." In the afternoon, as our train was nearing Rome, the kids were still trying to master the pronunciation of the name.

As we arrived, we found that a group of our friends, including James Yu, our Ambassador to Italy, Sie Shou-Kang, my predecessor at the Holy See, and Bishop Henry Valtorta of Hong Kong, who happened to be in Rome, had been waiting for more than two hours, because the train had been delayed. But the very first man who came to meet me was Monsignor Lokuang,[1] whose name, I learned, was Stanislaus! He was the Ecclesiastical Counselor of our Legation, who proved later to be my right-hand man. This happy coincidence has impressed me very much.

---

1. Now Archbishop of Taipei. [The author is referring to Stanislaus Lo Kuang (1911–2004), who was the ordinary of Taipei from 1966 to 1978— Editor.]

3. ST. AGNES

As January 21 was St. Agnes's day, I paid a visit on the same day to her Church on the Via Nomentana. I liked it because it was simple and homelike. What was my joy when I heard from Msgr. Lokuang that he had found a house about five minutes from the Church! We went to see the house the next day, but found the house full of refugees. I was given to understand that if a diplomat was to rent the house it would be as easy as pie to drive away the refugees. But I did not like the idea. My diplomacy was to be one of love, and it did not sound like love to use diplomatic privileges to drive away the poor. So I dropped the idea of renting that house. At the same time, I played the spoiled child with St. Agnes. I went again to the Church, I said, "St. Agnes, I like this church; and I want to be near you, so that I can come to Mass everyday." "That house?" "Yes, but how can I house my own family by making others home-less? The long and short of it is that you, O St. Agnes, have to find another house for me near this Church." I was so attached to that ancient Basilica for many reasons. First, I admired the Virgin-martyr. Secondly, St. Thérèse had visited it when she was fifteen. In her autobiography she wrote, addressing herself to her eldest sister Mother Agnès, "Our visit to the Church of St. Agnes was also a sweet experience, and there I found a friend of my childhood. At first I was unsuccessful in my endeavor to procure for you some little relic, dear Mother, but, when men refused me, God Himself came to my aid, for there fell at my feet a fragment of red marble from an ancient mosaic dating back to the time of the gentle Martyr. Was it not touching that St. Agnes herself should give me a keepsake from her house?" Thirdly, as we arrived on her Feast, we wanted to live in her Parish, thus making time and space meet in her. This is a typically Chinese fancy. The Chinese word for the universe is Yu-ch'ou (宇宙), Yu denoting space and ch'ou time; so that the universe means for us "spacetime." Last but not least, the present Holy Father Pius XII first decided to be a priest during a retreat in the premises of this Basilica. In fact, at the front door of the Church, there is a stone tablet on the wall recording this momentous event in the life of His Holiness:

In questa Canonica
Presso la tomba
Del candido angelico di Cristo Agnese,
Meditava e sequiva nell'agosto 1894
La chiamata di Dio
EUGENIO PACELLI
Che la divina providenza voleva
Pastore angelico del Mistico Gregge
Col nome di Pio XII
L'Anno del Signore 1942
Venticinquesimo del Suo Espiscopoto
I canonici regolari lateranensi
A perenne ricordo

———

(In this parish, near the tomb of the pure angel of Christ, Agnes, Eugenio Pacelli meditated on and followed the call of God in August 1894—he whom the divine providence willed to be the angelic pastor of the Mystical Flock with the name Pius XII. In the year of Our Lord 1942, the 25th of his episcopate, the Lateran canons regular [placed this inscription] in lasting memory.)

As I was to have many dealings with the Holy Father, I entrusted our diplomacy of love to the hands of St. Agnes.

We looked for a house for two weeks, but there was none. A friend from our Embassy informed us that there was a mansion about a two-minute walk from St. Agnes, called Villa Bianca. We went to see it and found it a palatial mansion with a large park around it. But the porter told us that it was not for rent, but for sale. We came back disappointed. After a few days, just as we were reciting our evening Rosary and praying to Our Lady to help us solve the housing problem, we received a telephone message from the owner of that mansion, saying that if we were willing to rent it subject to the contingency of an eventual sale, he would be glad to let us move in. Well, I said to myself, our life on earth is a contingent thing in any case. Besides, the house was so big, the contingency of a sale seemed very remote. So we moved in, and up to now our Legation is still there.

I often went to the latest Mass, at ten! The truth is, in whatever city I may find myself, the first thing I would do is to seek out a priest and ask him, "When is the last Mass said here?" And I would adjust my sleeping and rising accordingly. My spirit is willing to get up earlier, but my flesh prefers to stay in bed as long as it is compatible with daily communion. When I wash up in the morning and see the lazy bone in the mirror, I often draw a sigh and shake my head, saying, "John, you make me laugh!" However, no creature is entirely bad; even in me there is something good. Whenever I saw a priest offering the Holy Sacrifice of the Mass without an altar-boy to serve him, I simply could not forebear going to the Altar quietly to make the responses and to serve him, as I would serve Christ Himself. Sometimes the priest was visibly startled to hear such an unexpected voice behind him. I did it many times at St. Agnes. In the beginning my conduct became quite a talk in the diplomatic circles. "Just think of it!" they would say, "An envoy from a country of four hundred million people serving the Mass like an altar-boy!" A lady actually told me this at a cocktail party. She was not scandalized, but rather edified, which however scandalized me. What has official rank to do when you are before the Altar of God? No worldly honor can be compared with the supreme privilege open to a layman of serving the representative of Christ offering the same Sacrifice as He did at Calvary. The priest may not be a saintly man—I wish all priests were—but at the Mass he is another Christ. I expounded this view in all candidness to the good lady, and there was no more talk about it. Anyway, St. Agnes did not seem to be displeased at my serving the Mass.

4. THE DEAN OF CARDINALS

In accordance with Protocol, a new diplomat, after he has seen the Holy Father, is supposed to call on the Cardinals. So I began with the Dean, Cardinal Gennao Granito Pignatelli di Belmonte. I visited him on February 21, 1947. He was then ninety-six years old, but still very lively. Knowing of my special devotion to St. Thérèse of Lisieux, he spoke of her with great gusto. He told me a very touching story. In the early 1920's when he was already over seventy, he was afflicted with a grave sickness. The doctor said that an operation was necessary. However, the Cardinal was too old and weak to stand such an operation. In his distress, someone gave him a relic of Blessed Thérèse. (It was before her Canonization.) And he wore it on him. The next day, he was entirely cured! When the cause of her Canonization was before the Sacred College of Cardinals, Pope Pius XI asked each of the Cardinals if he had anything to say against the cause. None of them said anything. But Cardinal Granito stood up and said, "Your Holiness asks me whether I have anything to testify in favor of her?" He told them the whole story of his miraculous cure. In the midst of his narration, he was so moved that he cried for gratitude. Then the other Cardinals were so touched by his crying that they too cried. "Finally," the good Cardinal told me, "the Holy Father Himself cried!" I was tickled by this story. I thought that the little Thérèse's message of spiritual childhood must have inundated the Sacred College. Just imagine all these old men crying like babies, and they did it so liturgically!

On February 15, 1948, the good Cardinal passed away.

5. IN THE HOME OF ST. THÉRÈSE

Since I was settled down in Rome, I often desired to make a trip to Lisieux to visit the house where St. Thérèse was brought up and to see her two surviving sisters at the Carmel, Mother Agnès and Mother Geneviève (Pauline and Céline). However, being a diplomat, I was supposed to stay at the post and not to move around like a pilgrim. So I mortified my desire in the spirit of St. Thérèse herself. In the summer, I received an invitation from UNESCO in Paris to give a lecture on "Adolescence in China." I sent a telegram to the Foreign Ministry to ask for permission to go to Paris, and it was given immediately. I went to Paris in August accompanied by my boys Edward and Peter. After I had given the lecture at the UNESCO summer school, we went to Lisieux by motoring. The Papal Nuncio at Paris[2] had sent word to the Carmelites to receive me without veils. While we were driving, a thought came to my mind: it would be a good souvenir to take a picture of the elder sisters of the Saint, who was chiefly instrumental for my conversion. My reasoning was like this: since Saint Thérèse was my little Mother, her elder sisters were my aunts. So I asked Edward, "Have you brought your camera with you?" Yes, he had. I said, "Don't forget to take a snapshot of the Mothers when they come to the grille!" "Understood," Edward responded.

Upon our arrival at Lisieux, the first thing that impressed us was that it had been badly bombed during the War, but the Carmel was intact like an oasis in the midst of the desert. As soon as we announced ourselves at the Carmel, the Mothers came out to the grille and received us with truly maternal warmth. But suddenly Mother Geneviève saw what Edward was doing behind my back, and asked me, "What is he doing? It is forbidden!" I saw Mother Agnès making some gesture to her sister, as if saying, "Don't be so scrupulous." I the great rascal pretended not to know anything about it. Turning my head to Edward, I said, "Who asked you to do that?" Edward said, "But I have already done it!" Aside from this little episode, our conversation was one of the most pleasant I have had in my life. I explained to them in what sense they were my aunts; they understood it perfectly well, after all, for the French ideas about human relations are not so different from the Chinese. The Mothers had read the French translation of my *Science of Love*, which they liked very much.

We had a perfect day in Lisieux, visiting Les Buissonnets and the House of Souvenirs. We also met Msgr. Germain, the Pastor

2. Later he became Pope John XXIII.

of the Parish, and Father André Combes, who was called "The Thérèsian Doctor."

Upon our return to Paris, I asked Edward, "Did you really get the snapshot?" He said, "I surely did do it!" After a few days, we returned to Rome. One of the first things I wanted to do was to go to my confessor, Father Duchemin, Rector of Collegio Beda. As it was summer vacation he was away in England, but before he went he had recommended Father Williamson, saying, "I am sure he is a saint." Father Williamson was a man of eighty-four. He was the chaplain of the Clinic run by the Blue Sisters, where George Santayana, the Spanish American philosopher, has been staying and well taken care of for the last few years. The Father (God bless his memory) was one of the most holy men I have ever met. He was a great devotee of St. Thérèse, and had written quite a few books on her. Well, I confessed to him everything about the photographing, and said to him, "Father, don't you think that I should burn the negative?" You know what he said? "Don't burn it before you develop it," he advised, "After you have developed it, you can keep one picture for your album; and then burn the negative." He also undertook to write about it to the Mothers, with whom he was in constant correspondence.

In the spring of 1948, I received an invitation from the International Congress of the History of Literature, sponsored by the University of Paris, to be one of the four Honorary Presidents of the conference to be held at the Sorbonne in April. The letter stated that Gilbert Murray and Benedicto Croce were among those invited. It was a great temptation to me, as I wanted very much to meet them. After getting permission from my Foreign Ministry, I consented to go. This time I went in my private car. When I arrived at Paris, I was somewhat disappointed in finding that I was the only Honorary President that could come. The others were prevented from coming for one reason or another. However, I thoroughly enjoyed the learned papers read by the French, Italian, Belgian, and English scholars, discussing the inter-relations between the literatures of different nations. I was asked to give a closing message on the last day of the conference. The gist of my "message" was that the greatest works of literature are vessels of spiritual values. Any literary work that does not bring man nearer to God, the Supreme Beauty, is rubbish to me. It made quite a stir in the Parisian newspapers, such as *Le Monde* and *La Croix*. There was no adverse comment.

After the conference was over, we went again to Lisieux. As soon as the curtain was drawn aside, the first words that Mother Geneviève said were, "Please turn on the lights!" I thought I was luckier this time. A young sister, who accompanied the Mothers, discussed with me as to how to answer a recent book—the one by Van de Meersch—on St. Thérèse. All the Carmelites were displeased with that book, because it exaggerated the severity of Mother Gonzaga toward the Saint. I gave them quite a lecture on Thérèsian spirituality! "Let it alone," I said, "controversies will lead nowhere. The important thing is to expound the positive content of the doctrine of love. This is the true spirit of the Saint: whereas to enter into controversies is against her spirit. Today you come across an inaccuracy in a book, and you try to correct it: tomorrow you come across an inaccuracy in another book, and you try to correct it. You will be too busy tracking down errors. Think what the Saint herself would do!" The mothers nodded.

The most remarkable experience I have had of the Saint of Lisieux occurred on July 7, 1949. In those days we were preparing to leave Rome to come to Honolulu. I was busy taking leave of my friends, one after another. On that particular morning, after the Holy Mass, I prayed before the picture of St. Thérèse. I said to her, "I am going away from Rome. Am I going away from you? Shall I say good-bye to you also? Or are you going with me? If you will still be with me, give me a sign." I had never or seldom prayed like that. My spirit was in agony. Of course I was glad to come to America. That was my own choice. All the same, it was most painful for me to leave Rome, dearer to me than home: I had taken leave of the Holy Father, and of Msgr. Celso Constantini and Msgr. Montini, to mention but a few of my dearest friends. So you

can understand why I said these words to St. Thérèse. On my return
to the Legation, a letter was awaiting me, a letter from Céline!
It said:

Jésus Marie
Pax Christi
Carmel de Lisieux

Excellence,

Très touchées de l'envoi des deux notices sur Dom Lou, notre
Révérende Mère et moi exprimons à Votre Excellence notre
gratitude et notre admiration pour cette âme si Thérèsienne et
pour l'auteur qui a su en tracer un portrait saisissant.

Que notre chère petite Sainte continue à l'assister, en toutes
circonstances, par son aide et son affection fraternelle!

Avec ce souhait, excellence, et avec l'assurance de nos prières
pour la Chine, si chère, cette mère des sages, si éprouvée actuelle-
ment, je vous prie d'agréer l'expression de notre religieux et "af-
fectueux" respect.

Sr Geneviève de la Sainte Face et de Sainte Thérèse

Le 4 juillet dix neuf cent quarante neuf

———

(Excellency,

Our Reverend Mother and myself are very touched by your
sending us the pamphlets on Dom Lou. We would like to express to your Excellency our gratitude and admiration for his
soul, so Thérèsian, as well as for the author who succeeded in
painting such a gripping portrait of him.

May our dear little Saint continue in assisting Him, in all circumstances, with her help and fraternal affection!

Together with this wish, I beg your Excellency to accept our
religious and "affectionate" respect and our prayers for China,

this mother of the Wise, so dear to us, who is going now through so much hardship.

Sister Geneviève of the Holy Face and of St. Thérèse

July 4, 1949)

The wonderful thing about it is that I was not expecting any letter from Lisieux; I had not written to them for a long time; it was not I but Father Edouard Neut, the faithful secretary and friend of Dom Lou (陸微祥院長), who had sent them the two copies of my pamphlet on Dom Lou, which was a lecture I had given at the Abbey of St. Anselm in Rome. To receive such an unexpected letter from the most beloved sister and "echo" of the Saint immediately after I had asked for a sign from her—it was an almost baffling experience for me. My only explanation of the matter is that the prayer was infused from above.

6. HOSPITALITY OF ST. FRANCIS

Even before I was a Catholic, I had admired and loved the great Saint of Assisi. He appealed to me as the most oriental of Christian saints. Since my conversion, my love for him has grown with the years. I had a strong desire to visit Assisi, when I was in Rome. One day in the spring of 1947, two Italian gentlemen called on me. They had come from Assisi in order to invite me in the name of Bishop Giuseppe Placido Nicolini and Father Giovanni Rossi to go to Assisi to give a lecture in the Corso de Studi Cristiani to be held in September. My subject was to be "The Devotion to the Blessed Virgin in China." They told me that there would be a distinguished gathering of Cardinals, Bishops, and Professors of theology from all parts of Italy. At first I declined the invitation, because to talk to such a formidable audience on a religious subject did not seem to be an easy thing to do. Furthermore, I could not speak Italian. But they insisted upon my accepting, saying, "You can speak either in French or in English, and someone will translate your speech into Italian." We were still arguing back and forth when a thought suddenly crossed my mind: *It is St. Francis inviting you to visit his home and to talk on our Blessed Mother to the glory of Her Son; how dare you decline such a loving hiding?* "Bene, Bene!" I said, "I will accept."

I arrived at Assisi in the evening of September 3 together with four of my boys, including Francis. They put us up at Windsor Savoia. The next morning we went to Mass and received Communion at the Tomb of St. Francis. I was kneeling on the stone steps, and while my knees felt some pain, I was happy to imitate St. Francis, who used to sleep on a stone pillow, which we had seen the night before. I was glad to offer a little mortification. But a priest kindly gave me a cushion. I accepted it immediately, thinking that exterior mortification must yield to interior mortification.

My lecture was scheduled for half past four in the afternoon. At a little before four, there was a terrific thunderstorm raining cats and dogs. I was taking tea with my boys. I prayed to St. Francis, saying, "Now, Seraphic Saint, is this your hospitality? I have a car to go to the Theatre; but what about my audience? If you love me, stop it!" The storm stopped in five minutes; and my boys were greatly edified. At the appointed time we went to the Theatre, and we found it filled to its capacity. There must have been around three thousand people there. Of course, I do not claim that all of them had come to listen to me alone, for there was another speaker for the day, Cardinal Adeodata Piazza, the Patriarch of Venice. I was the first to speak. As the thunderstorm and St. Francis' prompt answer to my prayer were still fresh in my mind, I introduced my lecture by telling them the story, and I concluded the story by saying, "Such is the hospitality of the Saint of Assisi!" Immediately there came a thunderous applause from the audience. This is what I called "thunder for thunder!"

After my lecture a Bishop said to me, "You are the Ambassador of Our Lady!" Many people waited for me at the door of the Theatre. When I came out, they called, *"Viva Cina!"* I was so touched by the goodness of the Italians that I almost wept. But I summoned up my self-control, and told my boys to join me in saying, *"Viva Italia! Viva Italia!"* Apparently, our wishes for Italy have been more effective than their wishes for China.

7. THE CHARM OF ITALY

You have to stay in Italy for some time to realize how great a country she is and how rich is her culture. You feel as though you were looking at Time through a high-powered telescope. The events that happened in antiquity seem as though they had occurred only yesterday. "This is where St. Peter was crucified with his body upside down." "This is where St. John was thrown into the boiling oil and came out unscathed." "This is where the Martyrs were eaten by the wild beasts." "This is where Dante first met Beatrice." "This is where John Keats spent his last day." "This is where Shelley was drowned." "This is the Bridge of Sighs about which Lord Byron wrote." "This is where St. Benedict threw himself upon the thorns when he was tempted to impurity." "This is where St. Catherine lived." "This is the robe which St. Francis wore." "This is where St. Philip Neri said his Mass." "This is where Michelangelo spent fifteen years of his life in painting this magnificent fresco." "This is the tower where Galileo made his experiments." These words of the guides make you feel contemporaneous with the ancients.

It is impossible to record all the interesting experiences in my pilgrimages. I will only mention one or two. In Padua, I went to see the Church of St. Anthony. I saw many people praying at the tomb of the Saint. A pretty girl was weeping silently. I did not know what she was praying for. But I was so touched by her weeping that quite impulsively I threw myself upon my knees behind her and said, "I endorse all her petitions with my whole heart!" I was so bold because I trusted that Saint Anthony would only intervene in legitimate affairs. So there is method in my madness.

In Verona I saw the Sarcophagus in which the body of Juliet had lain. A Friar told me that the body had been stolen, leaving this empty case like an orphan. For a moment I was saturated with the pathos of life. No wonder Romeo said:

Hang up philosophy!
Unless philosophy can make a Juliet,
Displant a town, reverse a Prince's doom,
It helps not, it prevails not: talk no more.

I was also reminded of the words of Prospero (from *The Tempest*):

Our revels now are ended. These our actors,
As I foretold you, were all spirits and
Are melted into air, into thin air:
And like the baseless fabric of this vision,
The cloud-capp'd towers, the gorgeous palaces.
The solemn temples, the great globe itself,
Yea, all which it inherit, shall dissolve
And like this insubstantial pageant fade,
Leaving not a rack behind. We are such stuff
As dreams are made on, and our little life
Is rounded with a sleep.

8. ST. BENEDICT JOSEPH LABRE

When I was in Rome, my relations with Jacques Maritain, the French Ambassador to the Holy See, were among the most pleasant. I came also to know Madame Maritain and her sister Miss Oumancoff. They impressed me as being very spiritual, for although engaged actively in diplomatic life they seemed to me truly detached from the world and "poor in spirit." In fact, the very first time Jacques Maritain called on me, he mentioned St. Benedict Joseph Labre, "the Beggar of Rome," as one of those Saints to whom he had a special devotion. I had read about the Saint in Goodier's *Saints for Sinners*, and conceived a great love for him. Shortly after the visit of Maritain, I went to see the Church where his tomb is. People told me that where the Church now stands there was originally a rich man's mansion. The rich man was so kind as to take in the saintly "Beggar of Rome" in his last illness; with the result that the house was later turned into a Church! I have no way of checking up the truth of this legend, but it is beautiful.

Before the Tomb of the Saint I prayed for Maritain and my relations with him. On one occasion, we went together and offered
our prayers.

In the spring of 1948, when I was in Paris, I went with a French
professor, Charles Bedeyan, to visit the tomb of Léon Bloy, who
had converted the Maritains. On my return to Rome I wrote to
Maritain about my experience. He was so moved that he wrote me
a most beautiful letter, which I treasure and from which I beg to
reproduce a passage here:

> Comment vous remercier de votre si bonne lettre? Je suis pro-
> fondément touché de tout ce que vous m'écrivez de la France et
> de l'accueil que vous avez reçu et c'est avec un vif sentiment de
> gratitude et d'émotion que l'Ambassadrice et moi avons appris
> que vous êtes allés prier sur la tombe de notre cher parrain Léon
> Bloy. O parfait témoignage de cette communion des saints à
> laquelle il croyait de toute son âme! Le grand penseur chrétien
> qui représente si dignement la Chine près le Saint Siège Apos-
> tolique, et protégé au Ciel par Sainte Thérèse de Lisieux, va en
> terre de France à la rencontre du Pélerin de l'Absolu!

(How can I thank you for such a nice letter?! I am deeply
touched by everything you've written to me about France and
the welcome you have received. It is with a deep feeling of gratitude and emotion that the Ambassadress and I hear that you
went and prayed at the tomb of our dear godfather, Léon Bloy.
What a perfect testimony of this communion of saints in which
he believed with all his soul! The great Christian thinker who,
with such dignity, represents China to the Holy See, is going,
protected in Heaven by Saint Thérèse de Lisieux, to the land of
France to meet the Pilgrim of the Absolute!)

The letter was dated April 16, the Feast of St. Benedict Joseph
Labre! When I met Maritain the next time, I asked him, "Did you

realize that your letter was written on the Feast of the Beggar
Saint?" He was astounded because he had not thought of it at all!

9. MSGR. JOHN MONTINI

Msgr. Montini is the Acting Secretary of State at the Vatican.[3] All
my colleagues in the diplomatic Corps spoke highly of his spirituality. He is, perhaps, the busiest man in the Holy See, and yet there
is such a leisureliness about him that you feel as though you were
talking to a monk in his cell! I owe him a special debt of gratitude,
because he used to set apart July 1 of each year during my stay to
offer a special Mass for my country and my family. All my family
members, three carloads of them, would go to attend that Mass and
receive Holy Communion from his hands. The last time, on July 1,
1949, I served the Mass. At Thanksgiving he signaled to me to tell
my folks to recite together three Our Father's in Chinese.

On my leave-taking we had a very edifying talk together. Naturally we talked about current events. He expressed his profound re-
grets that China should have fallen such an easy prey to the
Communists. I said, "Monsignor, the Church is the center of
human history. She is so dear to the Heart of God that He has
arranged everything for her good. He permitted the Reformation
in order to stimulate her to purify herself from corruption. This
time, He has permitted the rise of Communism in order to stir us
to practice seriously the charity of Christ. *If we Christians had been
as charitable as we ought to have been there would have been no Communism.* It is our worldliness and snobbish attitude toward the poor
that has provoked the anger of God. Our enemy is not in the exterior, but in the interior. When will true Christian charitableness,
love and justice be revived once more to help humankind? Unless
we can love the poor more intensely than the Communists hate the
rich, the world will enjoy no peace. As I look at it, materialistic
Communism is a menace to the whole world, not merely China."
The good Monsignor was so pleased with these casual remarks of

3. Later Pope Paul VI.

mine that he turned to Msgr. Lokuang who was with us and said, "I am exceedingly happy to see that His Excellency always looks at things of the earth from the standpoint of God!"

10. A VISIT TO DOM LOU

Dom Lou is universally recognized as one of the greatest Catholics that China has produced. After a most brilliant political career, he became a Benedictine monk in 1927, when he was already fifty-six years old. He died on January 15, 1949, in the halo of sanctity. He has left two books: *Souvenir et Pensées*, which has been translated into English and published under the title, *Ways of Confucius and of Christ*, and *La Rencontre des Humanités (The Meeting of Civilizations)*, which has been published posthumously but has not yet been translated. There is already a good biography of Dom Lou in Chinese by his intimate friend Msgr. Lokuang.

But it is impossible here to give even a brief sketch of his life. I can only give some impressions of him during my visit to the Abbey of St. Andrew at Bruges in August of 1947. I found the old Abbot burning with apostolic zeal. He desired to go to China to establish a Benedictine Monastery in Peking. On account of the troubled conditions of the country, I had to put a damper on his project. "Beloved Abbot," I said, "do you remember what Our Lord said: *Unless the grain of wheat falls into the ground and dies, it remains alone. But if it dies, it brings forth much fruit*"? I don't know why I should have quoted these words; but somehow I had an idea that the mission of Dom Lou would begin only after his going to Heaven. Dom Lou, instead of being saddened by my words, smiled most affably and understandingly.

I stayed in the Abbey two days, but I enjoyed the privilege of serving the Old Abbot at Mass. The way he said the Mass revealed his profound spirituality. He read every word slowly, tenderly, and distinctly. It made you feel that every Mass for him was just as fresh as if it were his maiden Mass. When he recited: *Introibo ad altare Dei*, and I responded: *Ad Deum qui laetificat juventutem meum*, I felt such an ecstasy of joy that I will never forget it. Here is a man, I thought to myself, who has already lived three years longer than Confucius did, and yet you can still say of him: *Unto God who giveth joy to my youth!* Here is a truly great man, who, in the words of Mencius, has not lost the virginal heart he had as a child! I was reminded of the most touching verses of Psalm 71:

> Thou has taught me, O God, from my youth,
> And up to now I have proclaimed Thy wonders.
> And in my old age also and gray hair,
> O Lord, forsake me not,
> Until I shall show forth Thy arm to this generation,
> They might to all the generations to come,
> And Thy justice, O God, which touches the heavens,
> By which Thou hast done such great things:
> O God, who is like to Thee?

I met Dom Lou only this one time, but our friendship is sealed by the love of God. It is said in the Psalms:

> Truly, better is one day in Thy courts
> Than a thousand others.

We can also say that one day of friendship under the wings of God is better than a thousand days elsewhere.

After the demise of Dom Lou, the Abbey of St. Anselm at Tome invited me to give a talk on his spiritual life. I think one passage in which I spoke of the many mansions in the house of Our Lord may be worth reproducing in English.

> Happy those who, like Thomas Aquinas, can baptize the ancient philosophers in borrowing from them their riches! Happy those who, like Bonaventure and Teresa of Avila, are so sincerely and profoundly realistic that they cannot help aspiring toward God, supreme Reality! Happy those who, like John of the Cross, having renounced everything, have found the All! Happy those who,

like Benedict and his sister Scholastica, are so detached from all temporary affection that the all-merciful Father has instilled into them an everlasting affection! Happy those who, like Maurus and Anselm, attain the heights of sanctity by way of a heroic obedience!

Happy those who, like Ignatius of Loyola, work with all their energy and at the same time with the deep conviction that they do nothing but God does all! Happy those who, like Bernard and Francis de Sales, are so meek and docile to the Spirit that they become models of fortitude and moral courage! Happy those who, like Catherine of Siena, feed their spirituality upon the Humanity of the Son of God!

Happy those who, like Dominic, Alphonsus Liguori, Grignion of Montfort and Bernadette, in making themselves devoted sons and daughters of Mary, have become veritable children of God the Father, brothers of God the Son, and spouses of God the Holy Spirit, being made true gods by participation! Happy those who, like Thérèse of Lisieux, preserve with all care their virginity of body and of heart and yet feel infinitely grateful to the all-merciful Father as though they were another Magdalen or another prodigal son!

Happy those who, like Paul and Augustine, have such great sorrow for their past sins that God mercifully draws a great deal for good from them and deigns to employ them as vessels of election for extending His kingdom on earth, while keeping them ever humble and aware of their nothingness! Happy those who, like Thomas More and Contardo Ferrini, while living actively in the world, carry within themselves an interior cloister, in which they enjoy a continual rendezvous with their beloved Lord.

Happy those who, like our friend Dom Lou, having found *the one* thing necessary, can swim in the abundance of the universe without being drowned, can ascend and descend between the One and the many with the liberty of the children of God! When he ascends to heaven, it is for the love of his

Father. When he comes back to the earth, it is for love of his brothers.

Honolulu, Hawaii
January, 1950